STEPPING UP!

Stepping Up! offers inspiring suggestions for ways teachers and teacher educators can stand up and speak out for students to create welcoming classroom climates for LGBTQ and gender diverse youth. Building from ten years of collaborative longitudinal inquiry, including interviews with parents, students, teachers, and administrators, the authors share stories from different perspectives to support teachers with concrete examples of advocacy. The authors show teachers how to 'step up' by working with students, through and beyond curriculum, and by working with families and administrators to improve school culture for LGBTQ and gender diverse students. Additionally, they explore the potential constraints involved in such social justice work, and share strategies and resources for transforming schools to be more queer-friendly.

Mollie V. Blackburn is Professor in the Department of Teaching and Learning in the College of Education and Human Ecology at the Ohio State University.

Caroline T. Clark is Professor in the Department of Teaching and Learning in the College of Education and Human Ecology at the Ohio State University.

Ryan Schey is a doctoral candidate in Adolescent, Postsecondary, and Community Literacies in the Department of Teaching and Learning at the Ohio State University. He will soon begin his academic career as faculty at Auburn University.

STEPPING UP!

Teachers Advocating for Sexual and Gender Diversity in Schools

Mollie V. Blackburn, Caroline T. Clark, and Ryan Schey

with
Jenell Igeleke Penn, Courtney Johnson, Jill Williams, Dorothy Sutton, Kim Swensen, and Lane Vanderhule

NEW YORK AND LONDON

First published 2018
by Routledge
711 Third Avenue, New York, NY 10017

and by Routledge
2 Park Square, Milton Park, Abingdon, Oxon, OX14 4RN

Routledge is an imprint of the Taylor & Francis Group, an informa business

© 2018 Taylor & Francis

The right of Mollie V. Blackburn, Caroline T. Clark, and Ryan Schey to be identified as the authors of the editorial material, and of the authors for their individual chapters, has been asserted in accordance with sections 77 and 78 of the Copyright, Designs and Patents Act 1988.

All rights reserved. No part of this book may be reprinted or reproduced or utilised in any form or by any electronic, mechanical, or other means, now known or hereafter invented, including photocopying and recording, or in any information storage or retrieval system, without permission in writing from the publishers.

Trademark notice: Product or corporate names may be trademarks or registered trademarks, and are used only for identification and explanation without intent to infringe.

Library of Congress Cataloging-in-Publication Data
A catalog record for this book has been requested

ISBN: 978-1-138-56817-4 (hbk)
ISBN: 978-1-138-56819-8 (pbk)
ISBN: 978-0-203-70520-9 (ebk)

Typeset in Bembo
by Swales & Willis Ltd, Exeter, Devon, UK

To LGBTQ and gender diverse students everywhere.
We are inspired by your spirit and courage.
We see you, and we love you.

CONTENTS

Acknowledgements   *viii*

1. Stepping Up for LGBTQ and Gender Diverse Students   1
2. Stepping Up as Teachers: Seeing Possibilities in Teaching and Activism   19
3. Stepping Up as Teachers: Understanding Impact, Knowledge, and Vulnerability   38
4. Stepping Up With Parents of Queer Families in Schools   63
5. Queer High School Students on Stepping Up: Layered Lives and Layered Advocacy   103
6. Stepping Up Through Curriculum that Is Inclusive of Sexual and Gender Diversity   137
7. Stepping Up With School Leaders   159
8. Stepping Up: What It Takes and Why It Matters   189

References   *194*
List of Contributors   *199*
Index   *201*

ACKNOWLEDGEMENTS

This book has been a marathon in the best sense imaginable. We are grateful to the many individuals who made it possible.

First, the students, families, and educators who generously shared their stories and, truly, their lives with us. These individuals have inspired us and expanded our understandings of stepping up to make schools better for LGBTQ and gender diverse youth and their families.

We are also grateful for the American Educational Research Association's (AERA) Educational Research Service Projects (ERSP) and The Ohio State University's Office of Diversity and Inclusion for supporting portions of the project represented in this book.

Our friends and fellow TIGers, Ariel Uppstrom, Gail Griffith, Lauren Kenney, Liesa Klyn, and Megan Brown who even when they could not be with us in person supported us with their courage, wit, and writing expertise. No matter what else was going on, they always made time for us. Liesa and Gail conducted interviews for this project, in particular. Ariel, Gail, and Lauren read drafts of the complete manuscript and gave us significant feedback to guide our revisions. Megan presented some of the work at a national conference with us.

Our colleagues, who checked in on us, provided us with scholarship touchstones, and who showed up to our conference sessions with energy, love, and coffee. Your support has meant the world.

Also at these conference sessions were the discussants who pushed our thinking, including Cindy Cruz, Elizabeth Dutro, Kathy Schultz and Steve Athanases. Additionally, there were audience members who asked us tough questions that also provoked our thinking.

The hard work, time, and heart contributed by all of the Pink TIGers to make this book happen, with a special recognition to Drs. Mollie Blackburn and

Caroline Clark, two of the co-founders of the Pink TIGers. Their commitment to this work and to the TIGers has been the gift of a lifetime.

Finally, our family members and loved ones who have cheered us on, walked the dogs, and listened to our stories throughout this entire journey. As with our first book, we are deeply thankful and couldn't have done it without them.

1
STEPPING UP FOR LGBTQ AND GENDER DIVERSE STUDENTS

Schools in the United States continue to be antagonistic environments for students who embody and express sexual and gender identities beyond what Atkinson and DePalma (2009) call heterosexual hegemony. This is well and regularly documented by the Gay, Lesbian, Straight Education Network's (GLSEN) biannual nation-wide school climate survey of lesbian, gay, bisexual, transgender, and queer (LGBTQ) students. Even the most recent of these reports show that where LGBTQ youth persistently experience biased remarks, victimization, harassment, and assault, they exhibit pervasive absenteeism, lowered educational aspirations and academic achievement, and poor psychological well-being (Kosciw, Greytak, Giga, Villenas, & Danischewski, 2016). However, when teachers and other adults offer social support, protection from victimization, and active advocacy for LGBTQ youth in schools, including sponsoring or supporting the presence of Gay–Straight Alliances, developing and delivering inclusive curriculum, and providing comprehensive bullying and harassment policies that include enumerated language, these students' sense of school belonging, academic success, and overall psychological well-being are enhanced (Kosciw et al., 2016; Murdock & Bolch, 2005).

Unfortunately, though, GLSEN data also show us that, according to the students who responded to their most recent survey, only 36.5% of students who are harassed or assaulted because of their perceived sexual identities or gender expressions report these incidents to school staff. When they do report harassment or assault, 63.5% of the time, school staff, including but not limited to teachers, do nothing or, at most, tell students to ignore the behavior (Kosciw et al., 2016). To make matters even worse, school personnel actually contribute to such remarks. Over half (56.2%) of those surveyed reported "hearing homophobic remarks from their teachers or other school staff" (Kosciw et al., 2016, p. xvii) and even more (63.5%)

heard teachers or other staff make "negative remarks about gender expression" (Kosciw et al., 2016, p. xvii). We[1] repeat, not only are educators failing to interrupt homophobia and transphobia with any frequency, they are even contributing to the hostility LGBTQ students experience at schools with their own comments. This reality, and our combined frustration and curiosity about why any teacher or other adult in a school would fail to interrupt homophobia and transphobia, and even worse would contribute to it, was the impetus for this book.

As teachers ourselves, we argue that it is our responsibility to step up for LGBTQ and gender diverse students. And, as educational researchers, we claim that it is the job of teacher educators to provide guidance, support, and information for doing this work. We know that this work can be daunting and feel impossible. But we also know that it can be done, in part, because we've done it. Here, we aim to show that by working with students, through and beyond curriculum, as well as by working with families and administrators, any teacher, whether novice or experienced, elementary or secondary, can improve school culture for LGBTQ and gender diverse students. We understand this work to require information and courage rather than expertise. It can take the form of big acts but also everyday small acts. We also believe that there is no "right way" to take action. Instead, these acts of advocacy must be multiple, variable, flexible, and organic. It is through this work and these acts that teachers will make schools better places for LGBTQ and gender diverse people.

In this chapter, in particular, we introduce you to our teacher inquiry group, the Pink TIGers, by sharing a brief history of our group and the commitments and questions that drive our work. We then go into detail about the project, including some of its limitations, and delineate the theories that undergird the project that this book represents. Finally, we prepare you, as readers, for the rest of the book, by introducing you to the school contexts featured most prominently and laying out the organizational structure of the book.

First, though, we comment a bit on our use of terminology. We often use LGBTQ. We do not mean to exclude any people who may not see themselves in this acronym, but we also hope to represent accurately the people who shared their stories in this project. For us, LGBTQ means lesbian, gay, bisexual, trans, and queer. We use trans to capture the broad diversity of non-cisgender people who make up trans communities, and we use Q for queer to reflect people who experience their sexual and gender identities fluidly and/or prefer for these identities to remain suspended. On a related note, you will see that we use both Queer and queer. We use Queer with more precision, drawing on Queer Theory, that is to mean the disruption of norms in relation to sexuality and gender. We use queer, though, as an umbrella term, much like LGBTQ, but with more fluidity, variability, multiplicity, and even ambiguity (and a lot fewer syllables). We do not include asexual or intersex, as examples, because these were not identities that played a prominent role in our work. To include them, therefore, would be dishonest. Sometimes, though, you will notice we use a variation of the LGBTQ acronym.

Typically, this is because we are respecting someone else's choice, so, for example, GLSEN uses LGBT not LGBTQ in reports published before 2016. We therefore use LGBT when referencing these earlier reports. You will further note that we also include "gender diverse" (Nealy, 2017) in the list of gender expressions. This is a term that describes people who experience gender outside of the heterosexual matrix (Butler, 1990) but who have not, necessarily, claimed (or rejected) any particular sexual or gender identity. Our intention is to be as inclusive as possible without being dishonest.

The Pink TIGers

We know about the experiences of LGBTQ and gender diverse youth in U.S. schools not only from the GLSEN reports, but also from our own experiences in schools. We are all part of a group we call the Pink TIGers, pink for the pink triangle claimed as a symbol by many LGBTQ people, and TIGers as an acronym for our Teacher Inquiry Group and an indication of our aspired ferocity in fighting for equity and diversity. The Pink TIGers began meeting in 2004 with a commitment to interrogating heterosexism and homophobia in Central Ohio, with a belief that teacher professional learning could and should go beyond one-time, one-day, top-down professional development sessions in schools. By 2009 we were actively attending to transphobia as well. Fueled by these commitments and beliefs, the Pink TIGers, as an inquiry group, have been continually meeting and learning together for over 12 years. Three of the original members are still participating. And four members, who each contributed to our first Pink TIGer book *Acting Out!* (Blackburn, Clark, Kenney, & Smith, 2010), remain active group members. Others have moved away, or moved on to other phases of their teaching lives, with many new members joining; but to a person, we all remain committed to contesting heterosexual hegemony in schools and communities. The Pink TIGers, then, reflect the kind of sustained and sustaining professional learning and real change that we believe can occur when teachers work together, over time, around shared questions and commitments. With this history as a backdrop, we introduce you to the current group of Pink TIGers who wrote this book.

All of us have been teachers, and most of us still are. Our K-12 teaching experience has been predominantly in high school English language arts. One of us shifted from being a high school teacher to being a Library Media Specialist. Additionally, six of us have university teaching experience, mostly in education but also in women's studies. Some of us have held or continue to hold administrative positions, at both K-12 and post-secondary institutions, that have challenged us to consider how superintendents, and principals, among others, shape the climate and culture of a school and affect the lives of LGBTQ and gender diverse students. All of us have been students, and some of us still are, but now in graduate school. Although none of us were out as anything other than straight and cisgender when we were in K-12 schools, we have extensive experience working with those who are. Six of us have led, or still lead, our school's Gay Straight Alliances or Genders and Sexualities Alliances (GSAs).[2] Two of us volunteered at one or two LGBTQ youth centers. Many of us were parents, although only two of us were parenting children in schools with same-gender partners. In other words, we brought a vast range of experiences to the topics we explore in this book.

We have been in conversation with one another as well as additional Pink TIGers about the topics in this book since 2014. Three of us have been a part of the Pink TIGers in monthly meetings since its inception in 2004; one of us joined three years later, in 2007; two of us joined two years later, in 2009; two more in 2012 and one more in 2013. And these counts don't even include the Pink TIGers who elected not to participate in this book project, all of whom informed our work together. That is to say, we have been talking about the content in this book for a long time. From 2004–2014, we audiotaped all of our meetings. From time to time, we shared individual written reflections on these meetings and our experiences in this group. These materials add to the richness of what we have learned about working with LGBTQ and gender diverse students through our interactions with one another.

These conversations have been driven by the belief that, as Jill[3] said, "LGBTQ students deserve the best we've got, and we're simply not there yet." Together we, in Courtney's words, "inspire and challenge one another to be better allies." And, as Kim notes, we "enrich our own practice by sharing with others." We do this by bringing to the group what we are struggling with in our lives and, mostly but not entirely, in schools. For example, Jenell brought to the group the "challenges trans students have faced" in the schools at which she worked, which, in turn, brought to light the dearth of resources and the lack of preparation that educators have available to support trans students. Jill talked about how

> teaching at a large, diverse high school where, initially, no GSA existed gave me particular insight into what kinds of stories were valued in school and which ones weren't. LGBTQ people were everywhere in the school community, but these narratives were completely missing in the school. We had signs up about community and safety all over the school and yet this whole group of people was being made to feel invisible.

And through their work and stories of co-advising their school's GSA, Jenell and Courtney helped us to see the importance of these groups in schools, as well as their limitations. As Jenell puts it, a "GSA can support students socially and emotionally, and function as an extended family for kids . . . . GSA work has helped us shape students into advocates for themselves and agents of change." But, as Courtney notes, despite being these positive places for some students, we need to keep in mind that "GSA may not be a space where all queer kids feel

TABLE 1.1 The Pink TIGers

	Pink TIGers	K–12 teaching	Post-secondary teaching	Administration	GSA	LGBT youth center	Parent	Sexual Identity	Gender Expression	Race or ethnicity
Caroline	Since 2004	1986–90 ELA	1996–present Education	2011–15 Department Chair		2006–09	Yes	Bisexual	Cisgender woman	White
Courtney	Since 2012	2001–16 HS ELA 2016–present Library Media Specialist			2012–15		Yes	Straight	Cisgender woman	White
Dorothy	Since 2012	2011–present HS ELA			2014–16		No	Straight	Cisgender woman	White
Jenell	Since 2009	2007–16 HS ELA	2016–present Education		2009–2010, 2011–2016		Yes	Hetero	Cisgender woman	Nigerian & African American
Jill	Since 2004	1997–10 HS ELA	2011–present Education	2012–present Curriculum Specialist	2004–10		Yes	Straight	Cisgender woman	White
Kim	Since 2009	2008–present HS ELA	1997–99, 2001–07 Women's Studies		2010–present		Yes	Hetero	Cisgender woman	White
Lane	Since 2012	2013–present HS ELA			2013–present		Yes	Queer	Cisgender woman	White
Mollie	Since 2004	1991–97, 2015–16 MS & HS ELA	2001–present Education	2013–present Undergraduate Studies Chair		1997–2001, 2002–12	Yes	Queer/ gay/ lesbian	Cisgender woman	White
Ryan	Since 2007	2007–14 HS ELA	2014–present Education		2007–14		Yes	Straight	Cisgender man	White

safe and secure." Together, as Kim points out, we have come to understand the need to "embrace mistake-making as opportunities for growth and compassion." Our talking, writing, and reflecting together at meetings shapes how we now act in other places and spaces. As Courtney states, "When a queer kid needs a well-informed ally, I now ask myself, 'What would a Pink TIGer do?'" Our hope is that this book provokes you, as readers, to ask and prepares you to answer this same question.

That said, when we use the term "ally," we do so with some ambivalence. We wonder whether someone gets to claim that identity or whether it gets awarded, and if the latter, by whom. We also think that no one is always an ally. It is not a stagnant identity. One might always strive to be an ally, and sometimes achieve this goal and other times not. We appreciate the work of Schniedewind and Cathers (2003) on this point, whose work documents how people can be taught about and learn to be allies; that we are all always learning to do this in our lives, even when we mess up; and that being an ally can be hard. As they note, an ally is "someone who didn't have to be there, but they chose to act . . . they stand up for those being targeted because of any 'ism'" (pp. 188–189). Whether we use ally or advocate or something else, our challenge is the same, to choose to act.

While our work on *Acting Out!* made us keenly aware of the damage that homophobia and heterosexism can do, especially to young people in schools, we became concerned about potentially reinforcing rigid, heteronormative boundaries by focusing strictly on homophobia without attending to disrupting binaries related to sex and gender identities. Through sharing our stories and experiences as educators, we knew that gender binaries were being policed and reinforced beginning in pre-school and continuing on into K-12 and university classrooms.

Between 2009 and 2010, in the midst of our reading and learning about gender binaries and the impacts of heteronormativity, several young people across the U.S. committed suicide for either being gay or being perceived as gay. The quick succession of these suicides caught the attention of the media and shined a bright light on the issue of LGBTQ youth suicides and bullying. These events also prompted the gay columnist Dan Savage and his partner, Terry Miller, to start the "It Gets Better" project, a web-based collection of videos from celebrities and politicians to everyday adults and young people, aimed at communicating to LGBT youth, worldwide, that life gets better and is worth sticking around for, regardless of how terrible it may feel in the moment.

Even as we were shattered by each of these deaths, we noticed, too, that as the focus turned to bullying more generally, attention to homophobia, heterosexism, and LGBTQ students was dropped, creating a comfortable place for policy makers, legislators, and educators to stand against bullying without standing up for LGBTQ and gender diverse people. Witnessing these events and this turn toward bullying and away from its contextual causes surfaced new questions for inquiry and expanded the focus of our group. Together, we wondered why seemingly less powerful people, like early career teachers or students themselves, would go to extraordinary lengths to support LGBTQ and gender diverse students in schools while seemingly powerful people, like administrators, policy makers, or more experienced educators, would not. These wonderings propelled the project that is the focus of this book.

With respect to the project this book represents in particular, we were driven by our questions about why people in and around schools sometimes step up, and other times do not, as or on behalf of LGBTQ and gender diverse students. Why would teachers fail to intervene when a homophobic or negative comment about gender expression was said in their presence? Why on earth would they make such a comment themselves? These questions evolved into our research questions:

- What do teachers, students, their families, administrators, and other school personnel say about their experiences with advocacy for LGBTQ and gender diverse people in schools?
- In the stories they tell, when, where, how, and under what conditions do they understand themselves as experiencing support as LGBTQ and gender diverse people and/or supporting LGBTQ and gender diverse people in schools or not?

To answer these, we wanted more perspectives than our own, maybe people who were a little more ambivalent about how to navigate tensions created by homophobia and transphobia. We were used to gathering one another's stories in our monthly meetings, but we wanted the stories of other teachers who were not, necessarily, interested in making a long-term commitment to a teacher-inquiry group. Plus, we wanted stories of people besides teachers, such as students, parents, and administrators, and their participation in our teacher inquiry group would not even make sense. We wanted the stories of the students and parents with whom we shared friendships and the stories of teachers and administrators with whom we worked. We wanted to know more about these people and their work to inform our own but also to inform the work more broadly speaking. That is, we wanted to know their stories to inform how all stakeholders might work together to interrupt homophobia, heteronormativity, transphobia, and cisnormativity in classrooms and schools.

The Project

So, knowing the challenges LGBTQ and gender diverse youth experience in schools and striving to engage in humanizing research with the goal of making schools better for these young people, we engaged in a study different than any we had ever done before. Instead of inquiring into our own individual classrooms, as teacher researchers, and exploring how we might improve the lives of LGBTQ and gender diverse students through our curricula and pedagogy, as we did in our earlier book, this time we turned outward. We turned to students and parents, teachers and administrators, as well as other school personnel. We asked how they advocate for LGBTQ and gender diverse people in schools. We asked them when, where, how, and under what conditions they understand themselves as stepping up on behalf of LGBTQ and gender diverse people or not. We asked them, and, in our monthly meetings and through our writing and reflecting, we asked ourselves. In other words, this turn outward also required that we turn toward one another, as members of an inquiry group. These turns marked a significant investigatory and methodological shift in our work and required us to engage in more concerted and systematic data gathering, analysis, theorizing, and writing.

After collectively planning our new project in the autumn of 2012, the following spring we were funded to conduct the interviews that we imagined doing.[4] And, although all of us engaged in collecting interviews in different community spheres, for our initial analysis and writing, we divided the work according to our interests and backgrounds. Likewise, because of their positions as high school teachers working in a variety of spaces and places, including suburban, rural, and urban districts, as well as parochial and STEM-focused schools, Ryan, Dorothy, Kim, and Megan focused on teachers. Courtney and Jenell focused on students, since both were, at the time, actively leading their high school's GSA and had worked in several different schools, always in roles that supported LGBTQ and gender diverse students. Because of their positions as out, queer mothers of school-age children, Mollie and Lane focused on LGBTQ families. And, Jill and Caroline focused on school administrators and other non-instructional personnel, including coaches, counselors, social workers, and librarians, because of their time spent in administrative roles and their access to superintendents, principals, and other school leaders. Although each of us focused on one set of stakeholders, we sometimes interviewed people who represented other sets because we knew them better. Moreover, several other Pink TIGers beyond the authors of this book interviewed one or two other people[5] to contribute to these clusters of stakeholders.

There was so much data that it was tempting just to focus on these interviews in isolation, to forget their context or to disregard the fact that we had been working together in our teacher inquiry group for nine years before we conducted these interviews, and that in many cases we had been working in schools alongside and with the people we interviewed over the course of years as well. Had we done so, this project would be more solidly located with Brofenbrenner and Harding in that we focused on children, or, more specifically LGBTQ and gender diverse students and students who have same-gender or gender queer parents, in the contexts of their schools, homes, and communities; and we solicited multiple perspectives to inform our understandings of these students' experiences in schools. This is not, however, where we landed.

Instead, we continued our analysis at our monthly meetings across the next two years. We analyzed these data, wrote about what we were seeing in them, and then brought these findings to the group to contextualize them with our experiences with the people speaking in them and with our own experiences in these schools and communities. As such, we drew on the depth of our experiences and the breadth of the people we know, particularly those we interviewed—teachers, students, parents, administrators, among other stakeholders. It was when considering these interviews in the context of the teacher inquiry group and, more broadly, of each of our teacherly lives that our project can be understood as humanizing, striving to contribute to "solutions that support equality . . . in the lives of the young people and communities we learn from" (Paris & Winn, 2014, p. xix). And it is for these reasons that here, in this book, we immerse their stories in our own to offer insights about how we, all of us, might work together to make classrooms and schools better for all people, including but not limited to those who embody sexual identities and gender expressions beyond heterosexual hegemony.

Blind Spots

Although we brought to this inquiry a wide range of rich experiences, we still had some blind spots. These blind spots were tied to our privileges. We conceptualize privileges drawing on Ahmed (2013), who states,

> I think of social privilege as *an energy saving device*: less effort is required to pass through [an institution for bodies that fit]. For other some bodies so much more effort is required to get through, to stand up; to stay standing [emphasis in original].

Privileges, thus, might be defined by gender, sexuality, race, class, among many other identities.

With respect to us, as Pink TIGers and authors of this book, all of us are cisgender, with one of us identifying as a man. Most of us are straight; two of us identify as queer, and one as bisexual. Most of us are white and middle-class; only one of us identifies as a person of color, and she identifies as Nigerian and Black American. Our privileges, whether defined in terms of gender, sexuality, race, or any number of aspects of our identities, limited our insights. Castagno (2008) notes, with respect to race,

> white educators possess a strong desire for comfort and ideological safety within their classrooms and the school walls. White educators also tend to hold a shared allegiance to the status quo, presumably because it generally works for us. The sum total of these patterns is that race is not part of the accepted or expected discourse.
>
> (p. 315)

All of this is to say that we know our identities mattered as we engaged in our interviews with students, parents, administrators, and other educators, and we know that the identities of those we interviewed mattered too. If we were to understand how people in schools worked for queer students (or not), we needed to attend to our identities including and beyond sexual and gender identity. In short, we needed to attend to sexuality and gender not as isolated phenomena but to consider the interrelations among sexual, gender, racialized, and classed identities. Commonly, Black feminist (e.g., Collins, 1990; Crenshaw, 1991), queer of color (e.g., Cohen, 1997; Muñoz, 1999), and other scholars have used the terminology of intersectionality to refer to this perspective, as we do throughout this book. At the same time, we also recognize that others have troubled the metaphor of intersections by pointing out its limitations (e.g., Lugones, 2003), arguing that for identities to intersect, they must first be separate, which they never are. Taking up these perspectives, we attempted to pay attention to the interrelations among identities and the significance of these interrelations. Doing so helped us to notice exclusions and oppressions in the views of our participants (and ourselves). However, heeding Castagno's words, we acknowledge the possibility that the power and privilege that accompanied our whiteness, and privilege more broadly, likely shaped and even limited what our participants said to us and what we were able to hear from them.

Initially, we found it challenging to examine how intersections of race and class, with gender and sexuality, figured in the data we gathered. In part, this had to do with our participants. The majority of the people we interviewed – teachers, students, parents, administrators, and other educators—were white. This is not to say that participants only spoke about their own raced, classed, and gendered identities; of course they did not. And, this is not to say that their particular identities did not matter; of course they did. However, when most participants spoke about identities, their own or others, they did so in non-intersectional ways whether talking about themselves, their students, or their colleagues. Some people spoke about sexual identity but did not connect this at all to gender expression or gender identity. Similarly, when people spoke about race and class, they typically did so in isolation from sexual identity, gender expression, or gender identity. Indeed, these perspectives reinforce "ideologies of discreteness" (Ferguson, 2004, p. 4) and help reproduce the status quo of intersecting oppressions through masking these interrelations. And by and large, most people did not speak about race or class at all. As noted above, we know that part of this silence around race and class rests on us. Our shared interview questions did not ask participants about either race or class, directly, and often we did not probe for information on these. Moreover, we know that our positions in the process mattered and may have even stifled or silenced how participants spoke to us about gender, race, class, and sexual identity. As Jorgenson (2011) notes,

> participants' orientations to our research questions are shaped by their constructions of us. These constructions are often not revealed through anything explicitly said, but through what is not said or what is written 'between the lines,' in the research context or subtext as a whole.
>
> *(pp. 115–116)*

Our class status and especially our whiteness, then, in interviewing mostly white participants created a racialized subtext against which our elicitations around gender and sexuality must be read. With this in mind, we analyzed these interviews not only to look for explicit comments about race and class relative to sexuality and gender but also for instances of silencing around these issues through what Castagno (2008) calls "coded language" (p. 315) and citing Pollock (2004), "'color muteness' through 'the purposeful silencing of race words'" (p. 318). In these ways, we strived to check and recheck our blind spots and thus to be responsible researchers and educators.

Theories Undergirding the Project

It might be worth taking a moment to consider, too, some of the theories that undergird the work we do in this book. Here, we show you, as readers, how our thinking and theorizing have changed over time and the challenging reading and intense thinking we did to develop our ideas. We will also make explicit the place that theory holds in shaping both our research and our practice as teachers in K-12 and university settings.

Because of our interest in understanding how people in different spheres might impact the experiences of LGBTQ and gender diverse youth in schools, including parents, family members, peers, and educators, we initially turned to the work of Bronfenbrenner (1976) as a way to make sense of this study and our data. He offers an ecological systems theory of human development, which foregrounds the influence of the child's surroundings on them, including the context of schools. He conceptualizes these systems as five concentric circles: the child is nested inside of the family, for example, which is nested inside of neighbors and extended family, again, as examples, which are nested inside of cultural attitudes and ideologies, which are nested inside of time. This model was initially useful to us in that it draws attention to social and cultural contexts and recognizes differences in the spheres of influence that a person encounters over time. We also see it as important, because it is the theoretical model that is most often used to understand bullying in schools, and we know that LGBTQ and gender diverse youth are among the most bullied and harassed students in schools (Kosciw, et al., 2016; Swearer, Espelage, Vaillancourt, & Hymel, 2010).

That said, we also believe that it is limited in that it suggests that each "system" is separate; that is, the model accounts for the influence of each system on the individual, but not on the ways that ecological systems, themselves, overlap and influence one another. We also noticed that, in the context of work on bullying, the model focuses on "environmental conditions" that may either encourage or inhibit bullying. Additionally, the model joins these conditions with psychological factors, which locate the problems of bullying in either internalizing behaviors, that is, bullying behavior that may result in or be triggered by issues of depression or anxiety. Externalizing behaviors are also at play—that is, bullying behavior that may result in or be triggered by lower levels of school belonging or increased issues related to school misconduct (Swearer et al., 2010). For us, however, none of these fully explains or captures what we have seen or experienced in our work with LGBTQ and gender diverse people in or outside of schools. As Espelage (2014) notes, "although more comprehensive studies of the ecological model are emerging in the bully research literature, considerable efforts need to be made to conduct investigations that consider the complex interactions *within and across the ecological systems*" (p. 261, our emphasis added). Knowing that much of the discussion of LGBTQ and gender-creative young people in schools has been circumscribed by the discourse of "bullying," without naming or getting to the heart of the experiences of these particular students, we sought out theories to help us breakdown and destabilize structural theories, such as Bronfenbrenner's, and to account for the specific experiences of LGBTQ and gender diverse youth in schools.

We understand that knowledge grows from and is shaped by different social and cultural situations and places, and Bronfenbrenner's theory accounts for this to some extent. However, through our personal experiences, our research, and our teaching, we know that groups on the margins—including youth, sexual minorities, trans people, women, and people of color, among others—are often situated in ways that make them aware of inequities and oppression and better able to question norms. Given this, we believe that research, especially research that investigates questions of power and privilege, should take viewpoints from groups in these places as their starting point. As a developmental theory, Brofenbrenner's model assumes the child is at the center of the systems, which in some ways, aligns with our goal of centering groups on the margins. In our work with parents of queer families, however, we understand that sometimes, it is the parent, who may be marginalized and needs to be centered. Likewise, our experiences have shown us that if we focus solely on the child, we may miss the complexity and importance of overlapping and interacting systems and the experiences of people around the child. Reading and drawing on the work of Harding (1993) and Collins (1990) allowed us to address the importance of perspective and our desire to center different people from different groups at different times. But we continued to struggle with how to understand the complexity and importance of overlapping systems.

What happens when there is no real, clear center? Neither Bronfenbrenner nor Harding helped us to fully make sense of the overlaps and intersections in how we understood the experiences of LGBTQ and gender diverse students in schools, their agency, as well as the power of people who seemingly work for or against them. Foucault's (1995) work reminded us that, "the most intense point of a life, the point where its energy is concentrated, is where it comes against power, struggles with it, attempts to use its forces, and to evade its traps" (p. 162). This notion appealed to us. It suggested movement across systems and through time that resonated with the complex situations we had experienced or were seeing in our data. We discussed how many of us had experienced shifts, over time, in how we thought about our activism as moving from a stance of working *against cisheterosexism and cisheteronormativity* to, instead, *working for or on behalf of queer youth and communities*. Mollie suggested that the theories of Deleuze and Guattari (1987) might offer us a way to think about these shifts and this movement.

Deleuze and Guattari understand the world and the ways that people act, or can act, in it in terms of invisible "lines." Some of these are "lines of force," which aim to keep people acting in ways that are expected, taken-for-granted, or "normal." These invisible lines of force act on all of us, every day, at times even to our detriment. So, consider, for example, the practice of dividing students into two groups based on gender: boys and girls. This practice happens both for pedagogical purposes, like a quick and easy way to get students into groups, and for practical purposes, like getting students to restrooms or managing behavior in lunchrooms or on busses. This practice, though, is detrimental to students who identify as a gender different than the one listed on their birth certificate or suggested by the first name listed on the school's roster.

Sometimes, though, when these invisible "lines of force" cross, "lines of flight" emerge. For Deleuze and Guattari, intersecting lines of force and the resulting lines of flight are the points where we might access "vitalism," which Deleuze conceptualizes as, "the joy of wanting to destroy whatever mutilates life" (p. 85). So, to return to the practice of dividing students into groups of boys and girls, we might see "vitalism" when a child moves to the group with which they identify rather than the one the teacher and peers expect, or they stand in between the two groups, or refuse to get in one group or another. Or, we might see it when a teacher chooses to NOT divide students into groups of boys and girls, even when this is the expected and accepted school practice. The concept of vitalism, thus, resonated with many of us, suggesting a stance of working "for" versus "against." Further, Deleuze offered us the concept of "the fold" as one place from which to trouble tensions among systems and perspectives. As Atkinson (2001) defines it, the fold is "a place of coexistence for multiple and conflicting identities" (p. 309). However, as she notes, it is not an obvious space for change, writing

> this proposal that I would live in the slash, or the hyphen, or the fold, makes me feel very small indeed, and virtually invisible. Folds are where little things get lost, or where unwanted creatures, like moths, hide until they are shaken out. To escape from this feeling, and to see this place as a place of empowerment and discovery, I need a new image of the fold, as a sort of magical doorway into a world of infinite possibilities.
>
> *(Atkinson, 2001, p. 311)*

So, for the child who moves to the group that is aligned with their experienced rather than assigned gender and the child who rejects such categorization entirely, "the fold" could be one classroom, it could be our classrooms. As such, we were intrigued by this understanding of a fold as an empowering place to trouble tensions even as it is also a place of feeling lost and unwanted. As teachers advocating for real change in the lives of the LGBTQ and gender diverse students with whom we work and about whom we care, this seemed to capture the joy and vitalism of working *for* queer youth while simultaneously capturing the loneliness we sometimes feel working *against* hate in places that are so persistently heteronormative and homophobic, such as schools. While Deleuze helped us better understand these forces in our work, and the feelings that they conjured, the theoretical construct of the fold felt abstracted from our daily experiences with young people.

Seeking a way to center the perspectives of LGBTQ and gender diverse youth in our work, recognizing both their agency and the powerful forces and individual people working for and at times against them, we turned to a humanizing paradigm. A humanizing paradigm offers a way of teaching, researching, and being in the world that provokes us not only to center the perspectives of people on the margins, but also to "take as a starting point the humanity and dignity of all people" (Winn, 2014, p. 251) and, in doing so, to further our

> understanding[s] not only of how inequality happens across multiple communities and from multiple perspectives, but also how we can be part of solutions that support equality within our research [and teaching] practices and in the lives of the young people and communities we learn from.
> *(Paris & Winn, 2014, p. xix)*

Humanizing provided a nexus point for our prior theorizing, and added the critical need we felt to not only account for our work *against* hatred and *for* justice, but as a reminder that all of this work has real consequences for real people. This theoretical perspective requires that we continuously face decisions that challenge us to be parts of solutions in our research and teaching, and more broadly, by acting, reacting, and sometimes even failing to act in communities, with and on behalf of young people, always toward the goal of equity. Each decision provides us with an opportunity to research, teach, and be more (or less) humanizing. As a group, the Pink TIGers strove to be more humanizing, in our teaching, our research, and our lives more broadly speaking. It is this striving that served as the foundation of our data collection.

Contexts

You will notice, as you read the book, that several school contexts get featured extensively whereas others play less developed roles in the book. For those more prominent schools, we introduce them here. The others are described as you encounter them throughout the book.

Guthrie was a K-8 lottery school in an urban school district. All students in the district could attempt to lottery in, but there was always more of a demand than the school could accommodate. The student population was economically, racially, and ethnically diverse. The school also had a higher percentage of out LGBTQ parents with children who attended than most schools in the district. Teachers in the school strove to create engaging and authentic learning opportunities by drawing on students' interests as well as the district's curriculum. This child-centered approach also manifested itself in informal interactions between teachers and students. For example, most teachers encouraged students to address them by their first names. Classroom spaces were flexible, consisting of tables and movable furniture instead of rows of desks. Children were taught to be accountable for their learning and to self-advocate. In the early grades, teachers from general education classrooms collaborated with music, dance, and, visual arts teachers around thematic units to increase students' depth of learning and encourage student engagement. Parental involvement was active and strong at Guthrie.

In the same district but a different neighborhood, located north of downtown, Mount Jeffrey High School was on a large campus that it shared with a middle school and a career center. It was a magnet school for performing and visual arts, though students were not required to audition to get in; students entered the school through three avenues: a city-wide lottery, auditions, and a school-based feeder pattern. While the physical campus was large, the high school student body was only around 700 students. Most students in the school were economically disadvantaged. Because of the arts-focused curriculum, the school had a reputation for being a "safe" space for "artsy" students to attend. The school was also a safe haven for students who might not want to attend their own high schools for a variety of reasons including safety and academics. The climate for LGBTQ students was accepting, though there had been both adults and students who had not supported LGBTQ students. It was not unusual to see same-gender couples holding hands on campus, and it was also not unusual for GSA members to report incidents of name-calling and bullying.

Century was a small, early college high school with an enrollment of 400 students (9–12). When it originally opened, approximately 50% of the seats were filled by students in the same district as Guthrie and Mount Jeffrey, and the remaining seats were filled by students from all districts located in the same central Ohio county. However, more recently, the school was designated as a STEM Academy, and as such, admission to the school was open to any student in the state, with seats no longer reserved for students from specific districts. Student applicants were required to submit an essay and participate in an interview in order to be eligible for admission, via lottery. Entrance into the lottery was non-selective; any student could complete an application, regardless of academic standing. Century's student body was racially and economically diverse, with 58% identified as white, 28% as Black, 8% as Asian, and 8% as multiple ethnicities. 30% of the student body was economically disadvantaged. Century courses were taught in 90-minute block periods every day, so a year's worth of credit might be earned each semester. Students could therefore complete their requisite high school graduation requirements in two years. Century used a mastery system where students were required to earn 90% or higher in a course before moving on to the next in the sequence. After attaining most of their high school credits, students could choose to "gateway" in order to begin college coursework at the local university with a cohort of peers under the guidance and support of a Century teacher. During their gateway, students gave a presentation documenting how they had accomplished the "Century habits of mind" and demonstrating their maturity and readiness to take college courses. Century has historically had a 100% graduation rate. At times, the school has had a GSA, depending on student interest.

Williams High School was a mid-sized neighborhood high school of about 1,500 students located in a semi-rural town of a little over 35,000 people. Historically, agriculture was important to the town and continues to be an important part of life for a small sector of the students. More recently, there had been a revitalization in the town's historical downtown district along with growth in suburban style housing, attracting more middle class and professional families, with many professional families being connected to a small university located only a few minutes from the high school. The town also had a strong religious tradition, with a Christian seminary nearby. Christian churches continued to play an important role in the social and political life of the town, with many students participating in youth groups and other faith-based activities. With these different dimensions of the town's population, the school's social geography tended to be fairly segregated along lines of social class and race, mirroring the segregation in the town's physical geography. For instance, students who self-enrolled in honors and Advanced Placement courses tended to be predominantly white youth from middle class and professional families. They also were frequently—although not exclusively—the most active and visible students in school-sanctioned activities such as drama productions, homecoming court, and certain athletic activities. Students who self-enrolled or who school personnel enrolled in classes that were not advanced or who became involved in alternative or credit recovery programs tended to come from working class or poor families, with a higher percentage of rural families and students of color being represented than in the honors and AP programs. The school's environment had gradually changed for LGBTQ youth over the past decade. At the invitation of the high school, two teachers had co-founded a Gay–Straight Alliance (GSA) in 2007. At first, this group was highly visible in the school and well attended, serving as a touchstone for many LGB youth who had previously not connected with adults or activities in the school. However, after several years, the general environment of the school became less homophobic, although still remaining heteronormative and transphobic. Interest and attendance in the GSA declined at the same time as a lesbian couple ran for homecoming court and many students challenged the heterosexist framing of a Sadie Hawkins dance, suggesting a safer and more accepting environment for some LGB youth. For instance, lesbian women couples were commonly seen in the hallways holding hands or attending school dances together. However, few gay men were out at the school, with no gay men publicly dating each other. Similarly, trans youth were not out to the student body or administration but only to a trusted teacher or two. So, while the school environment for some LGBTQ youth had improved, these changes were uneven.

Hartville was a large, suburban, historically conservative district that had four middle schools and three high schools. It has a diverse population of students who come from a wide range of ethnic and socioeconomic backgrounds. Two of the high schools have strong, well-attended Gay–Straight Alliances and high visibility for LGBTQ students, teachers, and events such as Day of Silence, same-gender couples at prom, and photos of same-gender partners and spouses prominently displayed in work spaces. However, the overall culture of the district was heteronormative and homophobic incidents, while on the decline, were not entirely uncommon. Sometimes these incidents were acknowledged and addressed, sometimes they were not. With the exception of discussions related to President Obama's 2016 Executive Order that schools must provide equal access to formerly sex-segregated facilities like bathrooms and locker rooms, support for LGBTQ issues and students came largely from student, teacher, and staff initiatives and overall had been met with resistance from district administration. Despite this, LGBTQ students and teachers and their allies continued to find ways to make loud, proud, and fierce progress in Hartville.

You will encounter these particular schools and districts often throughout this book. They do not, however, serve as the organizational structure for the book. Instead, our analytic and crosscutting themes do. Chapters 2 and 3 explore the ways teachers can step up for LGBTQ and gender diverse students by grappling with possibilities and impossibilities, in Chapter 2, and understanding impact, knowledge, and vulnerability, in Chapter 3. The fourth chapter examines the ways teachers can work with queer families in schools. The fifth chapter dives into ways teachers can work with LGBTQ and gender diverse students in their advocacy efforts. The sixth chapter considers curriculum as a way teachers and students can work together in classrooms to combat homophobia and transphobia and interrogate heteronormativity and cisnormativity. Chapter 7 looks at how teachers can work with queer families and administrators, respectively, in this effort. Finally, in the eighth chapter, we challenge teachers to choose to act, or, in other words, to step up.

Notes

1 When we use "we," we mean the contributors to this book.
2 We know that since 2004, the meaning of the acronym GSA has changed. Although some of the groups facilitated by Pink TIGer teachers continue to understand GSA as "Gay–Straight Alliance," others now understand GSA in their school's context to mean "Genders and Sexualities Alliance." Throughout this book, we use the acronym GSA to stand for either of these.

3 When we use names of both people and places, we use pseudonyms. The exception to this rule are Pink TIGers.
4 We are grateful for the American Educational Research Association's (AERA) Educational Research Service Projects (ERSP) and The Ohio State University's Office of Diversity and Inclusion for supporting this portion of our project.
5 Gail Griffith and Liesa Klyn were Pink TIGers who conducted interviews but elected not to contribute to the writing of the book.

2
STEPPING UP AS TEACHERS

Seeing Possibilities in Teaching and Activism

What does it mean to step up as a teacher? What does it mean to step up for sexual and gender diversity? And, central to our work and the focus of this book, what does it mean to be a teacher who steps up in these ways in schools? The first question may seem easy. To many, to step up simply means to take action when they see a need or opportunity or when they are committed to a particular value. For many teachers, this is simply the act of teaching. Teachers act to support students in learning academic knowledge and skills. Occasionally, opportunities arise to teach in response to a student's question or something that happens unexpectedly. These "teachable moments" present opportunities to act educatively. But what about stepping up for social change by taking action for sexual and gender diversity? What about doing this work in schools, classrooms, and lessons? Is this part of teaching? And can you, as readers, imagine such work becoming a part, or a greater part, of your own teaching?

We understand stepping up as synonymous with activism. We draw on Mollie's previous work to define activism as "taking actions aligned with values that result in [cultural,] social and/or political change" (Blackburn, 2014, p. 2). Every day, we see needs and opportunities in schools to support LGBTQ and gender diverse youth in ways both large and small, in other words, to be activists. However, we recognize that you, as readers, might understand your work differently. Many of us haven't always seen teaching or activism in these ways, and learning to be activists and see activism in our teaching is an ongoing process (Blackburn, 2014; Blackburn, 2010). We have grappled with the tensions at the junctures of teaching and activism, with actions and decisions that feel possible in one moment and impossible in the next.

In this chapter, we explore ways teachers conceptualized two phenomena central to this book and our teacher inquiry group: teaching and activism. For the most part, teachers we interviewed didn't explicitly name their definitions of teaching or activism as factors that would limit or facilitate their efforts to step up to support sexual and gender diversity. Typically, neither did Pink TIGers explicitly discuss these ideas in monthly meetings. However, when we examined the interview data and reflected on our experiences working in schools with (and sometimes against) other educators, we discovered important differences in our fundamental assumptions about what counted as teaching and activism and the relationship between the two. Among the teachers we interviewed, their definitions of teaching and activism shaped what they perceived to be (im)possible when they considered supporting LGBTQ people. Moreover, these understandings also shaped how they perceived the impact, knowledge, and vulnerability involved in their choices, concepts that we explore in Chapter 3.

Here, we first discuss how the teachers defined teaching and activism. We then examine the interplay between each and how it affected their decisions to support LGBTQ and gender diverse youth. Finally, we close by reflecting on how these definitions of teaching and activism might help you to consider actions you might take to step up and cultivate your own stance as a teacher-activist/activist-teacher.

Definitions of Teaching

Across our interviews, teachers held diverse definitions of teaching and of what they believed counted, or didn't, as teaching. Some teachers defined teaching as the transmission of content-area knowledge and skills, implying that any deviations were a distraction from and in tension with their job responsibilities. Other teachers included a broader range of activities and responsibilities such as shaping the life trajectory of youth or educating about moral or civic responsibility. Underlying each perspective were teachers' notions of who possessed the authority to determine what could and should count as teaching

Staying within the official academic curriculum. Some teachers expressed that, for them, teaching entailed staying within content-area knowledge and skills, a view that was especially true for secondary teachers. State content-area standards, high-stakes testing, district curriculum guides, and lesson plans guided their actions as teachers. Anything outside these parameters didn't count as teaching. It's not that these teachers viewed things beyond official academics as unimportant. Many named a range of actions as being valuable for social change with respect to sexual and gender diversity in schools. For them, however, these other things did not count as teaching. When teachers characterized teaching this way, they described the stakes of their decisions to be about adding to or detracting from academic teaching and learning, which translated to doing or not doing their job and could subsequently increase or decrease individual vulnerability. These teachers experienced a tension between actions they saw as important and worthwhile, such as working against homophobia, and actions they felt were their obligations, such as completing the planned lesson for the day. Covering the given curriculum was paramount and activism held the potential to take teachers and students off-track.

Dave, an experienced English teacher at Williams High School and a straight, white, cisgender man, returned to this tension repeatedly during his interview. He described his efforts to support LGBTQ people in schools as contingent and varied. When discussing how he responded to students' homophobic behaviors during class, he explained:

> Obviously every situation is different, and I think in some ways it's kind of feeling your way through, if we're having a full class discussion, you can, I feel like you can get a sense of whether it's something that's going to take us completely off track and I guess the question becomes, is it worth possibly disrupting the learning for everyone, and maybe having a difficult time getting back to that, to make a point on this one comment or this one item, or is it better to say, "I want you [a student expressing homophobia] to talk to me, come see me after class" and just sort of redirect. And I think it's on a case-by-case basis.

Notice he didn't consider action vs. inaction. Rather, he addressed homophobia immediately, seeking the most productive use of instructional time, which aligned with his definition of teaching as covering subject-area content. He weighed the potential benefits of interrupting homophobia in ways that might educate the entire class against the potential losses of interrupting academic focus, time-on-task, and covering the official curriculum. Dave's decision to point out and silence one student's remarks provided some support to LGBTQ students while allowing him to remain consistent with his definition of teaching. For Dave, academic knowledge was privileged and sanctioned as teaching, whereas knowledge about sexual identity, gender expression, hurt, and responsibility to each other were relevant only in relation to how it might or might not disrupt the official curriculum. While he expressed valuing both, he missed an opportunity to educate students about the latter.

Dave's perspective reflected that of other teachers we interviewed, who, like Dave, believed that supporting LGBTQ and gender diverse youth was important work but not always congruent with the sanctioned, academic work of teaching. Justin, for instance, another straight, white, cisgender man who taught English at Williams, stated that curbing homophobic behavior was important and something he regularly "zapped" in his classroom by shutting down such talk. Spending more time on these issues:

although that's an important conversation to have, we might have to teach the use of semi-colons today, and you know, we make a judgment call of, of when a kid is looking at you, and you're having that con- is he receptive to what you're about to say. If not? Maybe it's time just to go, "Because I said so, and you'll figure it out later."

Justin suggested that conveying content, like semi-colons, was an obligatory part of his job as a teacher. Actively teaching against homophobia, while "important," was not his job, particularly if a student was not open to learning about the impact of their words on others.

A number of interviewed teachers shared the perspective that only delivering academic content counted as teaching. They implicitly expressed that administrators, curriculum directors, those who wrote the standards and created the tests, and community members—not teachers—had the authority to define teaching, so teachers couldn't deviate from their obligations to meet academic expectations.

Shaping youth as future community members. Other teachers defined teaching more expansively to include elements such as influencing the moral and political consciousness of youth as well as conveying content area knowledge and skills. For them, teaching included building relationships, teaching and learning about sexual and gender diversity, exploring the moral perspectives, and intervening educatively in hateful or oppressive interactions. Rather than distinguishing between covering the official curriculum as requisite and working for social change as important, but optional, these teachers expressed tensions in figuring out ways that their teaching could be used as a vehicle for social change while also including content-area knowledge and other traditional academic concerns. The subsequent tensions were about impact, knowledge, and vulnerability.

James, another Williams teacher, represents this perspective well. A straight, white, cisgender man who taught social studies, James usually taught senior-level government and economics courses. He discussed the important role that teachers play in students' lives, characterizing them as adults who shape the life courses of the youth with whom they work. As he defined it, teaching is not only about communicating content-area knowledge but also cultivating caring, thoughtful, and politically engaged citizens (a term that while inviting some youth into dialogue excluded others whose families lived and worked in the community). James also coached a number of sports, including boys' basketball and girls' softball. He understood his coaching and teaching as synonymous. He explained that he included representations of lesbian and gay people in his psychology and government courses by exploring "the psychology of same-sex attraction" and gay rights in relation to the U.S. constitution. He described the importance of LG-inclusive curricula in the following way:

I think that that's an important part of our job. And people that show up and they worry just about their subject and they forget that you have a platform to have a long-term impact on the kids for them, not for you. They're missing the boat on why [teaching] is a powerful job. Because I think, aside from being a parent, there's nobody in society that has a hundred and fifty malleable individuals that you get to see for 45–50 minutes for 180 days. And then they bring in a new batch and then you got it again.

James saw the significance of teaching in the uniqueness and expansiveness of the job. In his view, traditional academic knowledge and skills could seamlessly exist alongside teaching for social change. He explicitly critiqued more narrow definitions of teaching, implying that they foregrounded concerns of adult teachers rather than students. He sought to meet the needs of youth—to have "a long-term impact"—by making decisions for social change. Where public and visible discussions about sexual and gender diversity could detract from the learning for Dave and Justin, they *became* the learning for James.

At the time of the interviews, Dave, Justin, and James had worked in the same high school together for five years, teaching across the hall from each other for several of these years. They were well-liked and respected by other teachers, administrators, students, and families, although the school community generally saw that the three had distinct approaches to their jobs. Their differing definitions of teaching cannot easily be attributed to school context. That fact complicates questions about the (im)possibilities of working for social change regarding sexual and gender diversity. For instance, to what degree did Dave's worries about loss of academic focus reflect what consequences he would, or would not, encounter if he were to step up? School contexts, specifically what counts as teaching, are continually recreated as teachers, administrators, students, and families interact and co-construct the social relationships that we call schooling. We believe that in these continual repetitions there are possibilities for repeating with a difference and generating social change (Butler, 1990; 1993).

The official curriculum, youth lives, and (not) claiming authority. A number of interviewed teachers shared Dave's and Justin's perspective that only sticking to academic content counted as teaching. They implicitly expressed that administrators, curriculum directors, those who wrote the standards and created the tests, and community members—not teachers—had the authority to define teaching. Teachers did not have the authority to deviate from their obligations to meet academic expectations. While these teachers experienced these definitions as real and constraining, they rarely explicitly named the origin of their impression. It's worth comparing these teachers' perspectives about educational stakeholders' expectations with those articulated by those stakeholders we discuss elsewhere in this book.

James emphasized the possibilities of shaping students' lives. He understood authority differently than Dave or Justin. Where Dave and Justin located authority beyond the teacher, James claimed the authority of teachers to define teaching, an authority they shouldn't so easily dismiss. He drew a parallel between teachers and parents, suggesting that both have important, and complementary, decisions to make.

It is tempting to interpret these differences as a simple dichotomy. We instead argue that working for social change with respect to gender and sexual diversity is a complicated, ongoing process, as it involves claims to (not) having authority in order to turn an opportunity into a possibility or even a probability.

Without a doubt, teachers who insisted on staying within the official academic curriculum limited the range of opportunities to step up. Likewise, teachers who characterized teaching as a more robust set of actions opened an expansive array of possibilities for stepping up. However, expanding one's opportunities to strive for social change is not sufficient on its own to actually contributing to such change because an opportunity can be perceived as an impossibility. For teachers to step up, they need to claim the authority to take action when they see opportunities to teach for change and justice. Even expansive definitions of teaching can result in teachers not stepping up when they perceive themselves as lacking authority. In contrast, teachers who claimed authority could use an opportunity to step up for LGBTQ and gender diverse youth. We explore these dynamics by returning to Justin, discussed above, and reflecting on two elementary teachers, Mallory and Trisha.

Teachers often function in numerous roles, so even those with limiting definitions of teaching can be supportive of LGBTQ and gender diverse youth in schools. Recall that, to Justin, teaching meant staying within the official academic curriculum. His priority was to cover English language arts content knowledge such as semi-colons rather than to intervene educatively when students expressed homophobia. However, Justin also coached wrestling at Williams. Consider how, outside the classroom, he was described by Aiden, a passionate member of the wrestling team. She was a white cisgender woman who identified as a lesbian and frequently presented in quite masculine ways, often leading adults in the building to misgender her and even insist that she couldn't be a girl. In many ways, her high school experiences, both with adults and peers, were hard, but this shifted in her senior year. Aiden largely attributed this shift to Justin and described him as her biggest supporter, saying that he impacted her life in ways that other teachers, particularly those who were more generally recognized as "allies" in the school, hadn't, even when they tried. Other queer youth in the school didn't agree and experienced Justin as unsupportive. Nonetheless, Aiden cared deeply about him, was fiercely loyal, and frequently defended him from criticism. Though Justin often disavowed his authority to step up for LGBTQ students in his lessons and classroom, he did claim authority as a coach to step up for Aiden at school.

Mallory was a fourth-year teacher at Guthrie in a combined fourth/fifth grade classroom. White, straight, and a cisgender woman, she described herself as "an ally for sure" in terms of gender and sexual diversity and articulated a rather expansive definition of teaching. In referring to the ways that she understood gender and sexual diversity to be a part of her practices, she explained:

> I kind of feel like my job is to help kids who are either questioning or wondering now or will in the future and also to help grow people who aren't going to have to wonder or question into people who accept other people's wondering and questioning. My job is to take this chunk . . . and grow them to their next step.

Mallory's description of the work of teaching is in many ways similar to James. Both conceptualized teaching as shaping the life trajectories of youth, with Mallory specifically seeking to support young people who were questioning their sexual and/or gender identities and to teach students who weren't questioning to accept others who are. Yet, despite her claims to allyship and her explicitly stated expansive definition of teaching, LGBTQ youth and families in her school experienced her in ways that were ambivalent and mixed. She struggled with understanding non-cisgender people, especially trans and gender fluid parents at her school. She described meeting Elliot, a gender fluid parent of a gender diverse student, and feeling, "intimidated, uncomfortable, unsure with, by, or, or whatever, people whose gender I can't read, and I can't read hers. And I had seen her and honestly, the beard and the breasts. I don't know what to do with that." Mallory asserted that she didn't know or understand and didn't describe trying to learn either, enacting a stance distant from "accept[ing] other people's wondering and questioning," as she hoped her students would come to do.

Like Justin, she was more likely to cede her authority as a teacher to others, which limited the opportunities she saw for stepping up. In describing the ways that she decided to mostly exclude LGBTQ topics in history lessons, she said:

> My job is also to teach American history and Native Americans and so there is not enough time to do everything so I err on the side of what's going to give me the least parental backlash and what's in the actual curriculum and what's necessary and sometimes I feel that okay if we have these conversations I don't need to read a whole book about it.

Mallory named the importance of American and Native American history in her curriculum, highlighting how it's "necessary" and in the "actual curriculum" while LGBTQ topics lacked legitimacy. Moreover, because they lacked legitimacy, she could face pushback from parents, which she sought to avoid (however, we wonder if her concerns about "parental backlash" included parents such as Elliot). So, even as Mallory expressed a much more expansive definition of teaching than Justin, it didn't necessarily result in her stepping up more frequently or more effectively. Despite characterizing it as an integral part of her definition of teaching, she, like Justin, suggested that she frequently relinquished her authority to work for social change.

In contrast with Justin and Mallory, Trisha described her own tensions when working for social change much differently. She asserted her authority within her teaching. Like Mallory, she was a white straight cisgender woman who taught at Guthrie, yet more veteran as she was in her sixteenth year at the school. She understood teaching about "politics kinds of things" as part of her job as a sixth-grade teacher and did not feel constrained to stick with the given curriculum. She described how, "at the beginning of the year I often do a lot of read-alouds that have to do with self-identity kinds of things and so I always include stories that have to do with LGBTQ identity." In these ways, Trisha was clear that her teaching is both about conveying content and addressing the needs and identities of her students. Like James, she intertwined the two. However, even as she did so, she acknowledged that there were tensions in this work. For example, she explained that while she is "an advocate for human and civil rights" she couldn't assume that every young person in her classroom and their family would share her views. She expressed that this could result in "some cognitive dissonance" for students and some "uncomfortable" feelings for parents. In addition to tensions resulting from conflicting school–home values, Trisha explored others. While she sought to teach in ways that supported gender and sexual diversity, she wondered if this was the greatest need at her school and if she needed to focus more on other issues. She said:

> I feel like, in every classroom, these issues should be discussed or you know, part of the curriculum, but I don't necessarily think in our community that it's the greatest need maybe compared to . . . race, class just exceptions of people. I mean, our school is . . . the kings and queens of saying we accept everybody, but we don't. You know? So people are hurt all the time. I mean, I'm not saying we can keep people from hurting each other, but I think empathy building is the key to all of it, so when I step back from it, I think, that's what I feel like our total focus should be and within that . . . I feel comfortable with [sexual and gender diversity] being part of an umbrella and even if that is watering it down, I think that that is okay, that's pragmatic, because we have a lot of things we have to deal with, we can't just be dealing with LGBT and I wouldn't think that'd be right.

Trisha claimed her authority to decide what teaching means for her and to include content as well as moral, emotional, and civic knowledge as part of her work. She did not cede her authority to others, even to parents or students who might not be comfortable with her teaching and values; nor did she presume this work is already happening or unnecessary in her school. Rather, she included sexual and gender diversity as part of her class, but not over and above or to the exclusion of other "things we have to deal with." It's clear, however, that she means other kinds of human interactions and needs, not other required academic content. She suggested that this approach might be "watering it down," but we disagree. Rather than diluting the intensity of her work, she articulated that she strived to make it more responsive to the needs of her community, considering sexuality and gender in their intersections with and relations to other identity markers such as race and class. In this, she understood and took responsibility for her decisions, maintaining rather than refusing her own authority as a teacher, curriculum-maker, pedagogue, and caring adult in the lives of young people.

Justin, Mallory, and Trisha had differing definitions of teaching and authority, which resulted in them (not) acting to support gender and sexual diversity in very different ways. Importantly, a teacher's definition of teaching impacted what opportunities for stepping up that a teacher saw as existing; however, their perceptions of their own (lack of) authority were equally significant. Claiming authority helped teachers shift from merely noticing opportunities to using opportunities to act for social change. We encourage teachers to take up expansive definitions of the practice of teaching that include academic curricula along with sociopolitical and moral dimensions. The range of opportunities provided by such definitions become more possible, even probable, when teachers claim rather than disavow their professional, intellectual, and moral authority.

Definitions of Activism

Similar to teachers' differing definitions of teaching, teachers' definitions of activism also differed. In this section, we employ the definition of activism as taking actions aligned with values resulting in cultural, political, and/or social change to examine how teachers described taking these actions and what got to count as such an action, considering the stakes and tensions in these definitions.

Focusing on individuals. Some teachers characterized activism as actions focused on individual people. Stephen, a straight, white, cisgender man who taught social studies and coached at a Hartville High School, talked about his focus on individual youth, emphasizing their unique qualities without contextualizing them within broader patterns of oppression. He described these students as kind, smart, and loving, whose reactions to people who disrupted traditional gender roles or binary gender expressions were grounded not in hatred, but in curiosity. He explained that:

> Even when the teams show up in the gym with a male cheerleader, our kids are great. And they're polite. And they're nice. They don't heckle, and they don't say anything. And they don't—and they're not rude, but there's just that, you know, hushed murmur. Where, you know, like—and maybe they haven't seen it before . . . So, it's not necessarily a mean thing. It might just be an inquisitive thing.

Stephen assumed that all of his students were always part of privileged groups such as white, straight, and cisgender. He failed to consider what it might have been like for this cheerleader to show up to participate in a sporting event only to find that their gender expression had become the event, a spectacle for others. Similarly, as he implicitly characterized all of his students as always straight and cisgender, he failed to consider what it might be like for a student on his own team who might want to be like the "male cheerleader"—who in this discussion seems to symbolize some disruption of gender or sexual identity norms—yet observed the "hushed murmur" and feared being stigmatized and policed in a similar way.

For Stephen, his kids had individual characteristics—they're great, polite, and nice—that meant that their actions had a certain innocence and thus were innocuous. Encounters with people such as a "male cheerleader" provided opportunities to be inquisitive and gain information that could ameliorate previous ignorance. Elsewhere in his interview, Stephen explained that he thought this inquisitiveness "leads [students] to be more understanding because they've questioned and they've asked and they've gotten the answers they need, so they're more secure about it." From Stephen's point of view, the stakes in activism involved few tensions. Students—meaning privileged students—were inherently good people who needed opportunities to have their mistakes pointed out or to gain information that would smoothly lead to social change, or at least changes in their outward behavior.

Focusing on structures and patterns. When teachers defined activism beyond the confines of individual people, they considered structural or systemic patterns of oppression and marginalization across time and space. They looked to change not only individuals in this system but also the system itself. These teachers didn't characterize ignorance of sexual and gender diversity by straight cisgender youth as innocuous. Instead, they viewed it as a manifestation of schooling contexts that were cisheteronormative if not homophobic and transphobic. Students could be kind, polite, nice, great, and so forth while simultaneously perpetuating hatred, exclusion, harm, oppression, and other normative and phobic valences. Where individual definitions of activism commonly centered questions of intentions or the "goodness" of a student or students, structural definitions more often emphasized the patterned effects of the actions of students and educators in a school.

Anna discussed her structural understanding of activism in reference to her first year of teaching when she co-advised her school's Gay–Straight Alliance (GSA). A straight white cisgender woman who taught English at Williams High School, Anna was perceived by both staff and students as being a vocal and passionate activist for LGBTQ people. She reflected on her first year of co-advising the GSA as follows:

> I was a first-year teacher so I was gung-ho about everything. But we were really gung-ho about the GSA and getting it—which was great, because they needed more visibility because it was so underground. And so that was really good.

Here, Anna focused on the relationship between the GSA and the school. Before she started teaching in the district, there was a form of a GSA where several students met semi-regularly in the office of a guidance counselor after school, unbeknownst to the school as a whole save for a few with insider knowledge. She didn't devalue this individualized work but sought to expand it to create structural change. The previous pattern of the GSA's invisibility was troubling to her. In response, she worked to cultivate more visibility for the GSA rather than keeping it "underground," evaluating the increased public presence as "really good." For Anna, what was at stake in structural activism were the patterns of inclusion and exclusion, of visibility and invisibility, of normalization and marginalization.

Another Williams teacher, Terrence was a straight white cisgender man who taught English and was the faculty advisor for his school's student council. In his school, the student council was in charge of planning and making decisions for all of the dances and related activities such as homecoming week or school spirit week events. He explained how his teacher activism could be focused on changing dominant social structures, precisely because he had a pivotal role leading the system. He said:

> Two lesbian students wanted to run for homecoming king and queen in a culture in which that wasn't previously done or seemingly possible because the language of king and queen sort of disqualified same-sex couples. And so I was excited about the opportunity to try to help the climate of my school grow. Because, because the two girls were willing to, I think, step forward courageously to challenge the system, and because I was—I had a major role, if not in charge of the system, I had a major role in the structure of the system to be able to allow that to happen. It seemed like an exciting opportunity to grow the school.

Rather than denying his complicity in the system of schooling and its exclusions, he claimed his authority to take action to work for social change, which he described as an "exciting opportunity" and one that would result in desirable growth. When two lesbian students challenged the heterosexism inherent in this school tradition, Terrence saw an opportunity to change these structures. As faculty advisor, his decisions constituted the very system he wanted to change. His activism was focused on the school system itself and the culture that the system encouraged. Either way he would act, and the consequences of his actions would either work to reconsolidate and maintain heterosexual hegemony or to subvert and begin to change it. His activism was focused on changing the school system itself and the cultural values intertwined with that system. He pushed back against some of the administration in his school who wanted to change the homecoming rules to prevent the two young women from running together. Terrence resisted, saying that he wanted the school to grow. He said, "Here is an opportunity that other couples have. Why shouldn't [the two lesbian students] be able to have this opportunity as well? This is what it means to be a Williams student."

Against hatred and ignorance. Whether focusing on individual people or social structures, some teachers articulated that activism entailed actions working against something such as hatred or ignorance. One of the Pink TIGers, Caroline, has previously described this teacher approach as anti-work (i.e., anti-hatred, anti-ignorance) (Clark, 2010b). For Justin, the Williams English teacher described earlier, homophobic language was a clear and concrete instance where he could intervene in an attempt to work against hatred, if not ignorance. He stated that students might use language homophobically, insulting another student by saying:

> "You're gay." and I'll say, "Watch your language." Some of them won't even realize what they've done. They'll go, "What'd I say? What'd I say?" And maybe it's one of their peers that have to say, "You just said this!" and maybe then they don't even understand what's wrong with that. So it's a teaching moment. And there are other kids that are like, "Sorry" and they'll fix it right away, and they've got another word they can use, and they can express themselves more clearly in another way.

Similar to Stephen, Justin characterized students—implicitly straight cisgender students—as ignorant or unintentional in their homophobia. He saw such actions as an individual problem and his subsequent response was individualized, pointing out to a student that they used language inappropriately. If their reaction suggested that they didn't understand their mistake, he relied on peers to educate them, calling this a "teaching moment," and working toward clarity of language and expression, and against ignorance if not hatred, in the process. Unlike Stephen, however, his particular choice of the phrase "watch your language" suggests that this anti-approach for him entailed containment of homophobia through self-surveillance for self-protection. As Justin explains it:

> I think it is like anything else you teach. When you show them how it relates to their life, how it might affect them down the road, how you know, if you're calling your buddy a faggot in your social media, just playing around and you think it's pretty harmless, whatever you're using it for, you're calling him weak, you're calling him, you know, a coward, whatever. And you use that term, you know, maybe one day your boss is looking at your social media or somebody else, and you really don't know if you're in that habit, you're going to have to watch your back extra hard, you know? I mean because we can be in a position where it'll come back and zap yah, and maybe cost yah a job, cost yah a friend, cost yah an apology, some embarrassment down the road.

Here, even more so than Stephen, Justin clearly positions himself as working against homophobic language but, ultimately, doing this work in service of his straight, cisgender students so that they would not suffer more extreme consequences, in terms of social and material capital, in the future. While this approach enabled him to address overt and explicit instances of homophobic and potentially transphobic language, and may have offered some immediate protection to LGBTQ students in the moment, it mostly served to teach straight and cisgender students how to protect their privilege and maintain their entitlement in the future, and left heteronormative dimensions of his school context, among other social, cultural, and political factors, unquestioned and unchallenged.

For queerness. Other teachers described activist efforts that were focused on queerness, whether supporting LGBTQ and gender diverse students specifically or opening up space for queerness in their school contexts (on this last point, see Airton, 2013). Anna's work as a first-year teacher advising a GSA focused on LGBTQ and ally students. She discussed how her enthusiasm complemented a need for more visibility. So while her efforts did work against hatred and ignorance, her description of her efforts emphasized the needs and perspectives of GSA youth, a definition of activism that we will call queer-positive in contrast with anti-hatred or anti-ignorance definitions. In another moment in her interview, she described ways that she sought to open up space for queerness in her school through her English classes. She tried to interrupt heteronormativity by teaching ways of reading literature through a queer or gay lens. She said that in her classroom she works to have students:

> Looking at things through [a queer] perspective, or even offering it on material like when we're doing our literary analysis, talking about gender roles or sexual orientation. Looking at it through a gay lens and that sort of thing. Teaching the kids to look at it and just putting it as a listing of things. But then also being overt and obvious when I'm talking about an author's background or Shakespeare or whatever. And saying like, "This is a possibility of where they're coming from on this piece."

While her work in the GSA focused on specific GSA students, her work in her English classroom attempted to cultivate different ways of reading, ones that took up gender and sexuality as explicit categories of analysis and considered gay sexualities, for instance. She tried to teach her students to read through a queer analytic lens, discussed queer sexualities in authors' biographies, and offered students choices to take up these topics when she provided lists of potential topics for assignments. In contrast with Justin who sought to contain homophobic hatred or ignorance via surveillance, Anna attempted to interrogate heteronormativity and open up space for queerness. By having students read the words of the language arts curriculum differently, she strived to have them also read the world differently.

Universalizing experience. Finally, definitions of activism differed in terms of how teachers understood what it meant to be a human being in the world. Some teachers used a universalizing definition where all people were characterized as being fundamentally the same. Other teachers utilized a particularized definition where people were characterized as having important differences while still sharing a common humanity.

Teachers who defined activism via universalism emphasized that all people shared a core set of characteristics. They commonly argued that *all* students had the right to be safe and learn in schools regardless of any particular aspect of their identity. Their activist efforts were similarly universal and general. For example, they stressed open-minded tolerance and acceptance of all people.

Justin's conceptualization of activism represents this perspective. When asked how he included LGBTQ youth in his work, Justin replied:

> I don't think I do it specifically. You know? I just try to create a classroom environment specifically where no student is getting ostracized in anyway, that every student feels free to participate and to learn . . . I don't even know if I'm fully equipped to fight that battle on that sort of stage other than maybe "Hey, we accept all kinds," you know, and the tolerance piece.

Justin didn't intend or know how to step up for LGBTQ youth specifically. He relied on more general definitions of activism where non-dominant and minoritized youth should be tolerated, free to participate, and not ostracized. What was at stake was the *student* identity of LGBTQ and gender diverse students, but their sexual and gender identities were downplayed, if not erased, in emphasizing their student-ness. While some youth such as his wrestler Aiden benefitted from and were thankful for his efforts, this universalizing definition didn't recognize that LGBTQ and gender diverse students might have specific needs, desires, or experiences unlike those of straight and/or cisgender students, which might result in LGBTQ and gender diverse youth needing different and/or additional supports, or that they might have different needs and desires than one another. He regarded all types and categories of difference as essentially the same, interchangeable. This homogenizing perspective resonates with many anti-bullying, safety, and tolerance discourses, which fail to recognize the real state of emergency that bullying poses, particularly for queer students of color (Pritchard, 2013). Justin himself recognized some of the potential limitations of his approach, naming his lack of knowledge in that he wasn't "fully equipped" to participate in other types of activism.

Not all teachers employed universalizing as a way to deny differences. Instead, some teachers tactically used universalizing discourses to justify their activist efforts if they were challenged or questioned. For instance, Anna explained that if she were confronted by an administrator about teaching gay-inclusive lessons, she could respond by saying "Well, we're all here for the kids right?" She would go on to say:

Okay, well, here's the situation: I know I have gay students in my classrooms. Those are the students who never feel included, who are going to drop out of my class, who are not going to score well [on standardized tests because they missed instruction] and have no reason to come to school because they don't feel included. This is why I included that. Do you have any reason to tell me not to include that? Is this keeping anyone from coming to school by me including it? No, it's not . . . This is what I'm doing in order to keep [LGBTQ students] here. So I'm improving our test scores. I'm improving our graduation rate by doing these things.

Through her argument, Anna tactically drew on universalizing discourses to support her activism, using a familiar tool in a new and creative way. To disagree, an administrator would have to maintain a stance that not so subtly implied that the graduation rates, test scores, and daily attendance of students, and specifically LGBTQ students, didn't matter—a stance she implied was unsustainable for any school leader.

Valuing differences. Other teachers defined activism based on the unique experiences of LGBTQ students, considering their differences from other students while still recognizing a common humanity. Using such a definition of activism, teachers explored how they might modify their practices to be more responsive to and supportive of particular LGBTQ and gender diverse youth. Gail, an English and theater teacher and a frequent participant in Pink TIGer meetings, described some of her particularized efforts at activism as a straight, white, cisgender woman. She described various queer-specific efforts that she undertook in her school district. For example, she initiated an in-district workshop for teachers during a summer professional development session. In it, she educated them about LGBTQ-related language and terminology along with offering a series of suggestions for being a better ally. She planned to create a shorter version of the workshop that she could use at building-level staff meetings. She also shared LGBTQ-specific information with her building administration such as Teaching Tolerance's *Bullied* video. Gail's efforts highlighted the particular needs, desires, and experiences of LGBTQ students, understanding they couldn't be recognized by merely emphasizing a universal and shared humanity. The supposedly universal definition of a person masked the normative qualities of the definition, such as its straight, cisgender, and white center.

Relationships Between Teaching and Activism

Just as teachers articulated diverse definitions of teaching and activism, they described the relationships between teaching and activism differently. Some saw them as separate and competing while others saw them as overlapping and complementary. These views and relationships mattered for how students, especially LGBTQ and gender diverse students, were addressed in their teaching and further humanized, or not, through their activism.

Tension and competition. Teachers who defined teaching as limited to content-area knowledge and skills conceptualized activism, whatever their definition, as something separate and distinct from teaching. From this viewpoint, teaching and activism were in tension, even competition, with each other. Prioritizing teaching meant compromising their activism; prioritizing activism meant compromising their teaching. Some of these teachers expressed that they valued both teaching and activism. The resulting tension created a dynamic where they often felt frustrated and overburdened, even guilty, no matter what choice they made.

This tension was commonly expressed in terms of time. Time was a limited and valuable resource that teachers could invest either in their teaching or activism, but—since they understood these as distinct—they couldn't invest in both simultaneously. Justin perceived using time to address homophobic language educatively as taking time away from teaching about semi-colons. Although he stated that he valued conversations where people explored homophobia, he felt pressure to cover curriculum. The stakes were about being a teacher *or* activist, meeting one's professional responsibilities *or* one's moral responsibilities, using time in one way or a different way. Moreover, Justin foregrounded his own needs over those of youth, prioritizing what he needed to teach over what students needed to learn, whether content-area knowledge or personal values.

Mutual enrichment. Other teachers defined teaching and activism as overlapping and mutually complementary. They could be simultaneously activists and teachers rather than only one or the other. Time teaching could be time doing activism, the two intertwined. Being a better teacher could mean being a better activist and vice versa. When James discussed his rationale for including representations of lesbian and gay people in his social studies curriculum, he explained that teaching and activism were intermeshed for him. For him, if teachers reject opportunities to shape students in moral and political ways, then it doesn't matter

> how well you know your subject, you will always fail. And I think that our job is to create people that . . . have character first. And I know that's not supposed to be one of our jobs on paper. But it really has to be because you [the teacher interviewer] teach English, I teach social studies. The percentage of kids that are going to go teach English or teach social studies aren't that many. But we know that they're all going on in the world here very soon.

James valued his students' moral character first and foremost because quite soon they would be adults participating in the community at large. He suggested that much content-area knowledge is of secondary importance, if not somewhat trivial, because few students would go on to careers—such as being English or social studies teachers—where they would use that specific content-area information. He went on to explain that, "there's a lot of other ways that you can teach tolerance, especially in a class like government," and although he used the word "tolerance," we understand him to be teaching for understanding, empathy, and humanization. He gave multiple examples such as teaching the 5th and 14th amendments and engaging students in discussions about what people in the U.S. mean when they claim that "inclusiveness and respect and equality are a way of life" for the country. Generally, he wouldn't tell students his political stances such as his opinion of specific candidates. He did, however, share his stance on gay rights, arguing that even though the federal government didn't protect LGBTQ people, this would eventually change because it's morally right. To students expressing surprise or discomfort about his directness, he would respond: "I don't care if it makes you feel uncomfortable, it doesn't mean it's not right." For James, teaching and activism were inseparable. As he engaged his government students in discussions of civil rights, Constitutional amendments, and U.S. values such as inclusion and equality, he also facilitated conversations about sexual diversity and gay rights. He posited that exploring contemporary tensions in the U.S. democracy encouraged students to engage with his government course curriculum with more complexity and depth. He didn't have to trade one for the other but rather was able to do both and to do them more meaningfully, connecting content-area knowledge to developing students' moral character. He didn't shy away from discomfort, even expressing a willingness to explicitly address discomfort as part of learning.

Teaching and Activism as Humanizing Acts

When teachers understood their primary job as conveying content knowledge, they frequently attempted to engage in activism by centering students who were part of dominant groups, or by invoking the needs of "all students," universally. They saw activist work as primarily about working against ignorance and hatred. They worked to assure that privileged students didn't act homophobically or transphobically in the moment, as when Justin's students used homophobic language in the classroom or when Stephen's students encountered the male cheerleader. Justin and Stephen actively favored these privileged students, understanding their homophobia and transphobia as inadvertent, uninformed, or just "playing around." Justin even named the potential negative consequences for straight cisgender students in the future if they didn't learn to avoid public, homophobic remarks. These students were centered and directly addressed, often at the expense of LGBTQ and gender diverse students who, while likely present, were dehumanized and treated as the absent "other," reifying systemic oppression. In short, if activism is about social change, we question whether these well-intentioned actions actually contributed to such change. Instead, they seem to have reproduced heterosexual hegemony in modified ways, perhaps ones that were more palatable for those resistant to examining their own complicity in structures of domination.

In contrast, teachers who viewed teaching and activism as complementary and overlapping tended to view their activism as focused on structures and patterns, recognized and valued the students' intersecting identities, and saw their activist work as primarily about working for queerness. Instead of treating LGBTQ and gender diverse students as absent "others," these activist teachers worked to recognize and humanize their LGBTQ students. They worked to make queer students both more visible, as Anna did when she helped to bring the GSA more openly into her school and actively brought queer content into her classroom, but also less vulnerable, as Terrence did by changing cultural norms and social systems to work better for queer people rather than at their expense. In recognizing how these approaches to teaching and activism worked to humanize and dehumanize some students vs. others, our argument is not to suggest that any of these stances is necessarily all good or all bad. Stephen's actions will, we hope, do some good, since his students will probably be less overtly homophobic and transphobic, which should ultimately do some good for queer people in the world. And Justin's efforts to "zap" homophobic language in his classroom, aimed at helping already privileged kids stay out of trouble in the future, may offer some possible good, in the moment, for queer kids in his class. Furthermore, Anna highlights that even universalizing approaches, such as those associated with standardization and school accountability measures, can be tactically deployed to work for change. So, in this chapter we have sought to explore a range of definitions of teaching and activism in order to reflect on their affordances and constraints so that teachers might better understand the consequences—whether to reify, resist, contest, or transform oppressive social relations—of their daily teaching decisions. In doing so, we hope to shift away from a focus on teachers' intentions and toward the actual impact of their decisions. It is important to remember that actions, which may be liberatory in some ways, can also be dehumanizing in others.

In closing, we understand definitions of teaching, activism, and their relationships to be about what gets to count and be sanctioned, and who gets to be seen, addressed, and humanized, in the daily professional lives of teachers. These definitions are continually (re)negotiated as teachers, administrators, students, and families interact, and have different affordances and constraints depending on a teacher's context, knowledge, and experiences.

Nonetheless, teachers with broader definitions of teaching and activism positioned themselves as having more opportunities to work for social change. Those who claimed their authority to define what counts as teaching could work simultaneously as teachers and activists, without compromising one for the other. They could work in ways that were individual and structural, anti-oppressive and queer-positive, universalizing and particularizing. They could move across multiple definitions at different times for tactical reasons, remaining sensitive to the limitations and exclusions of any single definition, being vigilant in how they humanized some students and dehumanized others, and seeking to address these shortcomings. They were more willing to claim their authority as teachers and use old, conventional tools that have taken-for-granted purposes in more expansive, imaginative, and ultimately activist ways. We encourage teachers to open their teaching and activist imaginations as they reflect on their daily actions with respect to sexual and gender diversity in schools.

Teacher Take Aways

- Think about ways teaching can (and *does*) include moral, political, and relationship dimensions that enrich rather than detract from content-area knowledge and skills. Talk with students about how power and knowledge are mutually constitutive.
- Look for ways to utilize the authority that you have as a teacher in order to transform opportunities into possibilities; notice what it looks like when you claim this authority.
- Embrace a wide understanding of activism to open up as many opportunities as possible to support LGBTQ and gender diverse people and work for queer-friendly schools. Be tactical and purposeful as you take up these opportunities.
- Building individual relationships is a good way to support LGBTQ and gender diverse people and to work towards equity. When you notice broader patterns and structures that limit what you can do within these individual relationships, work towards changing the system.
- Strive to educate, enrich, and support. Think about how to move beyond exclusively engaging in "anti-work" (Clark, 2010b) toward queer-positive activism that is humanizing and reciprocal.
- Recognize and seek to understand the ways that LGBTQ and gender diverse youth in schools have different experiences, needs, and desires than straight and cisgender youth and from other LGBTQ and gender diverse youth; shift towards centering these particularities as you work for social change.
- See your teaching as activism and activism as teaching; reimagine how you can use your teaching tools for new purposes to work for social change for LGBTQ and gender diverse people.

3
STEPPING UP AS TEACHERS

Understanding Impact, Knowledge, and Vulnerability

As we outlined in the previous chapter, teachers conceptualized teaching and activism and the relationship between the two in different ways. These understandings framed the (im)possibilities that teachers saw for stepping up for sexual and gender diversity in schools. However, just because a teacher identified an opportunity for action didn't mean they always would see it as a possibility or probability. In this chapter, we take up the complexity around teachers' decisions to (not) step up for LGBTQ and gender diverse people. Specifically, we explore the nuances of decision-making and teachers learning to make choices. We hope to demonstrate how educators, more generally, can collaborate with colleagues, students, and families and leverage their choices to act as sites for social transformation, justice, and compassion. We begin by discussing three dimensions central to how teachers described their decision-making: the impact of their choices on different people; the knowledge they felt they did, or did not, have; and their vulnerabilities to different risks. We then focus on opportunities for learning named by teachers, exploring possibilities for expanding the ways they stepped up by increasing their knowledge and changing their practices. We close by offering suggestions for how teachers might step up in ways attuned to their contexts, recognizing that these must be variable, flexible, and organic to be the most impactful, informed, and collaborative.

Impact of Decisions

When teachers discussed stepping up for sexual and gender diversity, part of what they considered was the potential impact their actions would have on different groups of students. Sometimes they focused on straight cisgender students while at other times LGBTQ or gender diverse students. Teachers also explained how they navigated different types of student responses when they stepped up, often expressing uncertainty about how their efforts could be most effective. They questioned how they would determine whether or not their choices were impactful and to what degree. We discuss each of these themes next and then reflect on how you might step up more effectively in your own work.

Weighing the impact. Most frequently when weighing the impact of a decision, teachers focused on heteronormative and cisnormative youth,[1] the goal being to educate straight kids to not be homophobic and transphobic. They considered if they could contain or limit students' expressions of hatred, taking an anti-approach (i.e., anti-hate). For example, as mentioned before, whenever Justin heard students using homophobic and misogynistic language, he explained, "I zap it all the time," suggesting that, for him, this was a quick, direct, no-nonsense response. Other teachers focused more on educating than containing. Dave wanted his interventions with youth using homophobic language to be a "teachable moment" rather than a, "'we're-on-our-way-to-the-office' moment." While both of these approaches are reactive, Dave's goal was to change students' beliefs and mindsets whereas Justin focused on changing students' behavior. Importantly, these differences also suggest that teachers evaluated the impact of their decisions in relation to their underlying definitions of teaching and activism. Justin, for instance, understood his teaching to be about staying within the official curriculum, so he valued zapping any distractions. Other teachers focused on proactive rather than reactive approaches. They attempted to educate about the effects of homophobia on people in order to head off incidents before they occurred. Stephen, for instance, taught about others' experiences of oppression so students could make personal, human connections: "Just letting [students] know this type of stuff is real and how it affects people. And it's just me standing in front of them . . . I'm a person, and all of this stuff's real . . . It's easier listening to it on TV and hearing something about someone and tuning it out like that." At other times, teachers considered how a decision would impact LGBTQ and gender diverse students. The focus here was often on protecting LGBTQ and gender diverse students. Dave, for example, described an instance where one of his lesbian students experienced homophobic harassment. She had come to his class after lunch, "crying. She was a mess." Initially, he wanted "to know who did it, who said it." He wanted to protect her by holding the individual homophobe accountable. After this initial reaction however, he shifted his approach. He explained that "it doesn't need to be about going after whoever said what. It's about making her feel welcome, making her feel respected." Dave describes a shift in his understanding of how effectively to step up and support a lesbian student, at first reactively and then proactively.

Other teachers explained making decisions or taking actions that would help LGBTQ and gender diverse youth flourish in their lives. These teachers moved beyond attempting to impact queer youth by protecting them to supporting LGBTQ youth in asserting their own agency, a shift that also suggests that they drew on a perspective where teaching entailed shaping the lives of young people and not only covering curriculum. Jared, a trans man who taught high school arts classes, worked to provide mentoring and advice to his trans students even though he was not openly trans with them. While he used their correct names and pronouns,

> he also offered "concrete bits of advice," like . . . pointing them "in the direction of colleges that have good transition resources and health care available to trans students" and suggesting that they "get in touch with LGBT student services at . . . school to find out about dorm assignments and name changes."
>
> *(Blackburn, 2014, p. 10)*

Another teacher, Anna, struggled with the intersections of race and sexual identity, attempting but being uncertain as to how to support her Black gay and questioning students. She had previously worked extensively in extracurricular contexts such as the GSA and the school's African American Cultural Club to support LGBTQ students, both Black and non-Black. While this strategy was effective earlier in her career, she came to question its effectiveness later. She said:

> I have so many Black kids in my classes who are so outspoken about equality, not only for race, but also for gender and sexual orientation . . . There are lots of kids who are Black and gay or who are questioning, and they don't come to our [GSA] meetings. But they also don't go to the—and I know this because I go, I've been to the African American Cultural Club—and they don't go to that either.

Anna wanted to meaningfully support her Black gay and questioning students and recognized that she wasn't doing this well enough even as she was making space for them in her classroom, so she looked for new possibilities because she wanted to help them flourish in relation to both their race and sexuality.

Trisha, a straight white cisgender woman who taught at Guthrie, also considered the impact of her decisions with respect to race, sexual identity, and gender expression. However, while Anna was concerned about the intersections of these identity markers, Trisha perceived that her choices around each were in tension. Trisha worked in a school she believed to be relatively queer-friendly. She had included lesbian- and gay-themed literature in her classroom, but at the time of the interview "didn't see necessarily a need to focus in specifically on gender and sexuality issues." In her words: "what I see our kids feeling really uncomfortable talking about is race," Thus, she invested more effort into cultivating conversations about race rather than sexual and gender diversity. In contrast with Anna, who was considering the impact of her decisions at the intersections of race and sexuality, Trisha was grappling with what she experienced as a tradeoff between one or the other, but not both. She worried that continued focus on LGBTQ topics might not be supporting her students and families of color or helping her white students learn to talk about race. Overwhelmingly, teachers focused on straight cisgender youth, emphasizing reactive decisions that were alternatively containing and educative. When shifting focus to LGBTQ youth, teachers foregrounded their obligations to protect queer students, rather than support queer students in asserting their own agency. Teachers most frequently articulated anti perspectives, whether anti-hatred or anti-oppression. Queer-positive ones were uncommon, as were discussions of heteronormativity, cisnormativity, or homonormativity.

Navigating student responses. Teachers also described how, when they stepped up, they navigated different student responses and the tensions they felt around these responses. Kevin was a straight white cisgender man who taught social studies and used to coach football at a Hartville high school. He described how students might not take up a topic as he'd hoped. Depending on when he introduced sexual and gender diversity, it could lead to students trivializing these topics, undermining the effectiveness of curricular inclusion. Reflecting on one instance, he said:

> I probably didn't time it right you know, and the kids were like in the process of getting out of there, kind of getting ready, packing up or whatever. It's—and so you kind of feel like "Oh you know if only you guys would give this [the lesson] a chance" you know, "You'd really, really love it, you know we'd all be weeping together." Um, but you know I mean not everybody reacts the same way to every incident.

A high school librarian in Hartville, Meredith, a straight white cisgender woman, explained her struggle to find ways to follow through in stepping up when students were resistant and trivialized topics:

> you'll see somebody say something, and people will giggle like a lot of times it's the athletic team kids that sit with their friends, and they'll—they'll snicker about it. Or, mostly it's more than that. It's like rolling their eyes like that or, you know, "teachers are so liberal."

Both Kevin and Meredith wondered how best to build communication and dialogue, inviting students to rethink their beliefs, but feared that pushing too far or too quickly could damage relationships and close off possibilities for changing their schools and communities. At the same time, they didn't want students' resistance to remain unchallenged, worrying that silence could be a tacit approval of these stances or the hateful beliefs behind them.

Trisha worried that introducing some topics, such as sexual and gender diversity, could invite emotions into the classroom that she didn't know how to navigate. She stated:

what I always worry about as a teacher is bringing up topics that can be emotionally charged and not having—It's like the moment on the hotline, like not being able to help somebody cope with their emotions in a way that isn't going to—you know, in a way that everyone can feel respected and not traumatized by.

Here, Trisha referred to her prior work on a rape crisis hotline. In one call from a child, she worried that her response had done more harm than good. This experience shaped her teaching philosophy, grounded in a "do no harm" ethic. She worried that bringing up topics, such as sexual and gender diversity, might invite strong emotions into the classroom. These emotions, once circulating, could result in students—particularly LGBTQ students as a group and gender diverse students most poignantly—experiencing trauma, which contradicted her goal of stepping up for LGBTQ people. Trisha wasn't sure she could mediate these emotions in ways that were respectful, safe, and could contribute to social change. As a result, she said she was more likely to avoid this type of situation.

Other teachers expressed tensions regarding the intersections of sexuality, race, and religion. Fae, a straight African American cisgender woman who worked as an intervention specialist in a high school, had grown up in New York City during the 1960s, participating actively in political activism and theater. She was an ordained minister. A colleague to one of the Pink TIGers, Fae often shared stories about coming-of-age in the 60s amidst political rallies and theatre life. She described frequently meeting non-heteronormative people of different races in these contexts. In her interview, when asked about how she understood the intersections of her anti-homophobic and anti-racist work, she said the following of Black queer students in her school:

> Well, that's a student sub-group that I think needs a lot of this work. A lot of the African American student group can tend to be very super-religious and sometimes that makes them more homophobic than students that maybe don't go to church. So that's a mindset that needs a lot of this kind of sensitivity work.

Her concerns were not only about trivializing sexual and gender diversity or damaging relationships. She had an acute awareness of the related intersections especially to how racial and religious differences moved across schooling and some churches in her community, a relationship that is not simply about religious groups automatically being more homophobic as Marianne and Sally illustrate later in this chapter. Nonetheless, Fae named challenges of stepping up while being sensitive and responsive to straight cisgender and queer African American students.

In navigating the tensions in students' responses, teachers worried that their efforts to step up for sexual and gender diversity might result in the opposite by (re)entrenching homophobia, transphobia, heteronormativity, and cisnormativity.

Reflecting on decisions. Teachers commonly expressed uncertainty about whether their efforts to step up were effective. While uncertain, they used ways to determine whether they perceived that their choices were helpful or not. At times, teachers reflected on past experiences to learn and make changes to improve their practices, as Kevin and Meredith did. At other times, teachers struggled to determine whether stepping up might do more harm than good by inviting strong, even traumatic, emotions in the classroom, as Trisha expressed.

Some interpreted no response from parents as a good sign. Trisha, for instance, took silence from a family to signal that she had effectively supported their gender-nonconforming child: "I never heard from Melanie that Kai was unhappy with PE . . . Um . . . I think she really liked it" (a situation that readers can learn more about through Melanie's and Kai's perspectives in Chapter 4). Others presumed judgment and negativity from queer parents even prior to interacting with them. For example, Mallory, a straight white cisgender woman who taught elementary school, experienced great anxiety when she interacted with queer parents, worrying that they would critique her and make her feel like less of a person. She explained that there were:

> times that I see parents that intersect with my feelings of constant inadequacy and then I think that I didn't do enough in any given situation and so when I see parents at official parent events I'm always intimidated. Universally. So orientation. You are going to hate me. You're going to hate what I say.

She didn't experience such interactions as a way to evaluate how her decisions were experienced by parents or students, or with the goal of changing her practices. Instead, her own adequacy and sense of self were at stake. Rarely did teachers explicitly seek feedback from parents about their efforts or work to facilitate dialogue with students, families, or communities about how to support LGBTQ or gender diverse students.

Stepping up more effectively. Both proactive and reactive approaches can have value when stepping up, whether to contain straight, cisgender students' expressions of hatred or to educate against hatred—what Caroline has described as "anti-work" (Clark, 2010b)—or to protect or support LGBTQ and gender diverse students. We advocate particularly for educative, enriching, and supportive approaches to sustain mutually caring relationships. These humanizing actions move toward queer-positive teacher-activism and activist-teaching such as exemplified by Jared, who strived to do the same things that his teachers and administrators did when he transitioned during college. They "were thoughtful, receptive, and respectful and his classmates were good, kind, and open" (Blackburn, 2014, p. 9). He worked to listen to, learn with, and advocating for his LGBTQ and gender diverse students, both by supporting their sexual identities and gender expressions and their interests beyond these.

Such tactics also help teachers navigate some of the tensions found in this work, such as opening up rather than closing down dialogue across disagreements, trivializing new or different ideas, negotiating strong emotions, and sustaining cultural practices—such as those at the intersections of race, religion, and sexuality—in the midst of critiquing oppressive aspects of such practices (Paris & Alim, 2014). Finally, we urge teachers not to evaluate the effectiveness of their choices alone. Often teachers are their own worst critics. And, like Mallory, they know that it's easy to let their fears overwhelm them and lead toward silence and inaction. To counter this self-criticism and fear, we encourage teachers to seek input from multiple community members including queer families and young people and activist–teacher colleagues. Any or all of these can help increase understandings of how to contribute to the flourishing of LGBTQ and gender diverse youth in relation to their sexual identities, gender identities, and gender expressions but also in relation to their identities, passions, and desires beyond sexuality and gender, as Jared suggests.

Knowledge Rather than Expertise

Teachers talked about what they did, and didn't, know as influencing their choices to step up for sexual and gender diversity. Many expressed a lack of knowledge especially in relation to sexual, gender, and racial identities different from their own. Other teachers felt that they did have some knowledge, often articulating what they did to continue learning more as opposed to feeling the need to be an expert. When discussing being informed, they often named people in schools as key resources in helping them learn more. We explore each of these themes and then reflect on ways teachers might continue to learn more about stepping up.

Not knowing. Straight, cisgender teachers were the most apt to cite lack of knowledge or information about sexual and gender diversity as a barrier to supporting LGBTQ and gender diverse students. Uniformly, they didn't feel comfortable or confident to introduce representations of sexual and gender diversity into their curricula or to mediate these conversations among their students. Some teachers, like Trisha, felt their lack of knowledge could result in ineffective, even harmful, actions. Others named a lack of knowledge as limiting their possibilities for action. They desired to step up but wanted to make sure that they did so in ways that were responsible and accurate.

Sandra, a straight, white, cisgender woman who taught English at a Hartville high school, discussed not knowing. She was a visible supporter of LGB people in her school and had been identified by others as an ally. However, she felt more comfortable supporting LGB than trans and gender diverse people. She said:

> I feel ignorant and I don't want to present things [i.e., transgender topics] in a way that aren't, that isn't like, I don't want it to become a joke or because I don't know enough about it that if I say something

> like a man who likes to wear a woman's clothing, that becomes funny to them, or at least they talk about . . . my point there is that I don't know enough about it, so I just stay quiet because I feel ignorant and I don't want to open a discussion that I can't control when it's, not that I need to control the discussion, but that I feel like there's a potential for disrespect.

Sandra described not "know[ing] enough" and "feel[ing] ignorant," as contributing to her discomfort and uncertainty when she imagined including representations of gender diversity in her curriculum. In her reduction of trans people to "a man who likes to wear a woman's clothing" she performatively demonstrated a lack of knowledge that could trivialize trans communities or promulgate disrespect and transphobia. While we support the argument that LGBTQ-inclusive curricula are beneficial (Greytak & Kosciw, 2013; Kosciw, Greytak, Giga, Villenas, & Danischewski, 2016), Sandra's discussion points to teachers as critical components of curriculum. Not all teachers would be able to teach such curricula in ways that provided enough safety to LGBTQ and gender diverse students in those classrooms (see Blackburn, 2012), much less in ways that were nuanced, compassionate, or even accurate.

Trisha named a similar lack of knowing about transgender and gender diverse people. She explained that she had done read-alouds in her elementary classroom to facilitate conversations about sexuality but not about gender. When asked about discussing gender diversity, she reflected:

> I'm trying to think if I can even think of any literature that I've read actually that . . . besides *The New York Times* article, which is more about gender, but like all the things that I'm thinking of that are—whether it's a novel or a short story—that seems like it's more about sexuality.

In response, the Pink TIGer interviewer offered to put together a list of some resources, including titles of books with short descriptions and grade level suggestions. Trisha was open to this suggestion, saying it would be "really useful." While Sandra seems to have characterized not knowing as a reason not to step up, Trisha recognized not knowing as an opportunity to learn more. However, neither Sandra nor Trisha felt knowledgeable enough at the time to take up the topic of gender diversity in their curricula.

Other teachers named different types of "not knowing," ones that were grounded in pedagogy more than knowledge about queer people and communities. These teachers weren't sure how to mediate conversations about sexual and gender diversity once they were in the midst of them. For example, Meredith talked about not knowing how to respond to students who made hateful remarks yet would be polite and compliant when she intervened. She said:

Same way when you're talking with kids about remarks you overhear them make during their work time in here. They know enough to be quiet, and they pretty much a lot of times will just hear teachers out, like "Yeah, yeah. We've heard this before. I know. I know." Not realizing how important it really is. And I still have not found a really good way of talking to kids about remarks that they make.

Whereas Sandra worried that students would express disrespect, Meredith suggested that students used superficial displays of respect as subtle acts of resistance, to comply with a teacher's immediate statements because of their authority while maintaining an oppositional stance regarding their use of homophobic, transphobic, or hateful slurs. In contrast with Sandra, Meredith didn't use not knowing as a rationale for inaction but reflected on her practice because she wanted to improve it.

Anna, still striving to step up, explained how she didn't know enough about the intersections of race, sexuality, gender, and age, particularly for her Black students who were young men, echoing her previous questions about the effectiveness of extracurricular clubs as an activist step. She wondered about why fewer young men, compared to young women, in her high school publicly and visibly claimed LGBQ identities, particularly among students of color. She explained that she was unsure how to support these students, particularly young gay Black men as they negotiated the intersections of racism and homophobia, especially since they weren't participating in extracurricular clubs designed for queer or Black students (see also, McCready, 2010). In closing, she reflected: "I wonder about my purpose as an ally and a teacher and a GSA advisor." As the years of her career passed, she felt less equipped to respond to changing circumstances and youth culture and needed to gain more knowledge and skills.

Being informed rather than an expert. Some straight, cisgender teachers talked about what they knew, how they attained it, and how they drew upon it in their actions to support LGBTQ and gender diverse people. They didn't claim to be experts, but they knew enough to act in some ways. Anna, for example, recognized that while she didn't know some things—such as how to best support her Black gay and questioning students—she did know others, which enabled her to engage in an ongoing process of stepping up. She used several types of knowledge—her knowledge of LGBT-themed literature, her students' reading interests, and her relationships with students—to increase curricular visibility of LGBT people:

> My growing library, since my growing knowledge of LGBT materials, my growing shelf of LGBT books for kids to choose. And the likelihood of kids who will take them. When they come to me and ask for a book recommendation, I'll be like, "What kind of stuff do you like?" They'll be like, "Oh, I really like" a girl will ask me "Oh, I really like romance.

I really like—just sweet romance or whatever." And I'll be like, "Have you read *Annie on My Mind*? Oh my God, it's fantastic! You have to read it." And then they come to me and they're like, "I loved it!"

Using what she did know, she was able to make informed decisions that educated her students about sexual and gender diversity. In this particular case, she was able to challenge the heteronormative, if not heterosexist, literacy practices of her school through helping some students find lesbian-themed books that they came to love. For Anna, knowing and not knowing weren't fixed or absolute categories that a teacher wholly occupied. A teacher could know some things and not others but still participate in activism.

Queer families and students appreciated when teachers showed themselves as being informed enough to act even though the teachers didn't, and couldn't, know everything. When Mollie's children were in preschool, she and her family felt supported through the ways that the teachers were informed enough to make space for queer and gender diverse people, whether families or children. For instance, the teachers visibly displayed LG-inclusive literature such as the children's picture book *And Tango Makes Three* in the classroom and read such books aloud with the students. Within this queer-inclusive presentation of family structures, the teachers facilitated a discussion where the class counted and graphed the number of different people in the students' families by asking, for example, how many dads and moms, among other family members, that the children had. Mollie and her family experienced this framing as inviting and inclusive—since the children could share that they had two moms if they chose to do so—but as offering a degree of safety because children weren't obligated to explicitly name their family as queer. They could name whatever number they wanted to and having more than one mom didn't necessarily mean that a child was part of a queer family. Through these subtle yet significant actions, teachers showed that they knew enough to work toward supporting queer young people and families.

Other queer young people and families also valued when teachers were proactive. They didn't expect teachers to know everything in order to support their family. For example, Dakota, a child of queer parents, recounted an instance in her elementary school classroom where her classmates were asking other students if they liked dogs or cats better. The students didn't tell the others that the words *cats* and *dogs* were coded language for *girls* and *boys* respectively. If they answered in a way that implied same-gender desire (e.g., if a girl likes cats it also means she is attracted to girls), the students harassed them in homophobic ways. When Dakota informed her teacher, she intervened by holding a classroom discussion about the situation. What Dakota and her family valued was that the teacher felt informed enough to have an educative conversation with all of the students and that she attempted to create solutions while also making it clear that homophobia was unacceptable.

Not surprisingly, queer teachers—specifically cisgender lesbian and trans queer teachers in our interviews—tended to feel more knowledgeable in terms of supporting LGBTQ and gender diverse students. Knowing, however, did not always translate into stepping up. Tori, a white lesbian cisgender woman who was a high school intervention specialist, asserted that her lived experiences and lesbian identity resulted in abilities and knowledge that a straight person couldn't have. She said:

> A lesbian or a gay person does a better job [at leading the GSA] than a straight or a heterosexual person . . . I have wanted to do more with the GSA. But being a lesbian, I didn't know how that would shake out. And if students and people, if you're affiliated with it, you must be part of that group. So, I didn't really want to out myself. But yet, I thought I had something to offer.

For Tori, her knowledge, and hence her capacity to be supportive, rested with her identity as a lesbian, and she believed she was unable to step up without being out to the entire school community. Other queer teachers, however, took a different approach. For instance, Jared was able to support his trans students without being openly trans or exposing himself to greater vulnerability. He could share concrete advice that wasn't necessarily information that only a trans person could have. It was information that any teacher could learn if they were willing and interested. For Jared, "He had to be informed and be comfortable being explicit, but he did not have to be out to write himself into the world of this school as an activist" (Blackburn, 2014, p. 10).

Responsibility for knowing. At times, teachers expressed tension regarding who was responsible for teachers learning how to step up. There were also tensions surrounding trailblazers. By trailblazers, we mean teachers perceived by others in their schools to be leading the way in doing innovative activist work alongside and on behalf of LGBTQ and gender diverse people. While trailblazers could be models or even mentors, some teachers used trailblazers as a rationale to deny responsibility for knowing about queer activism. Some teachers recognized that they didn't know enough but weren't sure who should be responsible for changing this situation. Terrence talked about how teachers in his building felt that they lacked competency and therefore chose not to act for social change even though his principal repeatedly and explicitly directed teachers to be more active in addressing homophobic language and behavior. Terrence critiqued his principal's mandates because they weren't followed up by any support or substance. He stated:

> We don't have these kinds of conversations as staff members in the building. And so, even though our principal can say, "When you hear fag and gay," we don't have conversations about sexuality in our building.

Terrence's comment is partially about responsibility for knowing. He implied that knowledge about responding to homophobia and transphobia was a collective school-wide responsibility and that the school administration was obligated to ensure that teachers had access to such knowing, suggesting that teachers had neither the responsibility nor the capability to access information. Terrence's comments represent a thread common, where teachers struggled with questions of administrative and teacher—along with individual and collective—responsibilities for knowing.

Trailblazer teachers—those who stepped up to advocate for sexual and gender diversity in new, visible, and recognizable ways—often served as mentors who modeled activist decision-making, and actively supported others in early activist efforts. Terrence talked about Anna helping him continually grow in small ways:

> I appreciate having Anna two doors down, so that between classes, when, during a lesson when a word starts to come out of my mouth and I realize "Ah! I don't think I should use this," I can then run down between classes and ask her how does this language work. And then she can help me understand, and so having someone to bounce those ideas off on the hallways is helpful to me. Because if we didn't have [these] sort of mentors for understanding that difference in our building, I don't know who I would go to, or how I would think about it differently.

Terrence recognized he might be making a mistake, but he didn't always know how he could improve. He saw Anna as someone who was informed, so he could go to learn from her in small and immediate ways to mentor him in this area of his teaching.

While Anna's trailblazer status served as encouragement to some teachers in her building, others used it as a rationale for inaction. For example, Justin justified his inaction, saying: "there are other people in our school that fight that fight and are loud about it. And I think there's a different role that different people play! I don't need to try to." He implied that teachers fell into one of two fixed categories, ally or non-ally. He suggested that Anna would always "fight that fight," meaning that since she would always address homophobia, he didn't need to.

Other teachers named out-queer teachers as their reason for choosing to not step up. Mallory discussed Martha, an out lesbian colleague in her elementary school, who taught an LGBT-inclusive curriculum: "she does a full to some degree unit, she goes way into. It's a huge part of her curriculum and it isn't mine." Mallory explained that her classroom literature curriculum was already packed full, leaving no space for books that provided images of sexual and gender diversity. She commented: "there is so much other stuff I want to do as far as literature," implying that she valued representations of straight cisgender people more than those of queer people. Mallory disavowed her personal responsibility for knowing about, teaching about, and stepping up for queer people because others were already doing so. So, while trailblazers—whether straight and cisgender or queer—may serve as models or mentors for teachers such as Terrence, others may feel as though they can opt out rather than contest hatred, ignorance, and normativity.

Stepping up to know more. We argue for teachers to take up a stance that assumes everyone can and is responsible for learning about queer communities and activism. While teachers who refused to step up characterized knowing and not knowing as absolute and stable categories, teachers who participated in activism, in both large and small ways, described these categories as shifting and variable depending on time, place, or relationships. Educators who feel they do not know enough—whether about queer lives and queer-inclusive texts, teaching practices, or intersecting identities to step up for sexual and gender diversity—can always learn more about curriculum, pedagogy, and sociocultural context. Viewing categories of (not) knowing as fixed or as the exclusive possession of some people limits possibilities for teacher-activism and activist-teaching. It also clashes with a basic premise of the enterprise of schooling, namely that everyone can learn and that such learning is a continual lifelong process.

Vulnerability to Risks

Every teacher reflected on their vulnerabilities to various risks as part of stepping up. In teaching, we understand risks to involve situations where a person encounters some possibility of negative consequence resulting from an action, perceived identity, or (a lack of) knowledge, so we focus on the relationship dimensions of risk that are social and embodied. Some of these risks are quite profound, such as experiencing oppression across a lifetime or losing a teaching job. Others are less so, such as experiencing embarrassment or feeling ignored. Not all teachers were vulnerable, or equally vulnerable, to all risks, and some teachers did not even acknowledge the risks that existed for others. For instance, if privilege can be understood as an energy saving device (Ahmed, 2013), then a straight cisgender man who teaches would have more energy to draw on, and thus be less vulnerable, when navigating the risk of a parental complaint for teaching a curriculum inclusive of sexual and gender diversity, especially when he's compared with a queer teacher. The vulnerability of the queer teacher would be further compounded by their unique risk of being fired for simply being, since the region where we conducted interviews lacked legal protections from such discrimination. So while all teachers named their vulnerabilities to risks, the degrees of vulnerability and types of risks cannot and should not be equated. We explore these differences primarily with respect to teachers' identities. Straight white cisgender teachers felt vulnerable to administrative and community censure, criticism, and rejection. Straight cisgender teachers of color experienced vulnerability in relation to religion, intersectionality, and the different visibility of racial and sexual identities. LGBTQ teachers named vulnerability in relation to being out and living as one's authentic self. We explore each of these group's experiences next and then reflect on possibilities for sharing vulnerability and risk when stepping up.

Censure, criticism, and rejection. Straight white cisgender teachers named censure by administration and criticism, whether from the community or administration, as their two most significant risks. Kevin was vulnerable to this risk in his relationship with his principal. Kevin advocated for sexual and gender diversity in his Social Studies curriculum, which his principal did not like. While the principal wasn't able to change Kevin's teaching practices, he retaliated in a different way, not renewing his contract as a football coach. Kevin described his experiences:

> What are the consequences of doing this work? I was doing this work as a high school football coach and I switched schools and I went to a school that had an administrator that I would consider to be homophobic and very prejudiced in a lot of ways. We butted heads a lot and I never really understood why until maybe years later when all of a sudden I realized his problem was not with anything that I was doing on the football field, it was with everything that was going on in the classroom, you know? Sometimes if they don't like what's going on in the classroom, a consequence can be what happens on the football field, where everybody is on one-year contracts, they decide whether they want to keep you or not keep you. And if football coaching is important to you, like it is to many Social Studies male teachers that's for sure, they again can choose to not do anything risky at all that might interfere with their ability to continue coaching football at whatever school they're at.

Kevin experienced increased vulnerability because he coached football rather than another sport. In his community, football was a flagship for the school in the public's eye. It was also a space defined by a particularly aggressive heterosexual masculinity. These elements contributed to enormous pressure for Kevin to conform to community norms to stay employed as the face of the football team and, by extension, the school in public. This did not include, unfortunately, participating in queer activist work such as his choice to take students to the local Pride parade. This example highlights the complex web of personal and community politics that many teachers, especially those in larger school districts due to the expansive web of high stake and highly visible community relationships, must negotiate in stepping up to support queer people.

In the same district, Meredith, a librarian, discussed her fear as she compared the collection of books in her school's library to the collection of books in the other high schools in the district. She believed that if school curricula, including the library's book collection, wasn't inclusive, then it was exclusive. Based on this conviction, she worked to make her library inclusive, granting legitimacy and visibility to all people, including those who lived their lives beyond heterosexual hegemony. She experienced greater vulnerability to this risk because her library's online catalog was publicly available. Her high school library's catalog was much more liberal than those of other high school libraries in her district. In her view, the other librarians were afraid about community backlash. She said:

> And, it's not homophobic. It's more fear to have books that have a sexual content, or graphic content because our [online library catalog] is publicly searchable. And it is. I mean. It is. It is scary because our community's really conservative, and I fully expect, at some point, something I've included will come into question. And, people have lost their jobs over things like this. It seems crazy, but it's true.

It's important to note that, though Meredith describes the fear as not homophobic, but rather a reaction to books with sexual or graphic content, the conflation of sexual and gender diversity with sex acts and sexual behavior and the hypersexualization of queer people are common in heterosexist and cissexist contexts. In her community in particular, the conservative political presence was strong and organized. For example, it coordinated campaigns against school funding levies and even attempted to repeal a school levy via a recall vote after it had passed. Kevin and Meredith both were vulnerable to risks, though this vulnerability was not strong enough to deter them from stepping up or even, in Kevin's case, to stop once he experienced repercussions when his administrator did not renew his football coaching contract. Instead, they embraced their vulnerability, utilizing it as a resource to work for social change (see also, Blackburn & Schey, in review).

In contrast, Mallory, a Guthrie elementary teacher, feared parental criticism, but explained that she responded to past complaints by significantly limiting, rather than bravely maintaining or tactically reimagining, her teaching practices. When explaining why she did not teach her entire class a curriculum inclusive of sexual and gender diversity, she said:

> because I'm afraid of, I don't want to go too far. I realize that there are families in my classrooms, not this year in my class, but in the past there are families in my class who don't agree with my perspectives who are much more conservative politically, socially, whatever, and I have had some parents who have challenged me on my curriculum as far as why are you teaching it this way.

Her past experiences of being challenged led her to avoid rather than take up an inclusive whole-class curriculum. In her words: "I err on the side of what's going to give me the least parental backlash," a move that sought to minimize her individual vulnerability. She instead preferred to provide selected students with LGBTQ-themed texts such as the middle-grade graphic novel *Drama* for their individual reading, effectively increasing the vulnerability of her elementary students and putting them at risk for being stigmatized by their peers for choosing to engage with LGBTQ-themed literature (Blackburn, 2012).

Visibility, misrecognition, and religion. The dynamics of visibility operated differently with respect to race than sexuality. When attempting to advocate for sexual and gender diversity, some straight, cisgender teachers of color named additional risks beyond those of their white colleagues. At times, they engaged with audiences who were unable to recognize the ways in which racial and sexual identities intersected. For some teachers of color, religious dynamics added layers to their experiences of educational activism. In this section, we draw from interviews from Williams, a small, politically conservative and highly religious town, so we see this discussion of the intersections of race and sexuality to be just as much about place and religion.

In her interview, Fae, a straight, cisgender teacher, at times considered the intersections of race and sexuality and at times used race as an analogy for sexuality. For example, she discussed her experiences being the only African American teacher, and one of only two teachers of color, in Williams High School. She recounted a story where she was confronted by several young white women who were students. They pointed out that she was the only African American teacher in the school and asked her how that made her feel. She continued the story in her interview as follows:

Fae: And I turned it right back and I said, "How does it make you feel? That you don't have access to a diverse teaching staff? Is that a problem for you? If it's a problem for you, you need to go and talk to your parents and your parents need to talk to the school board and you need to have something be done about it." You know, because what are they missing if they don't have these multiple perspectives?

Interviewer: How'd the kids respond to that?

Fae: They got thoughtful. They got really quiet. And they got thoughtful. Like, I don't know. Were they trying to make me cry or something? It was like, "Oh, you're all by yourself hanging out out there. How does it make you feel?" I said, "But I'm very aware of the fact." And I said, "If Ms. F. decided to change jobs or retire, you'd have none. Mkay? Is that a problem for you? Is it?"

She contrasted the experiences of teachers of color with those of lesbian and gay staff members with respect to the dimensions of visibility, vulnerability, and risk. She described applying for a teaching job as different when the applicant is a sexual as opposed to racial or ethnic minority:

> I mean, it's not something that, not a line item you're going to have in an interview, you know. When you are a person of color or a different ethnicity, you show up and things are apparent. So that's a big difference. Who's to say we haven't had gay staff members? But, you know, if you're not living an out lifestyle.

Whether others did, or didn't, acknowledge the significance of her racial identity, Fae stated that she was "very aware of the fact," a perspective reinforced in her interview where she told several stories of how racism was always a present influence in any type of activist work she undertook. Her racial visibility and its impact on her teaching stood in contrast to what she perceived as some lesbian and gay teachers' potential to cover (Yoshino, 2006) or to pass as straight. While she explicitly posed the rhetorical question about the possibilities of gay staff members in her building, there was more going on in this moment. Both Fae and the teacher researcher who interviewed her were mutually aware—and aware of the other's knowledge—that there were lesbian and gay teachers at their school, both white and of color. However, these teachers were out only with a selective group of colleagues and not the school as a whole. This contrast further emphasized her point and the unique set of risks she experienced around racism, as a Black teacher participating in teacher activism that white teachers didn't experience or acknowledge.

Marianne was a recently retired white, cisgender teacher who had worked for over four decades both in schools and in out-of-school educational contexts, engaging in feminist, anti-racist, and queer activism. She described one instance where she had worked with a friend of hers, Sally, a straight African American woman who was a high school teacher, to respond to homophobia that some religious members of the community expressed as they critiqued her educational work. Sally was a longstanding participant in the civil rights movement in the community. For example, she had collaborated with others in the African American community in her town to protest the school district's curriculum, which resulted in the creation of some Black studies courses and extracurricular clubs at the high school. She taught the Black history course for many years. Sally also supported gay rights, vocally resigning from her AME church when anti-gay views were expressed from the pulpit. Marianne invited Sally to talk with a group of community members critiquing Marianne's queer-positive educational efforts. When Sally attended the event, Sally told her story:

> about leaving the church over this issue. The guys from this church, who were so angry with me, said, "We're not talking about racism here. Why is that Black woman here? We want to stay on topic."

While Sally experienced her racial and religious identities as intermeshed and inseparable from her perspectives on lesbian and gay sexualities, some people treated her Black identity as separate from all of her other identities, characterizing racism as isolated from other forms of hatred and oppression such as homophobia. The people she spoke with tried to use her Blackness to discredit her and dismiss her from the conversation. Sally's story echoes Fae's earlier comments about the intersections of race, sexuality, and religion in their small town, where they both worked to stay connected to the African American community, particularly through their ongoing commitment to Black churches, but at the same time publicly rejected homophobia in these contexts. They thus experienced tensions and risks in their activist work both in the broader small town of Williams where they lived and the smaller African American community within it. Their discussion of these vulnerabilities stands in stark contrast to the white teachers who didn't name dimensions of race and racism or acknowledge the role their white privilege played in affording them access to energy and resources they could leverage for social change.

Being Out, Living Authentically, and Staying Employed

LGBTQ teachers—specifically lesbian, Queer, and trans teachers—named being vulnerable to different risks than their straight cisgender colleagues, regardless of race (see also Melvin, 2010). Some lesbian and Queer teachers named vulnerabilities—ostracism and job security—about being out when advocating for sexual and gender diversity. Another trans teacher talked about his desire to live as his authentic self, not wanting to compromise this ability because he was stepping up.

Some lesbian and Queer teachers, such as Tori, worried that if they visibly stepped up for sexual and gender diversity, they would automatically be outed as "not straight." In her discussion of the unique knowledges of lesbian and gay teachers, she named her reluctance to regularly participate in the school's GSA, fearing ostracism and loss of job security. Sharon, a Queer white cisgender woman who taught at a mental and behavioral health family center, was worried about her job and ability to support her family but nonetheless was committed to advocating for sexual and gender diversity. She said:

> we all have families. And no one wants to lose their job. And everyone wants to stand up for what they believe in. But no one wants to lose their job. I mean, especially if they're the breadwinner of the family.

Sharon discussed the importance of straight people working for social change: "I think that we're going to keep relying on straight people and educators to talk for us because people listen to them." She also encouraged LGBQ educators to come out despite the consequences and discomfort: "Don't hide who you are. I, I feel like the more educators that come out, the better . . . it's uncomfortable. But I think in the long run, it will be more comfortable for everyone."

So while she recognized risks connected to her sexual identity, she also advocated for other LGBQ educators to be out as a form of activism.

The experiences of some queer families and students reinforce Sharon's perspectives. For example, Mollie recalls visiting her children's elementary school at the beginning of one year. During her visit, her daughter's teacher Eileen—who was an out lesbian—had her partner volunteering and helping in the room, putting up bulletin boards. Throughout the year, Eileen continued to talk about her partner with her students. Mollie and her family experienced this visibility as affirming and welcoming. Another queer family, in the same school, articulated a similar experience. The presence of multiple LG teachers who were out in the school was something their children said was "cool."

While coming out as a gay person was a way to be oneself, trans people named a different dynamic. For Jared, transitioning from woman to man marked his journey to becoming his authentic self. Once he was living and identifying as a man, he was truly himself, and to continually retell the story of his time as publicly identifying as a woman would be inauthentic. Hence, while being out might be activism for LGBQ people, he said:

> I think that in the gay community at least, there's this idea of being out is the way to be true to yourself.... Which yeah, if you're gay, okay. [But] because gay and trans get lumped in together so much, um, that gets extended to trans people.... Being out as a trans person and being out as a gay person is totally different.... For gay people, coming out is how you get to be seen as yourself. For trans people, I came out so that I could become myself. And now I am myself... if I were to disclose my true trans history now, that to me is like—That's not me.... for me, I am being my authentic self by being a man.
>
> *(Blackburn, 2014, p. 8)*

Jared's eschewal of publicly using his trans status as a way to step up should not be understood as a rejection of activism. Instead, he was a teacher activist in other ways, such as helping his queer students explore their interests and contribute to the world instead of only being "the gay kid" (Blackburn, 2014, p. 9), and these ways respected, rather than compromised, his sense of self.

Stepping up by embracing and sharing vulnerability and risk. We recognize that the different types of risks that teachers encountered were not the same and cannot be equated, whether these risks were about actions or (perceived) identities. Similarly, the degrees of vulnerability were different. These differential vulnerabilities and risks result in some teachers having greater amounts of energy to use in their activist efforts. Some teachers, such as Mallory, diverted their additional energy inward, seeking to use it to make themselves feel more comfortable and less vulnerable to smaller risks such as a parental complaint. Other teachers, such as Kevin, used their privilege and directed their energy outwards for social change. Still others were willing to embrace even greater degrees of vulnerability, such as Sharon, in relation to even greater risks. While we do not want to trivialize the very real experiences and anxieties of teachers' vulnerabilities, we argue that these vulnerabilities (and their related risks) cannot be the sole determining factor when teachers decide (not) to step up. Discomfort, uncertainty vulnerability, and risk are often, if not always (Fecho, 2001), part of teaching and learning. And, activism quite often requires even more of all of these. From our years of working in a collaborative teacher inquiry group, we've learned that acting collectively, in both small ways and large, can help people to have greater amounts of energy and resources to navigate these risks in sustainable, thoughtful, and compassionate ways. We encourage adults in schools, especially adults with multiple privileged identities, to seek to embrace vulnerability and be willing to use their energies to share risks across coalitions of difference such as sexual, gender, and racial identities, along with differences in age and institutional roles (on this point, see Blackburn & Schey, in review). Such coalitions might serve to mitigate risks, cultivate solidarity, and enable sustained and sustaining work for social change.

Opportunities for Learning and Inquiry

Stepping up as a continual process of knowing, doing, and learning more. Many teachers talked about not knowing enough to step up for gender and sexual diversity. Sometimes they didn't know enough about queer lives or about the intersections of sexuality, gender, race, place, and religion. Other times, they didn't know enough about pedagogical techniques that facilitated social change. The dynamics of determining when to act and when to wait to learn more are not simple or clear cut. Instead, the balance among learning, knowing, doing, and waiting is continually shifting. For instance, when a teacher chooses to not intervene because of a lack of knowledge, that teacher contributes to the reproduction of schools that marginalize queer youth, adults, and families. Such situations are far too common (e.g., Kosciw et al., 2016) and need to change. However, when a teacher chooses to intervene with good intentions but a lack of knowledge, this teacher might marginalize or jeopardize the safety of queer people. In Sandra's case, her decision not to teach trans-inclusive curricula was a responsible decision *in that moment*, but this momentary pause cannot become a habitual position, especially when 77% of transgender and gender non-conforming youth reported being harassed or having other negative experiences in K-12 settings and 24% reported being physically assaulted (James et al., 2016). As Sandra conceded, she needed to learn more about trans people and communities.

In his critique of his principal's mandates, Terrence suggested the process of such learning must have individual and collective aspects alongside teacher and administrative dimensions. Despite Justin and Mallory's assertions that they didn't need to step up, we argue that everyone has responsibilities and roles in social change because everyone has a part in (re)producing the set of social relationships called schooling. These social relationships are not given but are continually (re)created as teachers, administrators, students, and families interact, again and again, over time. These repetitions create opportunities for repeating differently, which is at the heart of learning. Learning involves change across time, which provides opportunities for people to ask new questions, to ask the same questions differently, and to develop different and more compassionate ways of being together. Based on our collective experiences, we believe that inquiry, and particularly collaborative inquiry, is a productive vehicle for such questioning and learning.

Teachers commonly talked about their own processes of learning. These processes involved a personal commitment to expanding one's knowledge and skills. While no single teacher or person can ever know everything about sexual and gender diversity, comprehensive knowledge isn't necessary in order to step up. Some of the responsibility for stepping up lies with teachers, such as Sandra. Teachers have the agency and tenacity for doing so, and some continually look to create opportunities for their learning through engaging in inquiry. For instance, Terrence talked about going to a trailblazer teacher, Anna, for help understanding language usage with respect to sexual and gender diversity. He understood trailblazer teachers to be resources rather than using them as rationales to discursively justify his inaction and the maintenance of exclusive schooling relationships. In seeking to learn, Terrence didn't expect others to teach him, although he did long for such community in activist work.

Anna described a continual process of inquiry through trial-and-error, as she explained:

> I think I've become confident in including LGBT material in my classroom that I don't even like question it. Like in the beginning it'd be like gearing up for it, "Oh, I'm going to include this and I'm just going to wait for that fucker who's going to say something." Now it doesn't even register that I'm including it, which I think is good. I think that's good. It's just a natural idea for me to include a David Sedaris piece in a collection of short stories or it's natural for me to talk about Lorraine Hansberry and how she identified as bisexual and had never really talked about it and then she died too young to really do anything about it. And like just having those conversations and making it seem like so much more like all the time sort of thing. And I think I've acquired so many more things in my repertoire of knowledge about authors or literature and things like that.

Anna's practice evolved over the years. She started with single lessons or texts where she included representations of LGBTQ people and saw these lessons in combative terms: her versus "that fucker" who would express homophobia.

Later, using LGBT-inclusive curricula became commonplace in her daily teaching. Teaching and activism were not mutually exclusive activities competing for space in her curriculum, as Mallory described, but were instead synonymous.

Time is always limited and teachers frequently have too much to do. Anna and others such as Terrence started to look for ways to do what they were already doing differently instead of doing more. Anna would teach a unit on short stories, so why not include work by David Sedaris? She would talk about Lorraine Hansberry when her class read *A Raisin in the Sun*, so why not discuss her queer sexuality? Terrence similarly thought about how to use language differently, catching the ways in which his current practices might be problematic or oppressive. Each understood that they would make a choice anyway: Anna would include representations of people's sexuality (whether queer or straight) and Terrence would use language in his classroom. Both enacted the stance that Meredith explicitly named: if something isn't inclusive, it's exclusive. Within this viewpoint, they tried to change and learn.

For Anna and Terrence, their efforts to step up were generative and self-reinforcing. They learned by doing, engaging in a recursive process of inquiry and action. For instance, as the student council advisor, Terrence wasn't sure how to navigate the situation when a lesbian couple was nominated for homecoming court, but he sought to learn in ways similar to Trisha. He asked the lesbian couple how they would like him to handle details of the situation such as the use of the language "king and queen" if they won, making sure to put in an inclusive order for the homecoming sash and flowers with the local florist in preparation for the event. He sought advice of other teachers in his building whose knowledge of sexual and gender diversity was greater than his. He also regularly met with the principal to discuss questions or address trouble that arose such as one student's homophobic graffiti on the lesbian couple's homecoming posters displayed in the hallways. He described his growing competency through inquiry and action:

> Now, I think that as I understand the issues, LGBTQ issues, as I understand that more, then I am more able to then have a conversation with students because of the homecoming events process. I have greater awareness, which then brings me greater comfort with addressing the issue with students, and the teachers who didn't have the opportunity to go through what I did with homecoming, they're probably even less likely to feel comfortable.

Terrence's story and comments depicted the self-reinforcing process of some teachers' involvement in attempts to make decisions to support LGBTQ people. Terrence knew he wasn't an expert. However, he was willing to take responsibility for his own learning, to have conversations with others including students, and to act when an opportunity arose. Kevin echoed this sentiment when he said: "I mean there's always more that you could do or ways that you can improve—when I get to the point where I feel like I can't improve my teaching I'll probably get out of teaching."

As Fae, Marianne, and Anna pointed out, such learning efforts must strive to recognize intersections and not treat sexual and gender diversity as discrete or separate from other identities such as race, ethnicity, age, religion, and place. We encourage all teacher activists to engage in the compassionate work of understanding these differences in both unique and intersecting ways.

Toward courageous teacher activism. We continue to learn ourselves, and encourage teachers to continue to inquire and learn about sexual and gender diversity. We advocate for such inquiry to be collective and collaborative, whether in schools or outside, among groups of educators with shared commitments. Over time, we have often learned the best by asking questions, jumping in, stepping up, doing, and reflecting together, and we would urge others to do the same. Acting is more apt to happen, and perhaps easier and less risky, when it occurs collectively rather than individually, attending to people's different vulnerabilities, risks, and privileges. We shouldn't expect ourselves to be experts or to get everything right the first time. Getting this work right all the time is impossible (see also Clark, 2010a). Different queer people have different needs, desires, and experiences, meaning that teachers will need to continually adjust and change how they step up. At times, you will make mistakes; we certainly have. But, rather than let this discourage you, we suggest acknowledging mistakes when they happen, asking for forgiveness if it's required, learning from the experience, and making a different decision in the future. An ethic of mistake making and forgiveness is generative and must be continually enacted alongside a profound commitment to learn in ways that are respectful of and responsive to others. It cannot be used to justify ways of being with others that are habitually harmful. Furthermore, not all risks are identical just as all people are not equally vulnerable to them, complicating dynamics around mistake making and forgiveness. So people with greater reserves of energy due to their privilege must direct this energy outwards towards learning how to do activism more effectively rather than inwards towards learning how to make themselves more comfortable.

We urge teachers to seek input from others regarding the impact of their decisions. Teachers' knowledge and experience is important and valuable, but by relying solely on their own judgments, they may miss things from their vantage points as people who, by and large, are in positions of power in schools and classrooms. Teachers' perceptions of (not) knowing, sense of identity, or (lack of) courage, cannot be the sole consideration in determining actions. Nor should teachers see critiques of schooling practices, their own pedagogy and curriculum included, as a personal attack on them, such as Mallory. Similarly, a lack of complaints from queer youth and families cannot be the measure of a job well done, as it was, in part, for Trisha. We encourage teachers to seek to learn from and with queer people and their allies to determine what actions are and are not effective for their school community. This means creating ongoing spaces and opportunities for dialogue and inquiry with queer young people, queer families, and other community members to help teachers develop queer-positive educational practices and build valuable relationships between schools and communities. Kevin described such a process of building relationships and trust as central to facilitating understanding across disagreements: "you hopefully develop relationships to the people and they can see what it is you're doing and see the motivations [of] why you're doing it."

In building such opportunities for dialogue, recognize intersectionality and build coalitions across different groups. Anna mentioned her work across the GSA and African American Cultural Club. Marianne described working with her friend Sally to consider the relationships between race, sexuality, and religion. This difficult but valuable work acknowledges and values the complexities of people's different lived experiences, positioning them as assets. In this way, teachers can value youth not just as students despite their other identities but can value them in each and every one of these unique differences.

While such efforts offer opportunities for learning involving knowledge and impact, we believe that they also matter for the risks that many teachers encounter. While not all educators or community members will agree with teachers advocating for sexual and gender diversity, relationships of mutual trust and respect can facilitate pluralism and responsiveness that can be early steps toward queer-friendly school communities. At the same time, teachers cannot control every variable or please everyone all of the time. Instead of exclusively seeking comfort and security, teachers should balance ethical actions pushing for immediate social change with strategic and longitudinal ones, choosing to have courageous resolve when it is productive and prioritizing justice and compassion over the pacification of critics.

We also encourage teachers to move beyond working *against* homophobia, transphobia, and racism and toward working *for* queer-friendly schools, a subtle but important shift. Activism looks different depending on the context and relationship. As Jared states, being openly queer can be activist just as not being out can lead to different ways of stepping up. Stepping up for sexual and gender diversity isn't a set of rules or steps to follow. It's flexible and organic, even as there are more and less considerate, responsive, and ethical ways of doing so. We hope that in these complex but necessary tensions among knowing, learning, and doing that teachers can find inspiration to work within their communities to advocate for sexual and gender diversity. We encourage all teachers to learn more about stepping up for sexual and gender diversity so that they can increase their impact while navigating vulnerability in ways that are sustaining and sustainable. Such collective and courageous activism must be grounded in loving, compassionate, and just relationships.

Teacher Take Aways

- Look for opportunities and reasons to step up for sexual and gender diversity rather than focusing on the barriers and reasons to not do so.
- Reflect on how your actions impact queer along with straight cisgender people; reflect on how different queer and straight cisgender people are impacted differently because of race, ethnicity, and religion among other identities.
- Seek out new knowledge about queer communities and topics with respect to curriculum, pedagogy, and your school and community context.
- Direct your energy outwards toward activism, and share risks while reflecting on your privilege, vulnerability, and risks.
- Initiate your own learning, be willing to learn from others, and support others' learning; strive to inquire, listen, reflect, and reevaluate what you thought you knew; find a balance among learning, knowing, doing, and waiting.
- Be willing to be held accountable and to hold others accountable. Offer criticism and praise in ways that are loving and sensitive; when someone holds you accountable listen to them and ask follow-up questions, receiving gifts of criticism and praise in ways that are humble and thankful.
- Acknowledge and seek to understand and value differences based on sexuality, gender, race, religion, and place, especially where these identities intersect; draw on differences as a resource and creative force. Attempt to share your own and others' vulnerabilities in coalitions; trust others; prioritize courageous and strategic resolve over fear.
- Be willing to make mistakes, acknowledge your mistakes, ask for (but do not expect) forgiveness, learn more, and make changes; be willing to forgive and support others; recognize uneven privileges, vulnerabilities, and risks in these dynamics.
- Put love, compassion, and justice at the center of your relationships as you embrace your activism.

Note

1 We use heteronormative and cisnormative to highlight that, generally, teachers perceived most of their students as straight and cisgender, whether they actually knew this information or not. This assumption fails to account for the possibility that LGBTQ and gender diverse youth may sometimes use homophobic or transphobic expressions themselves, either as a response to internalized homophobia or transphobia, or as a way to claim protection via the performance of (cis)heteronormativity.

4

STEPPING UP WITH PARENTS OF QUEER FAMILIES IN SCHOOLS

As teachers, you can work with queer families in schools as a way of learning to step up for LGBTQ and gender diverse students. By queer families, we mean families who have children who identify as something beyond heterosexual hegemony, such as but not limited to lesbian, gay, bisexual, transgender, queer, and gender diverse, or children who are questioning their sexual and gender identities.[1] But we also mean families in which the parents[2] identify in these ways. It is our contention that by paying attention to the ways that queer parents shape the experiences of their children in schools, teachers might be better equipped to serve these families.

Therefore, in this chapter, we briefly note how some parents' actions (straight or queer) may unintentionally harm children's experiences in schools, before diving into what queer parents describe as ideal schools for queer families and how queer parents looked for, got started at, and established presences in schools. We then explore a bit about the paradox of visibility for these parents and their families. Next, we examine how queer parents talked about acting, reacting, and helping improve the experiences of children in queer families in schools. Before shifting to how straight parents helped and struggled to help, we reflect on how heteronormativity and cisnormativity were sometimes used as protection in schools. Finally, we offer suggestions of how teachers and other stakeholders might contribute to the effort to improve the experiences of queer families in schools.

Parents who Unintentionally Harm the Experiences of Queer Families

Parents of LGBTQ and gender diverse students and LGBTQ parents' experiences of schools were, they reported, impacted by other parents who apparently held negative views of their families. For example, the Queer mother of a gender diverse child in elementary school talked about other parents policing gender rules and regulations that she was actively trying to dismantle for her child. She said,

> I can still hear conversations of parents, you know, where they say, "You can't do this," or "You can't do that" when it comes to like wearing costumes or . . . "You have to"—you know, "you have to"— You know, forcing them to play baseball or forcing them to do boy things.

Her suggestion was that by parents saying these kinds of things to their children, they were teaching their children gender rules and regulations that then got imposed on her child, even though those values were in conflict with hers and damaging to her child.

Some parents negatively impacted straight youth who happened to be in queer families, too. One of the adolescent children of two dads explained that usually the kids are OK with his parents being gay, but it's their parents who are less likely to be so. He said:

> Yeah, I think it's just like a generation thing like . . . Most of . . . my friends like that are kids . . . don't care and it's more their parents that care. I think you'll find this more often that the kids don't care and the parents do care.

One of the dads said that he wasn't too worried about other parents not liking his partner and him, as long as they were polite, especially to his children. He said:

> Well, we, I mean, any time you go to any of the functions, I mean, a lot of the other parents will come up to you and talk to you and just like you're anyone else. And, um, the ones that you know that, you know, there definitely are some that could care less about our family, [who] stay away. They, you know, they just know not to make it a big issue, which is nice . . . . You know, I don't care if you don't like me. Just don't be rude and crude in front of our family and . . . . especially in front of our kids. And that's basically been the, the way it's been.

He said, mostly, he hadn't even known when parents didn't like that he was gay until someone else had said something about it to him. This parent seemed to appreciate that other children's parents did not make their homophobia too visible in their affluent suburban community. This is in stark contrast to the parents who were actively trying to improve the experiences of schools for children in queer families, which we discuss for the remainder of this chapter.

Ideal Schools for Queer Parents

What was considered ideal in a school for one queer family was not necessarily ideal for another family. Certainly, all queer families wanted their families to be treated with respect in the schools their children attended. Beyond that, though, parents were looking for really different things, shaped, in part, by class, nationality, race, privilege, and intersections among these.

One white working-class parent, Reese, of a gender creative child, Dylan, explained that the child had no neighborhood friends because, "I don't live in the best part of town." According to this trans man, this was not a neighborhood where he felt like he could safely assume he or his child could make friendships. Implicit in this comment is a correlation between neighborhood values, which are both classed and raced, and perceived homophobia and transphobia. Rather than send his child to the neighborhood school there, he and his former partner, Blair, elected to use the lottery system to get into an alternative school. When this effort failed, they used Blair's address, instead of Reese's, to send Dylan to a neighborhood school in a more middle-class community.

This family was in no way alone. Most families were very strategic in identifying the schools where they would send their children, particularly working-class families and families comprising people of color. Another white working-class family selected their home based on the neighborhood schools. Liz said, "the school was part of the reason we started to live in our neighborhood," but, in her words, "it [the school] changed drastically." As a result, they considered two ways out of the school: using the lottery to get into an alternative school or using the gifted program to get into one of the schools with more developed services. They opted for the lottery school because the school that provided gifted services didn't offer after school care or transportation. Here the shortage of economic privilege, as suggested by the need for publicly funded transportation, constrained the family's opportunity to make use of the privileges offered to those identified with intellectual gifts. That is to say, in this case, class superseded intellectual privileges.

Many of the families with whom we talked successfully used the lottery system to access alternative schools. One Asian American middle-class parent said the lottery school was the best school in the area without commenting on their neighborhood school. An African American working-class parent simply named their neighborhood school as a way of explaining, without words, why they used the lottery system. A pair of white working-class parents started by just naming the school but then explained in more detail when asked. The parents, interviewed separately, said that they didn't consider their neighborhood school because of the significant immigrant population at the school. Their reasons for this being understood as an obstacle for their child attending that school were different. Elliot said that she thought it was appropriate for the school to "cater" to the immigrant population, but was worried that this might mean her child "would have gotten really lost." Kristin, however, made a connection between the population and homophobia through religion. She said not wanting to send the child to this school,

> has nothing to do with like international, you know, exposure, but it has more to do with like, uh, the [Islamic] religion and, you know, anti-gay stuff, you know, we were worried about other kids teasing her for having more than, you know, one mom, right, and not having a dad.

In other words, racial, ethnic, and religious differences correlated, for this parent, to perceived homophobia.

These queer families, comprising children of color, rejected schools located in poor or working-class communities as well as those that were all-white or overtly racist. Kai, for example, the child of a single, bisexual mom of Asian descent, described her neighborhood schools, schools that she did not attend, as schools "where, like, old white people send their children." Further, Simone described touring schools as a family—interracial parents with a biracial child. She said, "we were really looking at their reaction" to their family to know whether a school was going to be a good place for them to go. She said she had "gotten to this place of being able to use stereotypes and oppression . . . to [her] benefit." In other words, she would use people's racism, homophobia, and transphobia to help her know what school context would be best for her family. Even though families seemed to want schools that were both racially diverse and queer-friendly, Mason, a gay biracial adolescent, made it clear that the two characteristics do not, necessarily go hand-in-hand, when he described his school district as "really accepting" and another nearby community as "*really* accepting. [The nearby community] might not be that diverse, but it's really accepting anyway." The implication, here, was that the district that is more homogenous in terms of race (and class) was more accepting of gay people, like his parents and himself.

Mason's family, comprising white parents and multiracial children, left what Matthew, one of his fathers, described as a "rough area" as Mason approached school age. His other father explained that their leaving the school "was about the other parents . . . . It was just that we wanted our kids to be in an environment where college was not the exception." Here it seemed less about avoiding homophobia or racism and more about accessing privilege, which they had the option of accessing because of having enough money to move from one area of town to another. As they considered more affluent and suburban school districts, they sought racially diverse communities so their child would not be one of only a few people of color in his school. Because their family had, in Matthew's words, "not just a gay issue" but "the race issue" as well. Matthew said that in their child's school it, "doesn't matter what color you are, and that was important to us." Undergirding this comment is a color-blind mentality, which, of course, is problematic, but it is aligned with a similar mentality around being gay. As a result, these parents sought a school and community where assimilation was not only possible but also valued. Multiracial families, particularly those who include Black and biracial children, were not only looking for queer-friendly schools, they were also looking for anti-racist schools.

Queer Parents Seeking Welcoming Schools

In order to find the schools where they expected or hoped their families would be welcomed, queer parents toured schools, asked direct questions, and noticed subtleties in responses to their questions. In doing so, they tried to find schools that would meet their needs, but what counted as needs seemed to vary according to where they lived and ultimately sent their children to school.

Two white working-class Queer parents referred to the city, or at least the queer community therein, as a "bubble" that "insulated" their families. Sarah, a white middle-class lesbian parent described the neighborhood of Careytown as a "bubble" and referenced a working-class neighborhood in another part of the city as an "annex" to this neighborhood safe zone. That Careytown is a safe haven for queer families is further suggested by Sharon, a white middle-class Queer parent who explained that they would be going from their neighborhood, where few queer families lived, to Careytown, where many queer families lived, for schools. There is one school, in particular, Guthrie, in Careytown, that has a reputation for being relatively queer-friendly, considerably more queer-friendly than many schools in the district. One white middle-class lesbian mother of biracial sons said, "I feel like we're in a little bubble in [Guthrie].... It really feels safe and good."

Indeed, Guthrie was a place where queer families could go and find people like themselves. This is not to say all spaces in Guthrie always felt warm and welcoming; they did not. Still, it was a place where Simone and her partner, as a queer and interracial couple, "went in and, and presented the questions to the school that like we're going to like, 'Are there any other same-sex families?'" It was also a place where Elliot could go as a white working-class Queer parent of a gender queer elementary student and not be, in her words, "processed." She said:

> I remember looking around, and I was like, "oh my God there's like way bigger freaks than me here," you know and I didn't notice ... anybody looking at me ... cause you know when you're with a kid you kinda feel like you want to be invisible ... or not invisible ... but ... not in somebody's sights trying to process this.... So that was nice. I didn't feel like, you know, anybody was processing me.

Elliot was not the only Queer parent who talked about Guthrie in terms of its freak factor. Here, it can be assumed that a person's freak factor is based on how far away someone is from the standard of what it means to represent the heteronormative model of a parent. Susan, a white Queer parent, said she didn't feel like she was "even the biggest freak" there, even though at other lottery schools just being out was "clearly challenging just in the 10 second interviews. Like the very short time I was there, the people around me weren't comfortable." In other words, Guthrie was, for many queer parents, a bubble.

Although this sentiment was a widespread one, some queer parents who sent their children there saw the school in more pragmatic and less idealistic terms. For example, Lane said,

> this [school] community has been created by the family and the kids that are [Guthrie]. Not the teachers. Like, there's a lot of great teachers there, but somehow it's turned into what it's turned into because of the people who go there.

Similarly, Simone, a Queer African American parent, said, "talking about alternative families. When we find a safe haven in place it is important that we keep that consistency." In other words, the city had strong queer communities, Careytown had a strong lesbian presence in particular, and Guthrie was the school where many families in these communities sent their children, if they could lottery in (which, of course, was a tension). But the school community, at least, was like a bubble not only in that it was insulating but also in that it was tenuous. That is, it could have burst if the families and children who go there didn't continue to make it queer-friendly.

When visiting schools outside of Careytown, Sharon talked about sending her less visibly gay wife, Tess, who is also white and middle-class, in first to look at preschools for their son. Sharon said, "to get him into a five-star preschool did I send [Tess] instead of me? Yes." When Lane asked Sharon why, she simply answered, "[Tess] doesn't look gay." In this way, Sharon and Tess could get a sense of the quality of the school before putting Sharon's body on the line to determine whether the environment would be hostile to their family. Once they knew a school was a strong one and worth learning more about, then Sharon would go in, essentially outing the family as a queer one. Recall that Susan talked about sensing other people's discomfort in response to her being a visibly Queer parent. Sharon called this the "wince factor," which is a discrete reaction that offers at least a hint of disapproval. Sharon said, "if there's any wincing at all . . . . You know, then we just go somewhere else." In other words, she had no intention of sending her son to a school where someone representing that school even hinted at disapproval of their family. Being able to pick up on these subtle clues is one way some queer parents tried to avoid putting their children in schools where they were likely to encounter homophobia as a result of being the children of same-gender parents.

This situation, though, is all but inevitable, according to Sharon: "I know kids are going to say something, and at some point, I just don't want him to deal with, I don't want him to have to fight it." The tension between this knowledge and this desire put Sharon and Tess in a quandary. They really struggled with whether to choose a "five-star preschool" that was progressive enough and then "fix the stuff that [they] needed to fix afterwards" or to choose a "place where he doesn't have to defend us.... You know, in a place where he's safe." For them, it seemed like an either/or rather than both/and decision. Recall that it was Sharon who said, "we'll be going across the tracks to [Careytown] for schools."

Liz, however, lived in what Sarah called an "annex," as you may recall. She talked about visiting schools in her neighborhood, too, but she and her partner, Teri, always went together. According to Liz, "we made sure we went together so there weren't going to be any surprises." They ended up selecting a school where there were no other queer families that they knew of, but when they asked whether "[the school] had any experience with same-sex parents," the principal said

> that they would handle it, that they would certainly, you know, she teaches in a school that's all about community . . . bully-free zone, it's a where-everyone-is-different zone. I mean, they were very . . . . Kind of like, why are you asking me this? . . . . This wasn't something you need to be concerned about in these halls. This is a safe place to be, you know. Whoever you are, wherever you come from, or what you do.

For Liz and Teri, both white and working-class, they didn't need their child to be in a school where there were other families like theirs, or in Elliot and Susan's words, where there were bigger "freaks" than they were. Instead, they needed their child to be in a school that was a "bully-free zone . . . a safe place to be." For this family, though, safety seemed to be the most pressing concern.

When examining the talk about queer parents looking for schools in and out of the neighborhood of Careytown, or, more specifically, the school of Guthrie, we are struck by how those who were inside the school or neighborhood seemed to be looking for respect and community, whereas those who were outside of these seemed to be looking for safety and familiarity. So, for example, one Queer parent described Guthrie as a place that felt not only safe but also good, whereas Sharon and Tess stated that they were just looking for a safe place to send their children to school. They may have wanted it to be other things, like being "five-star," in Sharon's words, but those things were separate from and secondary to issues related to being a same-gender headed family. The distinction between inside and outside of the neighborhood and school is about respect. Inside, queer parents felt good; not just safe, but good. And, they felt respected, or at least they expected to. Outside, queer parents felt safe, and that was good enough.

Another distinction between inside and outside of the neighborhood and school is the expectation of community versus the expectation of familiarity. So, for example, Simone asked a Guthrie school representative whether there were any other same-gender families in the school. This is quite a different question than the one Liz and Teri asked at a different, non-Careytown school, which was, "do you have *any* experience with same-sex families." The former question was about whether their children would be the only ones in the school with same-gender parents, and whether they would be negotiating questions from students, teachers, or administrators, among others, about their parents alone or with others. The question Liz and Teri posed, however, just asked, in this case, the principal, whether she has *ever* had *any* students with same-gender parents in the school. The *assumption* was that their child would not have peers to support her as she negotiates questions about her parents, but the *question* was whether the principal would have her back as she did so. Was she prepared to interrupt any homophobia the child might encounter? The principal's answer seemed to be no and yes. No, she did not have any experience, but yes, she would have the child's back. For Liz and Teri, that seemed to be enough.

We do not think that these divides between inside and outside of the Careytown neighborhood and school and how they correlated with queer families' feelings of safety, community, and familiarity necessarily reflect all queer families' experiences in schools. In fact, people told us about unsafe situations in Careytown and at Guthrie, particularly around restrooms for gender diverse students. And we know from personal experience of situations in which Guthrie teachers seemed to have an absolute lack of familiarity of same-gender headed families, even in one case where there were four such families in the teacher's class. In other words, while queer parents might have expected respect and community at Guthrie and assumed this meant their children would be safe and their families familiar and welcome, this was not always the case. Similarly, queer parents who sent their children to schools outside of Careytown told stories of respect and community, even if not queer community. So, again, these divides were not neatly aligned with queer families' experiences.

They were, however, real divides, particularly in terms of expectations, that is what these parents might have expected, how they might have expected their children to be treated. And we worry that this might translate into how they believed they and their children *deserved* to be treated. This is particularly concerning given that these comments were from people who assert themselves in a school system. We worry further about what these real divides suggest about queer parents who do not assert themselves in school systems and further still about queer parents who are not in school systems that provide opportunities for such assertions. All queer parents and their children deserve safety and respect, familiarity and community. Rather than queer parents having to go on a quest to find such a school, it is our responsibility, as educators, to step up and provide such places in every school. Educators need to work to make every school safe, respectful, and welcoming to families with LGBTQ and gender diverse people in them by talking about diverse constructions of families with students and talking about diverse people more broadly.

Queer Parents Getting Started in Schools

Once queer families determined where their children would go to school, there became the issue of laying the groundwork for actually starting in a school. Part of this was about having legal paperwork in place and at the school that indicates who has custody of the children. While, on face of it, having such documentation might seem perfunctory, much like the myriad of forms that most parents fill out at the start of a school year, for queer parents, it was an additional burden. Often, producing such paperwork came with inordinate time commitments and significant legal fees, making such documentation a privilege that not all queer parents could afford. Unbeknownst to many, this is still the case, even after the 2015 *Obergefell versus Hodges* ruling of the Supreme Court legalizing same-sex marriages.

In addition to legal issues, there was the issue of making first impressions, not only the first year children go to a school but every year after that when children are assigned new teachers. Catherine, a white, middle-class, Queer parent, recalled being "really careful to explicitly talk to [her child's] kindergarten teacher about who all the adults were," so that the teacher would have the information needed to treat the family respectfully. Similarly, Ellen, also a white, middle-class Queer parent, said, "The first couple years . . . we would both go to the open house or first day . . . Introduction kind of thing. And say hello . . . . We are [Dakota's] parents." She recalled, the first year, her child's teacher, "didn't say hi to me and wouldn't shake my hand." This provoked this Queer parent to be more persistent in engaging with the teacher. She said,

> If I got off early at any point, I would come into the classroom to pick her up. Um, I . . . I'm pretty good at being very forward . . . . And, "Hi, I'm [Dakota's] mom." Um, and just being very present in that way.

We discuss this effort at and the importance of queer parents asserting a presence throughout the school year further in the next section of this chapter. First, though, we want to reflect more on the work of queer parents getting started in schools.

Similarly, Mollie remembered the first day her older child went to kindergarten. It was no accident that Mollie walked her daughter to school alone that day and her partner, who is more androgynous, stayed behind. The child was in a hyper pink, frilly, glittery phase, so when the two of them arrived at the classroom to see another parent and child—a woman in a tie with a girly-girl—Mollie felt relief. Admittedly working with stereotypes, she read the parent as a lesbian and the child as someone her child might connect with. She thought maybe her daughter would not be the only one in the classroom with same-gender parents, so if any difficult conversations arose, she could navigate them with a classmate. Mollie felt optimistic. At the end of that same day, however, the mom in the tie walked up to get her child before Mollie and the teacher called Mollie's daughter's name, as if to send her child home with the other lesbian. From Mollie's perception, the teacher had conflated her with another white lesbian parent rather than recognized her as the parent of her child.

Ginny, a white lesbian and teacher of students with special needs, also talked about the challenge of the first day of school, not only for her, as one of two moms, but also for her child. She said,

> I think at the beginning, like when you first go to new things, which is really hard for us as moms. . . . I don't think for [our child] as much, but I'm always got a little bit like, "okay when are they going to ask?" Because [at] dance [class] everybody knows, but at the beginning they were like, hm, took them awhile. Like, "okay, well, which one is your mom?" Kids now, like when she was in, I can't even remember, people say, "well, which one is your real mom?" That used to make her angry. She didn't like that. She said, "they are both my real moms. My real mom. They are both my real moms."

Ginny knew that people interacting with her family for the first time would be working to decipher her family and anticipated that they would ask some questions in their effort. She described this as "hard" on the moms but also anger-inducing for their child.

Sharon experienced something similar but went further to discuss the importance of responding to those questions. She recalled the first time she picked up her child from preschool:

> And this little girl runs up to me and says, "Are you [Trey]'s mom?" And I said, "Yeah." And he go—she goes, "Well, [Trey] has two moms and a dad." I'm like, "Yeah, yes he does." . . . . But there was a silence there for a second where I wanted to wait. And people who know me would probably not expect me to wait and see . . . . What his daycare provider would say . . . . You know, and I think that's just a softer version of me with my child. Uhm, so I said, "Yes," you know, "I am, uh, one of his moms." And, and then the little girl goes, "Well, I have a mom and dad, one mom and one dad." And then another little girl comes up— . . . . And says, "I just have one mom."

In this account, her open, honest, and "soft" answer invited classmates to name their family structures in a way that foregrounded the descriptive and backgrounded the evaluative. She asked the teacher about how the topic came up and how it went, and then,

> The kids came to us. And they wanted to know about it. They were like . . . "What is this whole two mom thing?" . . . . And so, we talked about it . . . . And, we talked about how some people and everyone has different families. Like— . . . she has a mom and a grandmamma, you know, and, um . . . so I think it's important to answer those questions as kids ask them. And not to confuse them with stuff . . . that bothers us.

Here, Sharon points to the importance of being in a context where a discussion can happen to educate families about their differences.

There are also times, however, when queer families want to bypass such discussions. Ginny, for example, said

> But now [that we've been in the school for several years] kids don't really ask questions. That is the beauty of this school. It is so small in classes, and they all know each other, and everybody knows every single thing about every single one of each other. So, I think it's good. That has been great.

In this case, once classmates came to know one another and their families, they did not need to ask questions that foregrounded one another's differences, or at least not the same ones they had asked when they first met one another, about their families. Mollie also described a teacher who was "just so much about teaching my kid, that it felt irrelevant . . . irrelevant in a really good way." That some parents appreciated the open discussion and others appreciated the absence of that discussion brings to mind Ryan's (2011) study of children of lesbian moms. In this study, a child at a progressive school felt some pressure to discuss her family, whereas children at an evangelical Christian school appreciated never being invited much less obligated to share details about their family. This tension points to the idea that there is no one correct way to welcome the children of queer parents into schools. Rather, educators need to get to know and understand the particular needs and desires of queer families, rather than generalize or make assumptions, by inviting queer families into conversations, listening to what they offer, and taking their requests and suggestions seriously.

Queer Parents Establishing a Presence in Schools

Once queer families' children get started at schools, these parents make decisions about who they will be in these spaces. Some worked to be visible, by being active or kind, whereas others strove to be invisible by blending in and being "normal."

Some families underscored the importance of their presence in their children's schools and classrooms. At the school level, several families talked about their roles in parent-teacher groups (PTGs). Elliot, for example, mentioned that she volunteered in her child's classroom her first year and then her partner at the time and she served as officers for the PTG for the following three years. Sarah also referenced both her partner and her serving as officers in their children's school's PTG. Liz and Teri talked about being active in their child's school's PTG as well.

These and other parents also talked about being present in their children's teachers' classrooms. Simone said that from the moment they arrived at their child's school, they had "always been very open about our unit." Similarly, Catherine said, "I think we've always all three been present. . . . I think we've just always felt comfortable just being present and it didn't feel like something we really had to think about." Some queer parents were more specific about their contributions to the schools and classrooms. Sarah said that her partner, "does copying like one day a week at the school." Ellen described offering to do a newspaper with her child's class, which she expected to last for a month but ended up lasting four months. Liz explained that they walked their child to her classroom every day and chaperoned field trips, and, as a result, "The teacher loves us." All of these ways of participating are wonderful contributions to schools and classrooms. Still, we worry that some queer parents in particular are feeling obligated to prove themselves as exceptional parents so they are not called into question, either as adequate parents or more disturbingly as not-parents at all. This is particularly an issue for non-biological parents at least some of whom we know did not have legal custody of the children they helped raise. In fact, one such parent, who named her lack of legal custody, said, "I think it's so much about visibility. It really is just like visibility and normalization." We discuss the topic of being normal later in this section, but for now, consider how parents' need for visibility reverberates against Sarah's assertion that these parents need to have legal paperwork in place. Then, reflect on the fact that getting that paperwork drawn up was a significant expense that not every family could manage, and even if they could, such paperwork was typically understood as an agreement among family members with little legal strength.

Further, whereas presence might seem to offer some security, it also comes with the risk that one's presence might be met with homophobia rather than the love that Liz named. Recall that when Ellen first went to her child's kindergarten classroom, the teacher dismissed her. Similarly, but later in the year, Mollie's partner went to a fall festival in one of their children's classrooms to facilitate an arts project, and the teacher failed to make eye contact with her the entire time she was in her room. Mollie started talking about this incident with some of the other queer parents, and "They were like, 'Oh yeah, she definitely has trouble with basically the butch one in the family, right? So, like, not saying anything [explicitly homophobic] but not making eye contact.'" So, there is a tension, particularly in terms of the visibility of the less heteronormative parents; it can be risky, which is less of an issue for the parents, who don't have to spend all day every day in these schools and classrooms, and more of an issue for their children who may suffer consequences from explicit homophobia or implicit bias (Anderson, 2016), whether it's their teachers' homophobia or someone else's, not because the children are perceived as queer but because their parents are. So even though one parent might point to the importance of being present, another stumbled, "Um, but anyway, so, I mean, we're not super visible," conjuring Yoshino's (2006) notion of covering. Families actively questioned how to present themselves in a manner that will cause the least amount of harm to their children. Choices that parents made directly impacted a family's visibility as queer. The impacts of such choices can affect students positively or negatively depending on the school environment.

Another tension around queer parents establishing a presence in their children's schools and classrooms is how their presence gets understood and experienced among queer parents. Some queer parents were eager to connect with one another, whereas others were not. Simone described this tension; she said:

> you know like you try to talk, you try to—you know, and at the same time the allies or the teachers there, they're not sure either because we don't know is it okay to say, "Listen if there are other families, is it okay if I connect you guys"? . . . Because some gay people don't want—some gay people don't want that, you know they want to be the furthest—they want to—they want to blend in. They don't want to—it's the same with any marginalized group I think . . . . You know? Like yes you need that networking and you all—it also at times is very important for you to feel like you're melding with . . . the rest of the people.

So, while Simone and her partner were asking, "Are there other same-sex families?" Ginny felt no need to connect with other same-gender parents, as examples for navigating the school. That is to say, same-gender parents underscored the importance of their normalcy in their children's schools and classrooms. For some parents, this seemed to mean normal as opposed to visibly gay. For example, after Ginny explained that her partner and she had "left that identification" in reference to LGBT communities and instead identified as "two women with a kid," Ginny said, "those people [who identify as part of an LGBT community] just lead different lives than I do. . . . I feel more like we just happen, we are a regular family we just happen to be two women." Less intensely, Liz explained that she didn't visibly assert her lesbian identity. She said,

> I don't walk in with a big rainbow flag on my shirt and say hey . . . I don't send my kid to school with you know . . . symbols on her t-shirt. They just go to school. We just live our everyday life.

For other parents, claiming normalcy seemed to mean being normal gay people, as distinct from perhaps more flamboyant or activist gay people. This is what we understood Sarah to mean when she said, "we've always been very out. You know, [and] very normal. You know what I mean. I mean. We're just like everybody else. We're very mainstream.... We're pretty boring." She further explained:

> We don't make a big deal out of [being same-sex parents]. It's just kinda that's the way it is. [Some] people have one parent. Some people have two that don't live together. Some people have two together that live of the same—the same gender, and that's just the way it is. And so we've never with the kids' friends, never made it an issue. You know what I mean? Just like treated it as normal as possible. It's always been normal for our kids.

Regardless of whether these parents are actively discarding their lesbian identities, just being more discrete with them, or asserting them but distinguishing them from some other LGBTQ identities, we understand all three points of view, which do not represent all of the parents we know and interviewed for this project, as supported by an assimilationist way of being in the world, specifically the world of their children's schools and classrooms.

Whereas we might at first assert that claim with some judgment, wanting more people to be visibly Queer and proud, that judgment is troubled when we consider Dylan's family. He was born into a two-mom household. Early in his life, they began to understand him as gender creative. Once he started school, he began suffering some negative consequences for his creativity. Additionally, shortly after starting school, one of his parents transitioned to living his life as a man. He conveyed that it was easier at school now that he could tell people he had a mom and a dad instead of two moms. His mom confirmed, "I'm sure it probably is a relief to him that now he does have a daddy and a mommy.... So, he's much more like other kids at school who have traditional families." In this situation, especially in school environments where adult personnel and educators do not step up and intervene, we can't help but want a little shield of normalcy for this young student. It is important for educators to pay attention to and respect families' needs and desires in terms of connecting with other families, both similar to and different than their own.

The Paradox of Visibility

With Dylan and his family in mind, we focus here on the paradox of visibility. This reflects what we see in the previous section, but magnifies it. To do so, we draw on interviews with queer parents raising gender diverse children because they have unique insights on being queer based on their own experiences that might inform their parenting of gender diverse children. This means we focused on a subset of the larger set of data: five interviews representing three families, each with one child, who we introduce below.

- Kai, who we mention earlier in this chapter, was the oldest of the young people of focus and was in between seventh and eighth grades. She was Asian American and middle class. Although assigned the gender of girl at birth, Kai had performed gender in ways that ranged from androgyny to masculinity ever since she had control of her clothes, shoes, and hairstyles. She was, however, in the process of reinventing her outward appearance and style. Kai's mother, Melanie, was the sole parent of Kai, was also Asian American and identified as bisexual.
- Libby was in fourth grade. She wore gender neutral clothing and generally expressed gender in ways that range from androgynous to masculine. She had two custodial parents, one of whom was Elliot, who was partnered with Kristin. Both Elliot and Kristin identified as Queer. In their household, Libby was a part of a working-class family.
- Dylan was in second grade and was the only child of Reese and Blair, both white, working-class individuals. Reese identified as a transsexual man. Blair identified as Queer. Reese and Blair had been separated and had shared custody for years.

All three of the students went to school in the same district, which, as we mention above, had a lottery system in which parents could enter their children to attend a school other than their neighborhood school. All three students participated in the lottery, and none of them attended their neighborhood school. Two of the three, Kai and Libby, attended Guthrie, which we discuss above as a lottery school. The third student, Dylan, attended a Careytown neighborhood school, just not the neighborhood school where his legal parent lived.

Both parents and students conveyed the desire to see people like themselves. Kristin, for example, Libby's stepparent, said,

> When we went, went, in our kindergarten, like first kindergarten day, um, there was another kid that had four moms. Not only four moms, but bio mom, non-bio mom, that had had her together and split and then they each had a girlfriend that was with them in the classroom just like . . . She had immediate like visibility of herself in someone else, yeah. . . . It was, we just felt like we already have this community.

Although all of these gender diverse youth did not articulate this wish for visible community as explicitly as Libby's parent, we heard the same message in Kai's desire for people like her, particularly when she compared camp and school. Emily was her friend at camp. According to Kai, Emily was the kind of person and the kind of friend that, in Kai's words, "if someone calls her a guy, she isn't just like, 'well, so is Kai.' She'd just be like, 'yeah I'm a guy, damn right.'" Kai and Emily changed in a private bathroom together before they went swimming at camp. When they were divided into lines based on gender they stood together at the back of and in between the two lines. Kai said the problem with school was that there was no one like Emily. Describing her school, she said, "I mean the people there are nice but they're not all like me, so I can't . . . I . . . yeah. I can never fully be open." Her mother mentioned one of her close friends, to which Kai replied, "Yeah she's accepting but she's not like me, so it's not the same." And when Mollie asked her what she wanted at school, she explained that she liked how things were at school, she just wished that "Emily or some other person was like her that went to my school." Thus, seeing people like themselves, having a visible community, was important for both queer parents and their gender diverse children.

The young people in particular, though, articulated the risks of being seen. Most commonly, these accounts were related to bathrooms and locker rooms. Both Kai and Libby's parents told about their being harassed by girls who perceive them as boys in girls' bathrooms to the extent of their refusing to drink water at school in order to avoid having to use the bathroom and be seen and therefore harassed in bathrooms. According to Melanie, Kai "did not like to go to the bathrooms at school because other girls would always tell her to get out." Similarly, Elliot reported that "a lot of times [Libby's] getting out of the car [coming home from school] like squeezing her legs, running to the bathroom." To be a student who other students perceive as a boy, whether that student identifies as such or not, in the girls' bathroom is to be seen as queer, at best, as predator, at worst. Either way, such visibility was avoided even when avoiding it came at great physical discomfort.

Being seen, though, as gender nonconforming even had consequences in spaces like the classroom, playground, bus, and synagogue as well. On Kai's bus, for example, "the bus driver decided to maintain order by separating . . . them out by gender." Then, according to Kai,

> when people got off and they were like . . . I mean like . . . I don't know anyone that, like, stares at you, but, like, if you're walking off the bus and you just, like, happen to look by a different row and you see, like, a boy on the side and then all these . . . and the rest of the girls.

The implication was that Kai felt vulnerable by her visibility as a not feminine person on the girls' side of the bus. According to Melanie, "you didn't want to ride on the bus anymore after that." Melanie remembered that Kai made herself sick to avoid the bus, although Kai remembered that differently. But even in a decidedly public space, like the bus, visibility as something other than gender conforming was avoided even when such avoidance required great effort.

Whereas visibility as queer was understood in relation to vulnerability, visibility as normative was understood in relation to security. Dylan, for example, called Reese "Mommy" when Dylan started school, even though "Reese has always projected butchness." When Reese started his transition, Dylan started calling him "Maddie" and then by first grade was calling him "Daddy." When classmates would reference Reese as Dylan's mom, Dylan would correct them, he said. Both Reese and Mollie tried to engage Dylan in a conversation about his experience of this transition

Reese: How do you feel about that? Mom becoming dad. You care?
Mollie: Does it make anything easier or harder?
Dylan: Easier.
Mollie: Why is it easier?
Reese: Why?
Dylan: Because . . .
Reese: You can cuddle on my chest now without these being in the way? [Laughter]
Reese: I don't know. Never mind. We can share clothes? We could do that before though.
Mollie: Is it easier telling people at school that you have a mom and a dad?
Dylan: Yeah.
Mollie: Than having two moms you think?
Dylan: Yeah.

The brevity of Dylan's contributions to this interaction make them difficult to interpret. Mollie understood Dylan's "yeah"s as earnest. If we assume this is correct, then we can understand that, for Dylan, it was easier to be visible as a child of a mom and a dad than it was as one of two moms. Visibility as normative was, for Dylan, more secure.

Kai seemed to agree. She was hoping that her life might be made easier by modifying her gender expression from gender queer to gender conforming. Kai's situation was distinct, though, in that her modification would require a different sort of effort. I asked her what she was hoping for in high school, and she said:

Well I'm plan . . . I mean, I don't really want to be like this . . . I don't really want to get, like, changed, um, I sort of just want to get out of this . . . like, I sort of just want to grow my hair out and I want to be able to go to the bathroom comfortably. And not have to worry about all this stuff. Like, most of my anx . . . like, anxiety is from problems that rise from this. So I sort of just . . . and it's not just because of the way people react, but it's also because I sort of just want to be more girly and grow my hair.

Kai thus explained that when she thought of high school, which would be her first school transition since she came to Guthrie for kindergarten, she could avoid the anxiety she experienced as a seventh grader by presenting in ways that are understood as more gender normative, that is more like a girl. Later, in the same discussion, her mom returned to this idea and said,

> I think you like to think that changing the way you dress is like the panacea. You know? It's like that's what's going to change everything. But I think it's like being in drag.... You'll be in drag every day of your life.

Kai resisted her mom's interpretation in a variety of ways, and then Mollie asked about the details of her plan:

Mollie: So are you imagining this happening, like, the summer between eighth grade and ninth grade?

Kai: I'm trying to. But then it would be like . . . like I can't come in one day and be like, I'm in a dress . . . er, not in a dress but I'm in this now. I don't know. So I don't know when I'm going to do it, but maybe over the summer between eighth grade and high school. But I sort of want to get it done before eighth grade.

Thus Kai communicated her intention to change her gender expression, her recognition of the challenges of such a change, and her commitment to overcoming the obstacles in order to "get it done." From Kai's point of view, being visible as gender normative would solve the most pronounced problems she was experiencing. Many of us have witnessed Kai's follow through on her intention. It has appeared thorough. Whether it has solved or created more problems, though, we do not know.

Queer parents and their gender diverse children expressed a desire to be a part of communities where they can see and be with other people like themselves. They, particularly the young people, though, understood a certain vulnerability with being seen as something other than gender conforming, whether they were being seen in private spaces like bathrooms and locker rooms or in public ones, like school buses. Moreover, they understood the security of being seen as part of a heteronormative family, in Dylan's case, or being seen as gender normative, in Kai's case. They, specifically Libby and Kai, are even willing to suffer consequences to avoid being seen, whether in the bathroom or more generally speaking, as gender non-conforming.

Queer parents and their gender diverse children do not want to be able to *see* people like themselves so much as *be* with people like them, to share in a community in which they are among others like themselves. It's not that they want those people to be vulnerable via their visibility but just to be available as supports, particularly for their children so they do not feel isolated or ostracized. Educators can support this effort by creating opportunities for parents to get to know one another.

An ideal community would be one where being seen as queer didn't come with penalties so severe that entirely changing one's gender expression feels like a reasonable change to make. In such a community, visibility as queer would not mean vulnerability, visibility as straight would not mean security, and, therefore, visibility would matter much less.

Queer Parents Acting

Once queer parents have established a presence in their children's schools, they started taking actions to make those schools the best they can be for their children, as well as other students who are impacted by biases against LGBTQ people. They noticed vulnerable students, provided teachers with resources, and even served as resources themselves.

Queer parents noticed vulnerable students, particularly gender diverse students. Simone, for example, noticed Libby at her child's school. She said,

> I've been noticing [Libby] doing some more girl-like things but she looks so unhappy . . . . That I wonder if she's just doing it because she can't deal with the pressure . . . . You know and I would think that it would be a safer place to work that out at [Guthrie]. But it doesn't seem to be.

Simone also noticed Kai at her child's school and described her as "taking a beating." She struggled with a desire to interact with this student. She said, "You know and I'm like how do I—what can I and I think that I'm also just sort of—I don't know, you know? It's like maybe you just want to say living in a transgender world, let's talk about it. You know?" Simone wanted to reach out to this young person, to talk about what it's like to live in a "transgender world," but was not, as far as we know, able to do so. Similarly, Mollie noticed that one of her children's classmates regularly disrupted gender norms and seemed to be experiencing some isolation at school. She always asked her child about this student and coached her child to be an ally on his behalf. Moreover, Mollie regularly saw this student at church and spoke to religious leaders about curtailing practices that reified dichotomous gender practices, like giving flowers to all girls and women on Mother's Day.

Queer parents also provided resources to teachers. When they saw that there were no books in their children's classrooms that represent families like theirs, for example, they recommended or even provided them. Liz, one of two moms of an elementary school student, talked about spending a lot of time in her daughter's classroom, and said,

> sometimes the kids have questions. We try to . . . we usually give teachers like a couple of ideas of maybe books they might want to share. . . . Like the Parr *[The] Family Book*, we talk about that, and um . . . you know just how our family is different.

Similarly, Mollie recommended that her child's childcare provider get that book, which states that it is OK to have all sorts of families, including but not limited to families with two moms or two dads, and Meyers and Frazee's *Everywhere Babies*, in which many kinds of families are represented in the illustrations, including interracial same-gender parents. Then, in preschool, Mollie suggested that teachers get Richardson and Parnell's *And Tango Makes Three*, which tells the true story of two male penguins pairing and adopting and raising a baby penguin. She found that these teachers were quite receptive to her suggestions. She later saw the books in the classroom, among other books about families and diversity. Moreover, providing such resources challenged teachers to engage in conversations about various family structures. For example, one time, Mollie walked into her child's preschool classroom to see a table on the wall that listed the students' names in the left-hand column and categories like mothers, fathers, brothers, sisters, dogs, cats, and other pets in the top row. Then in each block were tally marks. This invited but did not require children like Mollie's to name having two moms. Surprisingly, Mollie's child noted having two moms and six dads, which she later explained to Mollie was a count of significant men in her life, including her godfathers.

There were times that same-gender parents were positioned as experts by teachers, administrators, and other parents. For example, Sarah, one of two moms with two elementary school students, thought it was a "good thing" that the principal of one of the elementary schools her children attended positioned her as expert. In this case, Sarah and her partner were positioned as experts on the rights and responsibilities of same-gender parents. She told the story of a same-gender couple that broke up and then the "parent [who] was not the birth parent, and not the one where the kids were living, tr[ied] to pick the kids up, and it caused quite a . . . there was a big blow up." The principal called Sarah and her partner in "just to see if she was—to kind of bounce [ideas off of] how she was handling it." The principal explained that she didn't let the student go with the parent because the school did not have any paperwork on file. The principal had "never thought it, she didn't think it was . . . different than any other family." Sarah and her partner affirmed the principal's decision, stating, "if you check our kid's files, you'll see co-custodies . . . . You need it, so put it in there to cover your butt." In this case, these same-gender parents were brought in as experts if not to police other same-gender parents at least to support the principal in doing so.

This event raises questions regarding what is known about diversity within any given community. Sarah and her family had the economic privilege to obtain the legal paperwork that allowed both moms to pick up their children from school. Clearly, this is not the case with all same-gender parents. Moreover, in this situation, both the principal and the family was constrained by limits of their knowledge and experience. The principal declares her lack of knowledge and experience with queer families while asking a queer family to act as expert and advise a school administrator on the best course of action for another family. One family cannot speak well for all families just as no individual should be asked to speak for the entirety of any group of which they are a part. One might imagine an alternative suggestion for the principal to contact the parent with legal rights and ask about the family's intention and request that that parent submit supporting paperwork. So, while we question the judgment of the principal in this case, we also recognize that Sarah appreciated the principal reaching out to seek information that Sarah had and had likely worked hard to acquire.

As noted earlier, Elliot and Kristin were actively involved in their school's PTG and positioned as experts in their roles. They worked with other parents in the organization, including Caroline, to initiate and implement a weeklong curriculum that celebrated student individuality and diversity. Included in this curriculum was a viewing and discussion of the film *It's Elementary*, which features teachers and administrators exploring issues pertinent to lesbian and gay people with elementary and middle school students. Caroline did multiple screenings of the film first for Guthrie teachers, then for members of the PTG, and ultimately, for all of the middle grades students and all interested Guthrie parents. Initially, the PTG faced pushback from some Guthrie families who, although they had never seen the film, had concerns about its contents and about the curriculum plans in general. These parents contacted the Guthrie principal, who forwarded these concerns on to the PTG. PTG members, including the PTG president, a straight mother of three primary grade students, as well as Elliot, Kristin, and Caroline, a queer/bi- mother of a questioning sixth grader, invited these parents to meet with them at a local restaurant to share information about the film and to answer questions. This meeting required a great deal of extra time and effort on the part of queer parents, not to mention putting themselves in a situation where they would be vulnerable to other openly hostile parents while simultaneously being required to educate these same people about themselves and their children's experiences in school. Nonetheless, Elliot, Kristin, and Caroline made this choice in order to make it possible for the film and curriculum to be used at Guthrie. Kristen explained that they participated in the development of this curriculum because they knew that their child was "struggling with that and like bringing visual is, you know visual images of other types of women." Here, these parents brought their expertise as queer people to influence the school's curriculum.

By noticing vulnerable students, providing teachers with resources, and even serving as resources themselves, these queer parents acted in ways that improved the school experiences of children in queer families. Not unequivocally, though. One of Susan's children talked about how disorienting this week was. She spoke in particular about watching and discussing

> a movie about how it [being queer] is natural and it's fun, and then I was like watching kids who are like against it already. And I was like, that was the first real seeing I've had about people who did not approve of it, which really confused me because it was my life and I was this little kid.

In other words, she had been raised in a family where it was safe to be queer and did not really realize until this curricular event how contested her reality was. Thus, she experienced it as a place for people to articulate their homophobia rather than a space to combat it. Teachers can support queer parents who are willing to make curricular contributions, but they must, simultaneously understand queer families in all of their diversity.

Queer Parents Reacting

When queer parents were acting in their children's schools in an effort to make these contexts more friendly to queer families, they made some pretty positive contributions. When reacting to homophobia, heterosexism, and transphobia in these same contexts, though, their contributions were sometimes more troubling.

For example, when Sarah, a white middle-class lesbian mother, described a child calling her child a fag, she said,

> once in like first grade one little girl who was [a] retarded smart aleck called [Seth] a fag, but I don't think it had anything to do with [his having lesbian parents]. It was just her mouthing off on the playground, and that was the end of it. . . . I said, well, if it happens again, you tell me.

Here, when the child of a lesbian mom was called a homophobic slur, she reacted with another slur and additional dismissive language. Moreover, she understood it either as an isolated event to ignore or one that she would address. In this way, she missed opportunities to educate the girl who used the homophobic term about the harm in using words like fag or her son about how to navigate such interactions. Opportunities for humanizing discourses were, essentially, squashed.

Similarly, when queer parents encountered heterosexism from teachers they squashed opportunities for humanizing discourses by evading difficult conversations. This happened, for example, when a white, straight, and cisgender teacher in an elementary classroom with a handful of students with queer parents revealed her heterosexism in a class project. The class created a book of Greek gods and goddesses; each student was responsible for one page in the book. Parents were invited to purchase a bound version of the book. When the book came in, there was, according to Mollie, a "blank line [for a dedication] where kids could have filled it out, but [the teacher] wrote, 'to my mom and dad, the real goddess and god of my life,' or something like that." She said, "I was just, like, 'Ah!' And I was furious, like, I was furious about it. . . . But [the teacher] was proud of it. . . . The teacher put it in the display for parent/teacher conferences." Several queer parents described their negative reactions to this same event, but none of them talked to the teacher directly. Catherine said she "didn't want to like make it awkward for [our child] or bad for [him] in any way you know." Similarly, Simone said, "honestly the reason I didn't say anything is because I didn't want it to be more difficult.... For [my child] ... Or any of the other kids in here." Mollie expressed a similar apprehension. She said:

> I'm a teacher. I was a teacher. And like, parent/teacher conferences just completely stress me out. They—I feel like I get so little time with any given teacher that the consequences of that time are so, um, great, you know? Like if I screw it up, like, will she hate my kid for the rest of the year?

Despite these reservations, Mollie rehearsed what she would say to the teacher about the dedication page at the parent teacher conference, which was scheduled for the last time slot of the evening, but when the meeting happened, Mollie recounted that,

> the teacher couldn't go off her script. Like, she knew what she was going to say and that's what she was going to say, and then she was going to go home. And she seemed so flustered that I didn't feel like I could say—I was like, "She's going to cry. She's going to cry on me if I do anything wrong, or if I disrupt her plan."

As a result, Mollie said nothing about the dedication page to the teacher. Instead, Mollie spoke with her child and Martha, another white lesbian parent of a student in the teacher's class who was also a teacher in the school. Mollie noted that her child "understood when [she] said [she] was mad and why," and that Martha agreed to talk with the teacher as a colleague. According to Mollie, Martha said to the teacher,

> You know, I saw that this was out for parent conferences. You're going to ostracize some of your parents by this.... You know, not only families like mine who have two moms, but also people whose mom and dad are not in the picture, or a grandmother, all the depictions of family.

In response, Mollie was told that the teacher "just got weepy," and said, "Well, I never meant to do that." While Mollie appreciated Martha's talking to the teacher as her colleague, she wondered how things might have been different if, at the beginning of school, she had said something like,

> "We are both [Brooke]'s moms and you know, you should talk to both of us when we come." Like maybe [my partner] would have been more welcomed in that classroom. Maybe, um, maybe [the teacher] would have thought about it when she wrote that page. I don't know.

In other words, Mollie raised the question of what difference it might make if queer parents stepped into conversations with the teachers of their children rather than around them. That said, when some of these same parents, including Mollie, went to talk with the principal of the school about the need for a gender-neutral bathroom and locker room, the principal was kind in her response, listening, restating what she heard, and offering action steps, but ultimately ineffectual. That is to say, none of the action steps were actually taken, and ultimately, no changes were made to serve gender diverse students better with respect to bath rooms and locker rooms.

A more effective but no less problematic approach was hiding a concern of excluding gay people behind a concern of excluding other people, maybe a broader range of people, but decidedly not gay people. This was the approach taken by Liz and Teri when they were among parent leaders meeting to discuss the possibility of organizing a "daddy-daughter dance." Here's their account:

Liz: We have this little meeting about we wanted to do this Daddy-Daughter Dance . . . and we were all supposed to go home thinking about it, and I came back to the next meeting with statistics from our school, about why . . . because the principle was that they wanted everyone to be included, but I said "look, the first thing you're doing is you're cutting out over 60 percent of your school, because you're making it a Daddy-Daughter Dance, and all those boys, they've got nothing to do, so they are staying home. . . . So, now you have just these girls, less than half of your school is invited to this event. Now, within that, how many of these kids actually have a daddy at home?"

Teri: Or anywhere to be frank.

Liz: Right, so you don't have a daddy, so now another amount of these kids, are out of the equation. And then within that, how many of these kids are going to feel . . . how many of their parents are going to give them the money to go buy a special dress for this big gala? Now you have an economic reason. So now you've got . . . You want to do this so you can include everyone, and now you're way cutting them out . . . this tiny little sliver . . . and there was a parent on the board that was totally ticked at me the entire time, who thought I was making a gay thing out of it. I said, "I'm not making a gay thing out of it. Here are the statistics from our school. I have the specific statistics from our school about all the people that they were actually going to exclude from it." You know . . . and the answer . . . well . . . in February we are going to do a . . . or in March we are going to do a March Madness thing for boys. I'm just like . . . "Okay, so what about the little girls who like to play basketball who can't come? You know, because that's your boy thing. But you're doing all of this to be inclusionary . . . you want everyone to feel included, but you're wiping section after section after section out just from what you're calling it alone." . . . Then it ended up being called the sweetheart dance and everyone was like . . .

Teri: And it's still like that today, even though we are not there. . . .

Liz: But there was this one parent that was very adamant with me about how I was making it into a gay thing. I was like, "clearly, I'm not making it into a gay thing."

Liz and Teri clearly saw that their daughter would be excluded from a daddy-daughter dance because she had two mothers and no father, but rather than argue that case, they argued about how such an event would exclude all sons, daughters without dads, and daughters whose families could not provide fancy dresses. Although their approach raised the suspicion of at least one other person who insisted that their disapproval of the event was grounded in a "gay thing," it worked, perhaps in part because of their vehement refusal to acknowledge that their disapproval had anything to do with being gay. While effective, this approach was problematic in that it failed to address the implicit heterosexism in events like daddy-daughter dances, but also because it relied on stereotypes about others, such as who is raised in what sort of family construction, in articulating concerns about excluding people based on gender and class, and implicitly, race.

Of course, there were times when queer parents' reactions could be understood as troubling to some people but not to others. For example, we imagine many queer parents have had experiences like Sharon had in Trey's classroom; that is, when a classmate of their child had questions about their child's family. Sometimes these questions are coming from a place of earnest curiosity, as in Sharon's situation described earlier in this chapter, and other times from somewhere maybe a little less generous. For example, on multiple occasions, when Mollie volunteered in her child's kindergarten and first grade classes, for parties and field trips, students asked her questions about her child's family. At one class party, while decorating cookies, a student asked Mollie to confirm that her child was telling the truth regarding her parents. She explained, as briefly as possible, that her child had two moms, but she also had two godfathers, and that her sister had a biological father that this child sometimes claimed as her own. On one occasion Mollie followed up with a question about how many parents the inquiring student had, and he stated, "One mom, one dad, like normal." In this case, Mollie's reaction was to explain that normal is different for every family, and that his family might not seem normal to a child raised by only one parent or a grandparent or a parent with two moms or two dads. On another occasion, in the same class, this time on a field trip, a student told her that she knew how babies were made, and that she knew it took a mom and a dad. Mollie explained, again, as briefly as possible, that sometimes parents, even moms and dads, weren't able to give what was needed to make a baby, and for those people, they could get what was necessary from other people who were willing to share. Nervous about this conversation, Mollie contacted the child's parent, who she had met several times, and let her know what her child and Mollie had discussed. The parent explained that her husband and she try to be very open and honest with their child and thanked Mollie for answering her child's questions. In these situations, there was certainly a risk that Mollie's reactions might have been understood as troublesome, and although the latter example was not interpreted that way, the former might have been, she just didn't know the parents to follow up.

Just as queer parents reacted to homophobia, heterosexism, and transphobia in schools, they also reacted to racism and classism. For example, Simone's child attended Guthrie, and she yearned for connections among other multi-racial families there. She imagined

> Put[ting] up something and say[ing], you know, "Biracial, multi-racial, multi-ethnic, multi-cultured . . . . Want to talk about" and then . . . . See who shows up and then have a very clear idea that this, you know, this time that we meet you can air whatever you came here to air, when we meet again it's not going to be about that, we're going to move forward.

At the same time, she recognized that class diversity sometimes hindered connections. So, for example, she expressed frustration with "the classism in the way that you look at my SUV down your nose while you drive your bio car that costs $45,000." Even school practices were grounded in classism, such as the regular informal parent meetings at 9a.m. that cater to "that sort of stay at home mom thing." In other words, making connections in socioeconomically diverse schools, at least in this socioeconomically diverse school, was difficult because of the almost ubiquitous classism.

Teachers were also sometimes a part of the problem. In talking about her interactions with one of the teachers, Simone said:

> I do think that it's a color issue for her with us and the gay thing . . . . I think it's the both of those things you know? Right, and because I feel her physically withdraw . . . . And it doesn't feel like that it's just because she thinks I'm going to lean over and kiss her or something, you know? . . . . But I also think it's like the Black thing, I do.

Here, Simone conveyed how a Queer person of color is required to sort through which micro-aggressions are provoked by what features. She knew the teacher was repulsed by her and could imagine a homophobic reason for it but was certain there was also a racist reason behind it. This effort is considerably more labor intensive than the work a white Queer person has to do. For instance, Mollie recounted a similar experience with the same teacher refusing to make eye contact with her; she, however, did not have to wonder whether the response was about sexuality or race.

The impacts of a teacher's racism, homophobia, and transphobia, though, are not limited to the parent; the child suffers the consequences as well. According to Simone,

> In [the teacher's] eyes, I mean, you know, look, I am a dark skinned, Black kid from the country, queer, trans you know all of these things, Christian. I'm a little used to seeing people have difficulty with what to do with all of this greatness . . . . [But] I don't always think that of everybody, you know, so I'm trying to get my mind around, like, what can be done here, because [the teacher is] not comfortable and I feel like maybe [she and I] need to have a conversation because I'm not sure why [she's] not comfortable . . . . But if [she's] not comfortable, my kid has to be able to feel that and when people around are getting cues on how to stay in that from [her].

Thus, the child not only experienced biases from her teacher but also others, likely students, who were being implicitly taught by the teacher to reject people of color in queer families (Anderson, 2016). Simone worried about this enough to consider having a conversation with the teacher, but, in her words, "sometimes I just feel so worn out by everything because I know how much it will take." In other words, the work of making allies out of teachers who are not doing the work themselves is exhausting. Instead, Simone prepared her child for "what people might say;" she prepared her for what she called "this whole Civil Rights activism and whatnot."

Like Simone, Matthew prepared his biracial children for the impacts of racism along with homophobia. He said,

> I mean the one thing that we've taught our boys . . . is that there's, there's always going to be somebody that's gonna, not gonna like something about you—not gonna like your hair, not gonna like your color, not gonna like the fact that you have two parents, you have gay parents. You, there's going to be something. Your feet are too big . . . whatever. So forget about the people that are like that and gravitate toward the people that like you and that have friends that are like you. That, that's life. I mean it's just the way life is.

Although both Simone and Matthew talked about preparing their biracial children raised by same-gender parents for racism and homophobia, their approaches were really quite different. Simone, as an African America parent, drew on "Civil Rights activism" to explain her intentions. In doing so, she took a sort of intersectional approach; that is, an approach that honors intersecting identities. Matthew, on the other hand, as a white middle-class parent, considered all sorts of differences in parallel terms, from race and sexuality to foot size. His partner underscored this understanding of diversity by saying, "if you just put everybody on equal footing all the way around, that would be nice." The approach relies on an understanding of identities as parallel rather than intersecting. Although it is not surprising, it is still disheartening to find more evidence pointing to racism, classism, and xenophobia within LGBTQ communities. As teachers interested in supporting queer families, understanding intersectional identities and becoming aware of their own implicit biases is one important step toward disrupting this hatred in classrooms rather than perpetuating it.

Queer Parents Helping Their Children

Ultimately, it is not enough for queer parents to act (and react) in their children's schools. They must also help their children navigate schools in particular but also the world more broadly where they often encounter homophobia, transphobia, and heterosexism. We first focus on the ways that queer parents help their own queer children, and then examine how they support their children more generally, since even the most heteronormative of children are made vulnerable to homophobia and transphobia because they have queer parents.

When queer parents came to understand at least the possibility that their children might not conform to heteronormative expectations, whether that is because they express same-gender desire or perform gender diversity, these parents tried not to impose their experiences as queer youth on their children. Elliot, for example, you recall was a Queer parent of a gender queer elementary student, Libby. Elliot explained,

> I ended up with a pretty big chip on my shoulder.... I can't tell you how many times I've had security guards... waiting for me [outside of bathrooms]. Police officers waiting for me, like, and so it's hard not to—you know the armor starts to... ge[t] heavy... and I wanted to make sure that I didn't pass that to her.

Elliot expressed a concern that she would hand the weight of her experiences having grown up gender non-conforming in a homophobic and transphobic environment onto her child. As a way of interrupting this possible action, Elliot had to remind herself that she and her child grew up in entirely different contexts. She said,

> I have to realize... that she's living in a completely different world than I ever did... and I have to make sure that I'm not... seeing anything through my eyes when I was her age... because I know the world's changed. I can see it... so I have to make sure that when I'm talking to her about these things that I'm not talking to her with my child's eyes.

Coming to understand her child's environment as distinct from her own childhood context was crucial for Elliot. Seeing this difference allowed her to guide Libby in navigating the world as it is today, not as Elliot experienced it decades ago.

In addition to recognizing the differences between past and current contexts, queer parents of queer children also engaged their children in frank discussions about what it means to be queer in heterosexist if not homophobic and transphobic communities, recognizing that while their experiences of the world are not the same, such hatred is still a persistent presence. Libby's stepparent and one of her parents took different approaches in their conversations with her about her performance of masculinity. One said,

> You look like a boy. All the visual markers that you are displaying are boy. So, you really are going to have to tell people, unless you want to do something, unless you want to wear pink t-shirts or grow your hair out and have a ponytail. I mean, you can choose to look different so people will identify you differently, but the fact is if I saw you on the street and I didn't know you, I would think you were a boy until I learned differently.

The focus here is on what the young person did or could have done to inform others of the pronouns with which she identified, whether through clothes, like wearing pink; hair, like having a pony tail; or just telling people. The idea was that this child could take control of whether she was misgendered.

Other advice Libby received was less about what she could do to shape other people's interpretations of her and more about how she could make sense of their interpretations. This parent said:

> I've spent a lot of time, you know, like really trying to instill in her that it's not personal . . . it really, really, really isn't that. It's gender markers . . . you know and it's not specific to her. I mean if . . . a boy has long hair and somebody glances up . . . you know I'm like you don't really look at each other . . . so there's so many of us [people]. . . . so people just use gender markers . . . they're just like, you know . . . boy or girl? . . . You know it's just simple. It's just simple and it's not personal . . . so I really spend a lot of time just trying to like you know . . . just instill that in her that it really is not personal.

Although both adults were trying to be direct, explicit, and helpful, one focused on how the child might better accommodate her social context and the other focused on how the child might better understand her social context so that it is not so harmful to her. We are not suggesting that one approach is better than the other, but that the two approaches accomplish really different work. We imagine, though, it was of some use for Libby to hear both approaches so that she could consider the options and the related consequences to decide what was right for her in different contexts.

Similarly, Blair, the parent of Dylan, a gender queer elementary student you met earlier, explained, "we try really hard to get him to understand that difference is okay." Like Libby's parents, Blair had explicit conversations with Dylan. She said he and I have this conversation all the time . . . why would anybody want to be exactly the same. . . . And it's okay if you're different. . . . You know, so we have that discussion a lot. And I've heard him like—overheard him talking to people and like [say]—like word for word saying those same things . . . . "It's boring [not] to be different." And you know, so like, you know, as long as he understands.

By being explicit in her conversations with Dylan, Blair made it clear that Dylan was OK the way he was not in spite of being different but *because* of being different.

Just as Blair tried to teach Dylan to be comfortable with himself, other queer parents tried to teach their children, and not just queer children, to be comfortable with their families. They did so by teaching them about same-gender headed families in books, having their children spend time with similarly constructed families, and discussing with their children how there are a wide array of families, not just traditional families and theirs. Ginny's family, for example, read a variety of books to teach her child about their family. She said:

Ginny: We had a lot of books. A lot. We had a few books and then we talked. Like those Todd Parr books about families are diff—whatever, I can't remember . . .
Kim: *The Family Book.*
Ginny: Yes. We had those all the time. And we had some specifically about two moms, which was kind of awful, but it did explain it—because it the pictures are horrible. Could the women look dykier? I am always like oh man they are always stereotypical roles . . . . It explained us, but it wasn't really us. Not who we were.
Kim: Right. Right. *Heather Has Two [Mommies]*
Ginny: You know? So we—we would read that to her and so I mean, we, we did Todd Parr mostly. We'd be like, "Some families have two moms. Yay! Like me."

While this family used books to show their child other same-gender headed families, others made a concerted effort to connect with other families, particularly through a local social support group for same-gender headed families, a privilege not available for many people who live outside of cities.

There was also an effort to contextualize their "different" family among other kinds of differences in families, particularly with respect to the children their children know. One parent said,

We try to talk with [our child] about the different families that are in his class to kind of highlight it. . . . [Recently,] he said something about . . . how most kids have a mom and a dad. And I'm like, "Really?" I'm like, "Do you think that's true?" He's like, "Well, yeah, that's what most kids have." And I'm like, "Well let's think about your friends." And then we kind of went through his friends, and we talked about it.

This was certainly a pattern among queer parents. Teri, one of two moms, asked her child:

> Do you remember some of the conversations we have had when . . . [we] would give you some examples of other families, like some who have just a grandma, some who have just a dad. Remember? . . . because of where we live, there are lots of different families and we see it . . . there were numerous examples of Grandma's having their kids . . . We, of course, have you know two dad families, two mom families, four mom families, whatever. . . . So, we just give examples and go from there.

Then, her partner Liz turned to Mollie and said,

> We used to talk about how we have different families, but everybody has a different family and it isn't any more different than someone else's different, because different is different. . . . Everybody has a different family. What makes a family is love, and we have lots of love.

Here we see that queer parents wanted their children to know not only were they not the only family to be constructed as theirs was but also that there were all sorts of constructions of families. Moreover, they conveyed that what made a family was not structure so much as love.

Having their children feel comfortable with their families as different than some families, but similar to other families, was one thing queer parents wanted. But they also wanted their children to feel prepared to respond to questions about their families' differences if need be. And, they wanted this not only for what it would do for their child, but also for other queer families. Simone, for example, said,

> I feel like sometimes we—the negative situations happen because we don't have the language for how to really communicate about it. It's not—it doesn't matter if someone says, "Oh you have two moms"? Your response can be "Yeah I do, you want to talk about it"? . . . If we can try and give that language of being able to communicate; it's okay for somebody to ask you about your different; isn't that what we're—we've been fighting for . . . . So you know in this whole Civil Rights activism and whatnot, it's really about managing the conversation. So I wanted my daughter to be somewhat prepared for what people might say. . . . And to say "Hey"—it might be tough sometimes. I'm not setting an emotion; I'm being realistic about the world. It might be tough sometimes but remember we love you; you know? And not everybody has two moms, you know?

Simone believed that if her child could manage conversations about her family, then she would be a part of making the world a better place for other people who have two moms.

Similarly, some queer parents believed that teaching their children about gender and sexual fluidity could help make the world a better place. For example, Dakota and her family told a story about her as a preschooler. Dakota, a white, middle-class girl had classmates who would ask, repeatedly, "'Are you a boy or a girl?'" Dakota said she walked up to them and said, "'You don't have to be one or the other. You can be whatever you want to be. . . . A girl-boy or a boy-girl.' [And then] I threw my hands up in the air. I was like, 'Seriously.' So, and then nobody asked again." Understanding gender in these terms allowed this young person, when she was very young, to interrupt cisgender norms, a mindset she continued to carry and be proud of.

Queer parents helped their children navigate homophobia, transphobia, and heterosexism in schools in particular but also in the world more broadly in a variety of ways. When their children embodied sexualities and gender beyond the hegemonic heteronormative, they had to reflect deeply on their experiences and contain those experiences such that they did not inappropriately impose them on their children. Moreover, they had to engage in explicit and honest discussions about how their children might accommodate their social contexts, interpret their social contexts, and come to understand difference, their own and others, as valuable.

Regardless of their children's sexual identities and gender expressions, queer parents had to teach their children to be comfortable with their families in social contexts that often fail to support such a lesson. They drew on books about families and difference as well as other families who were anything other than the all but fictional traditional family to teach their children to be comfortable in their families that were different but not alone in their difference. That is to say, parents wanted their children to acknowledge their families' difference with an understanding that difference is not only OK but, like sameness, difference is also ubiquitous. Moreover, they prepared their children to respond to questions about their families in ways that invited open discussion rather than provoked something less productive, like silent tension. Finally, some parents strove to teach their children about sexual and gender fluidity with the idea that if sexual identity and gender expression can change over time and across spaces, then the question of whether one's parents are same-gender or not is much less significant and so too is the question of a young person's sexual identity or gender expression. Just because it is one way here and now doesn't mean it will not be another way later, somewhere else. What's the big deal, "seriously"?

Queer parents not only help their children navigate schools and the world, they work to make schools and the world more understanding of queer people. For example, when one parent at Guthrie was struggling with her child's gender creativity, a small group of queer parents came together to talk with her about their experiences with gender diverse children, mostly their children. This group met on and off over two school years to explore various ways they might make their school and perhaps even their school district more inviting places for gender diverse children. They launched an ongoing effort to propose and implement a trans-inclusive policy, drawing on GLSEN's policy, so that there would be accessible bathrooms and locker rooms in all schools in the district. In doing so, they reached out for support from local queer organizations, which prompted a training conducted by a local trans organization, which the group opened up to local teachers and parents. Over time, members of this group continued to be called on by the district as the policy effort inches forward.

Teachers can be informed of such efforts. They can support them by offering to answer any questions parents might have about what changes might work well in the school, by informing parents about school and district policies and procedures for making changes, and by serving as liaisons between parents and administration.

Heteronormativity as Protection

As much work as queer parents do to prepare their children for and protect them from homophobia and transphobia in and beyond schools, we acknowledge, almost with grief, the degree of protection inherent in heteronormativity. That is, parents understood and experienced their children's performances of heteronormativity as ways of protecting themselves from homophobia and transphobia, not flawlessly but fairly reliably. In some cases, young people performed heteronormativity by embodying hegemonic masculinity, which Blaise (2005), drawing on Connell, describes as the "cultural expression of the dominant form of masculinity that regulates and subordinates other patterns of masculinity and femininity" (p. 21). In another case, a young person performed heteronormativity by embodying emphasized femininity, which Blaise characterizes as "compliance with subordination . . . oriented around accommodating the interests and desires of men" (p. 21). In some cases, these children were victims or potential victims of homophobia because of their parents' sexual identities, in other cases because of their perceived sexual identities, and in others because of their actual sexual identities and gender expressions. Here we focus less on the form of the performance of heteronormativity or even the reason such performances were useful or necessary and instead focus on how parents reported making sense of these heteronormative performances.

For Sarah such performances seemed like a relief. When she talked about her oldest son, Seth, who was going into fifth grade, she said:

> We're lucky, I always joke that if, if two women are going to have little boys they should be big boys, and, you know Seth's uh, Seth's about 5' 2" runs about 115 [pounds] now at 10 [years old]. So he's a stocky kid, and

people don't mess with him. You know he's not. He's as gentle as gentle Ben. But he's a big-big kid, and so I think people hopefully it'll, hopefully that'll protect him a little bit.

The assumption undergirding this story is that the children of same-gender parents are made vulnerable to homophobia because of their parents, regardless of their own sexual identities or gender expressions. If, however, their sexual identities and gender expressions are normative, so, in this case, if a boy embodies hegemonic masculinity (Blaise, 2005) by being big in a way that "people don't mess with him," then he is "protect[ed]." In other words, when there is the threat of homophobia impacting the child of two mothers, then that child's heteronormativity may alleviate the impact. More explicitly, he is protected by his heteronormativity because it is unlikely that anyone will assume he is gay, but even if someone does, that person wouldn't bother him because, as a large kid, he is likely to be understood as tough, even violent.

Recall, though, Kai, who we discuss in the "Paradox of Visibility" section of this chapter. Kai deliberately planned and implemented her transition from gender queer to gender conforming to solve her problems. In short, she consciously shifted to performing heteronormativity. Since then, Kai has grown out her hair; and at her eighth grade graduation, she wore a dress. In the summer leading into high school, Mollie saw her at the pool in a bikini, tightly clutching a towel, and then again in a tennis skirt. In other words, Kai has performed heteronormativity by embodying femininity, even if not emphasized femininity. But unlike Sarah, Melanie was more worried than relieved. In an anonymous letter addressed to parents in the district she wrote,

> Now my child's a high schooler. I think she chose the school she's in because very few of her middle school classmates went there. It was an opportunity to reinvent herself. For now, she is cloaking herself in the protective cocoon of femininity. . . . She has removed all family photos from the downstairs that show her in her more "boyish" look from elementary and middle school years . . . she has friends over occasionally, and doesn't want them to see what she used to look like. . . . My sense at this point is that she may return to her more gender creative core once she's in college. But for now she's doing what she feels she needs to do to protect herself.

Before, in the interview, Melanie attended less to the homophobia, or transphobia in this case, that the child might suffer from as a result of her gender expression and more to the misery she might experience if she were to conform her gender performances to a heteronormative notion of what a girl should look like. She believed that her child would be happier if she could perform gender authentically rather than normatively. Later, in the letter, Melanie grappled with the tensions among wanting her child to be happy in her authentic gender expressions, understanding her child's need to protect herself, and believing that eventually she might be able to do both.

A final account of parents making sense of their children's performances of heteronormativity shows more evidence of a struggle between safety via heteronormativity and happiness via authenticity above normativity. For Barbara, a white middle-class mother, this struggle was profound. She and her husband were raising two boys: one was in between his sophomore and junior years of high school, and the other was between fifth and sixth grades. Ezra, the older of the two boys, was perceived as gay and experienced severe homophobic abuse as a result of this perception. Heteronormativity was not, it seemed, available to him as protection, or even if it was, it was not an option he elected to pursue.

His brother, Gabriel, though, did have access to such protection, even though he "firmly" identified as gay and had freely expressed, to his immediate family, his attractions to other boys since he was eight years old. He kept his gay identity a secret at school, where he once told one friend who had, as far as Barbara knew, kept it a secret. This maintained the possibility of using heteronormativity as protection. This possibility was made further accessible to Gabriel because he was, in his mother's words, "fairly popular. . . . He's a good athlete, you know, . . . he g[ot] along fine with boys and boys culture." And if this was not enough, Gabriel actively performed hegemonic masculinity at school. Barbara described walking Gabriel to the bus stop, and at first, "he'd be my like soft little bunny, . . . he'd be my like sweetheart, and then as we walk closer to the bus stop, he'd like— . . . physically transform into this like kind of weird swagger." He talked to her about this transformation explicitly. He said that at his school,

> I really need to be like a tough guy all the time, like the fit—like every morning when I go there, I have to like become like the guy, the guy— . . . that just, you know, like is really, really callous and like—like you know threatens to beat people up.

Moreover, when he encountered homophobia he would "get really angry and actually hi[t] people." In other words, asserting hegemonic masculinity by concealing gayness, assuming a swagger, positioning himself as a tough guy, behaving in callous ways, threatening to beat people up, and following through on those threats provided Gabriel with protection from homophobia. In other words, he, unlike Ezra, actively used heteronormativity, specifically hegemonic masculinity, as protection against homophobia.

This is not, however, what Gabriel wanted. According to Barbara, he was "put off" by what he understood as a fact that his friends would "drop him . . . like a hot potato," if they knew he was gay and he didn't like to make the transformation he felt he had to make in going to school. In fact, he chose his middle school because he believed that he could go there and be "'kind of nerdy and more queer and it'll just—like it'll feel more comfortable to me.'" Barbara wanted her sons to be safe and knew that Gabriel's heteronormative performances offered him protection, protection that Ezra lacked, but she also knew that Ezra's gender performances were more authentic than Gabriel's, and wished for Gabriel the opportunity to experience such authenticity, as Gabriel wished for himself, as well.

We see these three accounts on a sort of continuum defined by young people in particular contexts. On one end, there is Seth. While his size and stature did not fully reflect his gentle nature, we have no reason to believe that his mother, Sarah, understood his performance of heteronormativity as inauthentic, so for her, as a parent, there was no tension between the two. Rather, Sarah valued the protection it afforded. On the other end of the continuum, there is Kai, who lived in Careytown and attended Guthrie, both of which were described repeatedly as queer-positive bubbles. For Kai, and her mother Melanie, any tensions around her non-heteronormative identity were less tangible in this context, despite some of the homophobia and transphobia the Kai experienced at times. However, when Kai moved into high school, and assumed a more feminine, gender-conforming look, Melanie's worries were compounded, not relieved. Although she understood and valued Kai's desire for the protection afforded by her performance of heteronormativity, she was profoundly saddened and worried that Kai could not have both authenticity and protection in school. Like Kai, neither Ezra nor Gabriel's authentic gender performances were authentically heteronormative, at least according to their mother, even though they lived in the "bubble" of Careytown but did not go to Guthrie. For Ezra, this resulted in an authentic performance of sexual and gender identity that, due to the excessive demands of heteronormativity, subjected him to extreme homophobia and afforded him no protection. Conversely, for Gabriel, the opposite was true. Although he was authentically gay and comfortably out to his family, his overt masculinity and athleticism allowed him to conceal this identity from his school mates, affording him the protection of heteronormativity at the cost of his authenticity. Thus, there was increased tension between the young people and their contexts, from Seth to Gabriel to Ezra to Kai, which provoked more of a struggle for their parents as they wished both safety and happiness for their children.

In her response to a presentation of this work, Elizabeth Dutro, as our discussant, picked up on this tension, this tension of a straight parent wanting her queer children to be safe and happy, and added another. She talked about the inevitable partiality of parents' understandings of the children's experiences of school. She said,

> [I] wonder what I, as a parent, inevitably do not know, the various ways I might express my knowing and not knowing and how they are not separable. I think about what I interpret differently from my children about their negotiations of gender and sexual identity at school, and how my long view of their lives may offer them insights and, of course, how their lived

experience of school is something I can never fully know, no matter how close we may be, no matter how much we may talk with each other, no matter how much I may strive to be the parent ally they most need me to be. Because, always at play too is their love for me, their concern about my well-being, and what they may not say in order to protect me. Because, of course, a child wants his parent to be happy.

(Dutro, 2015)

Straight Parents Helping and Struggling to Help Their Queer Children

Considering Elizabeth's words and insights, we turn to other straight parents who help, and sometimes struggle to help, their queer children. One thing that seemed to help communicate a parent's support was when the parent had gay friends and included those friends among the child's support network. Barbara, for example, talked about how the children's godfathers were gay men who had been a couple for decades. In this way, her children experienced their parents' love and respect for gay men, at least, long before they claimed any queer identities. So, when the children were older and expressed same-gender desire or claimed non-heteronormative identities, they could do so with at least some confidence that they would be received well, as they were. For example, she described walking with one of her sons by a jogger and her son would say, "oh my god he's good looking," and she would say, "yeah, I know." And with her other child, she described being so proud of him as he expressed his identity and helped to start his school's gay straight alliance (GSA). She said,

> he was so out with—with his identity . . . . I was just kind of really proud, I mean really proud actually . . . and I think he's really proud of [starting the GSA], especially when he found out like from a lot of kids that it was something that meant a lot to them, you know something that he is really happy about.

She also surrounded her children with other people who were also proud of them. For example, one of the godfathers' parents is

> still really active and starting like P flags and all sorts of things . . . . And when she found out about [Ezra] she was like—made me sit down and like talked about the GSA and she was like, she kept coming up to me at this party that we were at, she was like, I'm so proud of him, I'm so proud of him.

Moreover, there is no secrecy that might communicate shame around Barbara's children's sexuality. She said, "both kids are out to all their family members, so there's no, I mean like all extended." Some of the extended family used to be homophobic, but they have, in her words, "become very—very gay proud." When she sent her children to camps, she sought out camps that she believed would be accepting of her children, and when one of them needed counseling, she found a counselor who was accepting of LGBTQ people.

But not all straight parents enter parenting with such insight and comfort around sexualities and gender expressions beyond heterosexual hegemony. This does not mean they do not love their children dearly and want what is best for them, but they might struggle to know what is, in fact, best for them. Consider Chandler's story. Chandler was a white, poor, high school student who was assigned the gender of boy at her birth and was raised by her great-grandmother as a boy. As such, her school records indicated that she was a boy. By the time she was in high school, though, she was presenting as herself, that is, as a girl. When she tried out for color guard, which was a real passion of hers, she was forced to try out as a boy, even though she knew she was a girl and wished to participate on the color guard as a girl. The great-grandmother spoke with school officials about the problem and ascertained that the way to resolve the problem was to take Chandler to a doctor who could provide documentation indicating that Chandler was, in fact, a girl. The great-grandmother said,

> I thought maybe we could get the doctor up there [a nearby city with active LGBT communities] . . . to go ahead and do a physical too. I hope we can. I don't see why [not] because a physical for that stuff, is just a matter of blood pressure and heart and-and check her ears. . . . My son had physicals, and they never checked down below.

It seemed the great-grandmother was hoping for Chandler's expression of femininity to be enough for a doctor to identify Chandler as female, and if the doctor didn't, then, "so be it." But Chandler protested, saying, "I can't go to a regular doctor, and be like OK. Check me." Moreover, she asserted, "I don't need proof because I'm living proof." The great-grandmother believed that by talking to school officials and offering to take Chandler to the doctor, she had done what she could do. She said, "I can't go no further than I went. . . . There's nothing I can do." But Chandler wanted her to do more. She wanted her great-grandmother to fight for her rights as a trans girl. She said to her great-grandmother,

> Mamaw, you don't understand that there's cases like this all the time that are fighting the schools, and I'm just sitting back, like, "oh, just run over my life, it's okay. Just come on in. Stomp on me with your muddy boots." . . . You can fight with [a center for LGBTQ youth]! We can get [the youth center] in there. I've said that a million times, and you said, "well, I don't know how to do that, I'm not going against the rules." They've already told me "bluh, bluh, bluh, bluh, bluh," because you're being a pushover. They're walking all over me, and everyone's just letting it happen. My mom moved. My-my dad doesn't care. . . . I only have one person, and that's you.

It seems that Chandler was appropriately afraid of her great-grandmother's plan with the doctor, but, also, she resented the idea that the doctor's perspective carried more weight than her own. She also resented her great-grandmother's failure to fight on her behalf, which was particularly important, since she understood her great-grandmother as her sole advocate. But there was another concern of Chandler's, which was that she did not believe that, even if she got the doctor's documentation, anything would change. She said,

> Everyone thinks that once I get proof, everything is going to change. It's not. . . . Unless I-I draw everyone's attention, I stand up on the table in front of everyone with an intercom, and say, "I have proof. I have a letter like do you want to read it? I'll read it out loud." Until I do that, I don't. I probably still know they'll be like, "faggot."

She asserted that when things like that happened, when people "yelled 'faggot' at [her]," she worked harder to "prove to them, that they're not gonna bring [her] down." But then, she said, "sometimes, you know, whenever I'm in my room, and I'll break down. And, I can break down right now, but I'm not, because I'm, it's my armor." Chandler needed her great-grandmother's support, but what her great-grandmother understood as support and what Chandler experienced as support were two different things. As a result of this discrepancy, Chandler suffered from homophobic abuse, even though she was not gay.

It is tempting to praise Barbara and shame Chandler's great-grandmother, but instead, we revisit Elizabeth's insights and remember the discrepancy of consequences has to do, in part, with the partialities of understandings. Certainly, Barbara's understandings are more comprehensive than Chandler's great-grandmother's, and the consequences are dire. But framing it in terms of partial understanding rather than, say, allies or not provokes parents to recognize their own partial understandings, where ever they and we are in their and our understandings. This is important because it reminds us to see ourselves in one another, so that we may both challenge and empathize with one another rather than simply villainize or celebrate. We can challenge one another to learn more, to do better, but we might also empathize with one another, forgive one another, knowing we, too, do not know the full story.

Teacher Take Aways

- Don't assume all students are part of heteronormative family structures. Double check to make sure that on letters and forms, of course, but also in everyday interactions with students and their parents that language and tone reflects inclusion of queer family structures (e.g. two moms).
- Talk about diverse constructions of families with students. Talk about diverse people. Use curriculum to facilitate such conversations.

- Provide opportunities not obligations for students to talk about their families and themselves.
- Listen to queer parents. Take their requests and suggestions seriously.
- Recognize the diversity and even oppression within and among queer families. Just like any groups of people, they have biases that need to be named, called out, and fought against. Recognize all families' efforts and contributions, not just those who manage to be visibly super helpful.
- Be informed and generous enough to offer feedback, even negative feedback, to parents, as if it is a gift (because it is!).
- Create opportunities for all parents to get to know one another.
- Don't be afraid of talking about queer families. Do so with love and respect. Know you'll get it wrong sometimes. Commit to doing better.

Notes

1 It is worth noting that the children in the families represented in this chapter are mostly younger, in other words there are more families speaking to the experiences of elementary school than those speaking to high school. This was not a deliberate choice, but it is not surprising since parents typically play a more active role in the school life of younger children and less so as these children get older. This imbalance here gets balanced out in the chapter focused on students, which attends primarily to high school students.

2 We recognize parents who identify themselves as such. This, of course, is not limited to biological or legal definitions of parents. Mostly, there is consensus among families about who the parents are, but sometimes, there are discrepancies and evolving roles, with breakups and new relationships, just like in families that do not identify in any way as queer, but a little more complicated since many of the families we interviewed do not enjoy the privilege of institutionalized support. (Marriage between same-sex couples was legalized after the interviews were conducted.) In the case of contested parental status, we honor the claimed identities of the person or people we are representing. We recognize the tensions in making this decision and forge ahead.

5
QUEER HIGH SCHOOL STUDENTS ON STEPPING UP

Layered Lives and Layered Advocacy

LGBTQ and gender diverse high school students[1] experience and participate in various levels of advocacy in school spaces. We use the words "advocate" and "advocacy" as opposed to "activist" and "activism," which are used in other chapters, to express what students need, as opposed to what teachers need to do. We begin by examining the factors and contexts that influence LGBTQ and gender diverse students' decisions to come out or not, and we show how our heteronormativity, homophobia, and transphobia contribute to oppressive, hostile educational spaces. Next, we explore the contexts in which LGBTQ and gender diverse youth desire to or are forced to advocate for themselves and their peers. In particular, we examine in what contexts they feel a sense of agency. We discuss this in connection to the lack of adult advocacy they experience, whether due to adults' intentions or ignorance. To close, we discuss the complexities and power of advocacy by sharing how students talked about the contexts and spaces that empowered and validated their identities. In this, we push for better advocacy for LGBTQ and gender diverse students.

The Complexities of Coming and/or Being Out at School

When discussing coming out experiences, one student participant said, "Being in the closet is the most exhausting thing I've ever done in my life." Being straight and cisgender is assumed and does not require an announcement. Herein lies a paradox of visibility: the desire to be true to oneself (present oneself fully) versus the realities of being out in the heteronormative, transphobic, heterosexist world of high school. The decision to come out is rarely an easy one, especially for students. Even though many LGBTQ and gender diverse students later said they wish they had come out sooner, the act of coming out at school is complex, as students come out in a variety of ways and sometimes several times. Visibility and recognition as an LGBTQ student can come with difficult realities.

To label or not to label? We begin with complicating the idea of labels. No one has to say, "Today I'm coming out as heterosexual and cisgender." The only time one has to identify themselves is when they are outside dominant norms. However, choosing a label limits opportunities for further questioning, exploration, or fluidity. The labels adults use to name young people's identities in academic work, like this book, are not always the ones used by students. Many of the students in our research eschew labels. Some embrace them. They all represent human beings, young people who have questioned, explored, and even changed their gender and/or sexual identities.

As we think about our students, we know they experience pressure to identify in particular ways. Sometimes the pressure comes from within LGBTQ communities and is framed as being "truthful." Well-intentioned educators involved in advocacy work may want or feel they need to know how a student identifies in order to be supportive, specifically because knowing a label can help adults feel they know some things the student might be experiencing and therefore might need. This desire to know often comes from a place of caring, not because teachers are trying to put undue pressure on the student. However, what we as educators need and oftentimes require of LGBTQ and gender diverse youth does not always align with how they choose and need to operate. It is unfair for educators to expect students to categorize themselves through a verbal declaration of sexual or gender identities. Doing so is especially difficult as it is already the heteronormative nature of schools to categorize kids in terms of sexual identity, gender identity, and desire.

We might look to the sports industry for a parallel. In this context, pressure has been placed on gay athletes, like NBA star Jason Collins, to either publicly announce and address their sexuality, or to answer questions about why they have been keeping it a secret. In hypermasculine arenas, such as professional sports, the assumption is that all of the athletes are straight and that there is no other way to be. So, when an athlete, specifically a cisgender man, comes out, the feeling is that he's been "passing." The question, "Why didn't you tell?" becomes an accusation that indicates that the queer athlete has somehow misled people by remaining in the closet.

This sort of questioning is not sports specific, as our students experience similar pressure to announce their sexual and gender identities at school; however, our experiences and research show that the majority of students do not "come out" this way. For example, Kenyatta, a lesbian Black girl student at Mount Jeffery, came out as a lesbian to Jenell, who was her English teacher at the time, by choosing "lesbian torture chambers" as her human welfare topic for her tenth-grade capstone research project. Because students were instructed to choose a topic that spoke to them on a personal level, Jenell knew that Kenyatta was sharing something very important with her. And, we know from experiences with other LGBTQ students that Kenyatta's method of coming out—one of using small subtle signals to communicate with and test out potentially supportive peers and adults—is not unusual.

Though we don't know all the reasons why some students are steering clear of labels, we wonder if they avoid the label because of the risk of homophobia and/or transphobia that may come with the label. For example, Rose, a bisexual, cisgender White girl, stated that she believes that her generation doesn't need to label themselves with a particular identity, and "really doesn't care" what people call her. She cited a poll at her gay-friendly charter school in which 40% of students reported that they are "other," which she and her mother interpreted as the students not wanting to "classify themselves," with a rigid label. When we asked another one of our student participants, Chandler, to define herself within the LGBTQ community, she replied,

> I'm just a very special person. I don't want to be put under any label. I just want to be a human being just like everyone else. It's been kinda complicated with growing up, and seeing how people react to you know, little boy wanting to do girl things, and it's confusing to me, but it's also confusing to everyone else because they don't understand. And, once you do something that's out of the norm, people want to, you know, make fun of or pick on that individual because they're just being themselves, and they can't help it, so that's how I look at myself, as just a person.

Kind-hearted Chandler, a white student from a rural, small town, forgave her own confusion and that of others all the while hoping to just be treated like a human being. The truth is that, at the time of this interview Chandler didn't know what to call herself, but what she did know was that she is and has always been a girl. Chandler's refusal to identify herself at that moment stemmed from a lifetime of forced invisibility. Tate, a white, young man, cisgender student, who self-identified as queer in his interview, offered this explanation about labels:

> The crux being that there should be no limits. The understanding being that the total possibilities of the human body to perform and to exist and to be materialized are almost infinite. They're rooted in the body, but there's the limited categories of gay, of one man and another man identifying as such, scripted through sexual orientation, may not be the best answer for everyone, and how even . . . trans may not be the best, the best way to describe bodies that don't conform. That's why I think queer is a much better working expansive broad category, whereas the LGBTQ, I think that whereas there's a certain comfort and an undeniability with labels, and how you're able to claim that and claim identity, and use that as a way to root yourself within a community.

Here, Tate expresses the tension between labeling oneself in order to be a part of a community, but also not wanting to limit himself to a label in order to be a part of that community. For some students, there was no single label that adequately described who they were or several labels did. Tate stressed this point and the tension between being one's whole self or identifying for the sake of being part of something and being acknowledged. In schools, however, despite these students telling us that labels cause harm and additional evidence supporting their experiences (Kosciw, et al., 2016), we educators continue to impose labels, and the norms and expectations that go along with them.

In this section, Rose, Chandler, and Tate all challenged the idea of rigid labels. But schools, which are shaped by the heteronormative, homophobic, and transphobic society in which we all live, continue to create socially constructed obstacles for young people who do not fit neatly into heteronormative gender or sexuality boxes. This is even more complicated for students who do not ascribe to a specific sexuality or gender, or who see themselves as agender or pansexual, for example.

What these students have taught us, as educators, is that they should be at the center of each decision regarding how to support and advocate for them. It has been our experience that what worked for one youth may not work for every youth and how one youth understands and expresses themselves in terms of gender or sexuality may not be the way another student does. We know that to treat every student fairly may seem impossible because it takes time, energy, and commitment to get to know each student as an individual. It is simpler, much easier, and may seem fairer to treat all kids the same. We contend, however, that like zero tolerance policies, treating all kids the same in our classrooms is not fair. Zero tolerance policies fail to account for particular students' histories, contexts, or needs. Sometimes, what one student needs in terms of "discipline" is not what another student needs. In schools, however, the response to each student is generally not individualized at all. Everyone, presumably, gets the same punishment no matter the circumstance. As is evident in the different needs and responses of Rose, Chandler, and Tate, above, there is no one size fits all way to support, encourage, or advocate for LGBTQ and gender diverse youth; the individual student must be at the center of advocacy. They must have the opportunity to label themselves, or not, as they see fit.

Even if students do decide to come out and claim a particular label, the process is still complicated, particularly in school settings. Sometimes, students remain silent about their sexual and/or gender identities to avoid having their identities stripped down to a single factor. Even if classmates and teachers are generally supportive, no one wants to be just "THE gay kid." For example, Leslie, a cisgender lesbian student at Williams High School who waited until the last few months of her senior year to be out because it was after her swim season had ended, stated:

I did not want to ever be remembered as, "Oh, that girl was a lesbian, right?" I want it to be like, "That girl was a good swimmer, wasn't she?" Like, if people in other classes were talking about me, or someday when I come back for a ten-year reunion, I didn't want it to be like, "Oh, that girl was gay." I want it to be like, "Oh, she was a good athlete," or "a good student," or something.

Like Leslie, other students we interviewed didn't want to be solely known for their gender and/or sexual identities. In contrast to Kenyatta, above for example, Rose talked about listing gay rights as her *third* option for a research project because she "didn't want to be known as the gay girl that does everything about gay rights." As with all people, sexual and gender identities are only one part of whom these students are. Leslie just wanted to be herself, an average young person with many facets. Unfortunately, when kids do not meet heteronormative expectations, the process of claiming a labeled identity for themselves not only highlights their difference, especially in settings where there are few other visible LGBTQ people, but also reduces their rich complex lives to a single dimension. And that can lead to difficult and potentially damaging experiences.

Sometimes, adults in schools ask LGBTQ students to represent, speak, or work on behalf of all queer students. David a gay, white, cisgender student at Williams, for instance, was a member of his high school volleyball team, and his PE teacher asked him to look out for a gay freshman student, Andy, who had just joined the team. This was tricky for David, as he was out to his teacher, but not out to his teammates. Though the teacher made this request in order to be supportive of Andy, the situation proved to be more difficult when Andy outed David. David shared,

> Well I know at a time there was a point in the season at the beginning where Andy was starting to try and start rumors about me, and I remember starting to get really upset and you know for about two weeks I was—kind of shoved him, I pushed him away, I'm like don't talk to me. My friends were starting to you know be mean toward him and once I saw that happening I was just kind of like okay, putting my own personal feelings aside. I'll be here for this kid, even though he's hurt me and kind of taken my trust away.

Here we see the negative consequences of being positioned as "the gay kid" by an adult who doesn't fully recognize the risks of that identity in schools. Despite the possible repercussions, David put himself on the line to help another gay student at the request of a trusted teacher. His teacher assumed he would be an ally to Andy simply because he was gay, but he never considered that David might not be out to his peers. Though the teacher may have meant well in his attempts to support Andy, he failed to consider the costs to David that resulted from seeing him as a "gay kid."

In other instances, however, we have experienced LGBTQ and gender diverse students choosing to make more verbal and explicit declarations about their sexual and/or gender identities. For some, such declarations are necessary in order to be seen and treated in ways that align with who they are and how they define themselves. Often, this may entail declaring new names and pronouns for themselves, either verbally or through written communication. Sometimes, but not always, students do so in order to assume a trans label. For example, Cal sent the following email to his teacher:

> ok so personally this is hard for me because i have not shared this with any adult not even parents in fear of rejection . . .
>
> Dear Mrs. J.,
>
> My name is Cal A. and I am currently attending your class. I am trans and have not legally changed my name. On your roster is my legal name, Miranda A.. I would greatly appreciate it if you refer to me as Cal and you [use] He/him pronouns when referring to me. Thank you for understanding.
>
> Sincerely,
>
> Cal A.

Cal chose a more formal method to declare his new name and pronouns. His transition required a reintroduction of himself to Courtney, and subsequently, the rest of the class. On the other hand, Sammie used the gender inclusive pronouns "they" and "them" though they had never explicitly labeled themselves in terms of gender.

Even though most of the students we interviewed were teenagers, some shared stories of having to navigate labels and identities as far back as preschool. Chandler, a teen girl who was misidentified as a boy at birth shared that she was bullied in Head Start because she loved *The Little Mermaid*. Another young girl visited Chandler at her home one day and saw *The Little Mermaid* toys and told the rest of the students during lunch. Students ridiculed Chandler and when she wore her Little Mermaid shirt, she was told by adults not to wear it so that she would not be picked on. Instead of supporting Chandler and creating a safer school, adults pushed her to hide that part of herself. To highlight how she navigated this suppression of her gender expression, Chandler added:

Chandler: . . . There was this favorite sequins outfit that I would love to get in. It was red and sequins. I would say that I was being a wrestler just so I could wear it, so I wouldn't get picked on.

Courtney: Because wrestlers can be flamboyant?

Chandler: Exactly! That's why I was like, so I went with that. I went with . . . I was just being a wrestler. But they didn't know what—what gender wrestler. I could be a girl wrestler. I could be a boy wrestler.

Through this story of transphobia, Chandler demonstrates that, even at a very young age, she was aware of the vitriol that comes with challenging the gender binary. This experience of transphobia and gender normativity in preschool could be part of the reason Chandler refused to submit to a label at the time of her interview.

What is clear from the stories of Leslie, Rose, David, Cal, and Chandler, is that every student has a different story. There is no checklist or timeframe; there is no right or wrong way to share gender and sexual identity with the world. As educators, we simply need to give our students the space for sharing only what they want to share when they want to share it. And when they do want to share it, we need to honor and respect their needs and choices. Unlike David's teacher, we should never make students feel obligated to share their identity or take on particular labor because of it. The sharing belongs to the students, not to us educators. We can listen, learn, support, and encourage, but because we don't have to navigate the heterosexual hegemony of schools, we should never be push students to do more or say more than they wish to themselves. In the next section, we describe what navigating these environments was like for the students we interviewed.

The realities of being out. As discussed in the introduction of this book, schools continue to be hostile for the majority of LGBTQ and gender diverse young people. For many of our student participants, the type and level of hostility is deeply connected to and compounded by other marginalized identity markers, such as a student's geographical location, race, economic status, or what's more accepted within LGBTQ communities (lesbian as opposed to trans). The less privilege a student has in a particular space in a particular school in a particular place, the more hostility and harassment they are likely to encounter.

In several of the interviews, students indicated that being out in school was "easier" and more socially acceptable for cisgender girls than for cisgender boys. Sylvia, a white, cisgender, out lesbian at Williams, said:

> [W]hen [girls] express something about themselves, like being gay, I think they're very aware of what could come at them and have their— you know, the ways that they can sort of fight that off just seem to be more acceptable within society for girls than boys . . . Like if a girl went to the administration to complain, you know, fine. And if a boy did though, the student body, as a whole, would not take that well. "Oh, he's a sissy. He needs to man up . . ."

Sylvia's words indicate that lesbian and bisexual girls are often seen as less threatening to the dominant norms of heterosexuality. Therefore, the ways in which girls are able to "fight that off" are "more acceptable," more accessible, and perhaps less susceptible to violence. Leslie echoed this perspective when discussing her gay friends:

> I don't know of very many boys who are gay that are out. I know boys who have told me that they're gay, but haven't told the whole rest of the population that they are? And so I feel like, to be alone in that would be really difficult, and that that's probably why more don't come out, because it feels like you would be like, the first one, or like, basically the only one. And, I mean, I'm sure that there are some, but I can't think of any off the top of my head who are out. And I don't know. I feel like boys are more likely to get harassed, probably? Like, in a locker room, or something like that. Just in general.

Leslie knew that there were several gay boys at her school, but that the school was not safe enough for gay boys to be out even if they wanted to be.

Students also cited the common trope that two girls together is "sexy" while two boys together is "gross." During her interview, Rose, who was inadvertently outed as bisexual after a social media post, recounted a conversation with a fellow student. In her school, there was some controversy over reading *The Catcher in the Rye*, specifically the chapter in which Holden Caulfield wonders if he might be gay. During the class discussion, a young man said, "Gay guys shouldn't marry." Rose recounted the rest of the discussion:

> And I was like, astonished that he [would] say that, especially to me . . . and he says, "Two guys kissing is disgusting and I hate it so much." And I said, "Well, what if it's two girls kissing? How do you feel about that?" And he's like, "Oh that's hot! That's awesome!" And I'm like, "So you think lesbians are OK?" And he's like, "I still don't think they should get married, but I think it's hot." And I'm like, "You're ridiculous." This is the image that the media has about lesbians is that they're two hot girls making out for a guy's pleasure. And that's completely ridiculous because that's not true.

Though Rose's experiences as a bisexual student in high school were far from easy, her conclusion that even the most homophobic students see queer girl students as more acceptable than queer boy students was consistent with what other students shared and with what we've seen in schools. Girls, especially white cisgender ones, are often given more leeway to perform gender and express sexuality beyond heterosexual hegemony, while boys are more likely to be harassed or worse for not performing heteronormative masculinity.

Jake, a Black and out gay student at Century High School, experienced a school environment laced with blatant discrimination and harassment, even from adults. He shared:

> I really had an obsession with high heels. That being said, I'm still a boy. I dress as a boy but I like high heels. So for about, I want to say all of sophomore year . . . I had gotten a lot of kind of negative feedback from the

administration and . . . it's not within dress code and, um, it's not very professional looking . . . or in the norm . . . I think that it was really, I don't want to say like a dirty thing to do but it was very disheartening in a sense that I couldn't wear whatever shoe I wanted and then I got so much kind of flak for it . . . The following year, my junior . . . the dress code language was changed to be a lot more gender specific . . . and I think a big part of that was when I was here [at the school], and this was in the four years that I was here, that I felt that I kind of felt alone in the fight . . . I was the only openly gay student and I was also the only student that was as flamboyant as I am . . . which kind of put a target on my back when it came down to our community's needs or our community's insight.

These school experiences left Jake feeling socially isolated and emotionally unsupported even by the adults in his school who were presumably there to educate him and enable his social, emotional, and academic success. This is compounded for Jake because not only was he not "the right kind of gay" (i.e., cisgender and white), but his outspokenness and flamboyance also served as barriers to being accepted in his alternative urban high school.

Likewise, Tate, a white, queer high school student, experienced violence in the conservative, suburban school he originally attended, including being pushed against lockers, harassed in gendered spaces, and knocked down in the hallways, because he was too flamboyant. The violence escalated when he was jumped during school, and he eventually transferred to a gay friendly charter school.

Chandler was also surrounded by blatant discrimination, harassment, and violence in her rural school:

> They say that high school's you know, the best years of your life, and for some kids it's not . . . . I don't even sometimes wanna get up to go to school. I don't wanna go there. I'd rather just be home schooled or something. Because I can just be myself here [at home], and not be picked on for it. Just relax in my makeup and weave and have fun and just, you know, listen to Britney Spears, and just do my homework, and study, and just have fun. That'd be so much easier than going to school, and as soon as you walk in you feel like every eyeball is on you because you're different.

Similar to Jake, Chandler's school experience led to chronic absenteeism, academic struggles, and isolation. The school often cited Chandler's school records, in which she was marked as a boy, as the basis for their decision-making. In her interview, Chandler said that she "never goes to the bathroom," and that she was "so glad [she] got gym class over with." During her freshman year, she would change in a private bathroom stall in the boys' locker room until some boys started locking the stall door making it so that she would have to crawl under the door. That year was the beginning of her transition, and the adults in the school were adamant that she used the boys' spaces. However, this was complicated, as Chandler dressed and looked like a girl, and one administrator we interviewed reported "jump[ing] on" her for being in the boys' bathroom. The administrator, who was a man, thought she had been in the bathroom with two boys. This same administrator was on the staff that demanded she only be allowed to use spaces designated for boys. Chandler was simply following the directives put in place for her, yet in doing so, she was still reprimanded, and even "slut-shamed" by adults. Chandler couldn't win. During her sophomore year, a friend encouraged her to use the girls' locker room to change for gym, and she did so for a time without any problems until a single girl student complained. After that, the gym teacher told her she could use either the boys' locker room or the private bathroom down a separate hallway. Chandler ended up using that gender neutral, stand-alone rest room for the rest of her high school years. For some students, their high school years go by too fast, but for Chandler, they went by too slowly. She was chained to the daily torture of school attendance in order to avoid truancy charges and also to get the high school diploma she needed to get out of her small town. No young person should have to go through these types of experiences, but our research shows that they are happening, in every type of school space from rural to suburban to urban. Chandler was not the only student we interviewed to report the difficulty that restrooms and locker rooms caused her on a daily basis (see Chapter 4, this volume). These stories remind us that, while the intellectual and emotional spaces that schools create for students are critical, the physical spaces schools open up for them are just as important.

Not all students suffered the same level of torment experienced by Chandler. Rose, for instance, saw her generation as more accepting of fluidity in sexual identity. Still, her experiences at Granthaven, a wealthy suburban school district that had a reputation for being "progressive," showed a grim reality. During her freshman year, Rose posted "Love is not defined by the gender of the person, but [by] the feelings," on a social media site, and that was the beginning of a very difficult year. Rose stated, "I never like came out. I was outed" when another student confronted her by saying, "Somebody told me you like girls." When Rose replied, "OK, I don't really care," the girl questioned her integrity by asking "Are you sure, or are you just saying that?" Rose, who was still questioning when and if she would label herself bisexual or otherwise, says the harassment from other students escalated from that day forward. Students from this tight-knit community started using homophobic language on social media and calling Rose a "dyke and faggot." Girls who had been her friends wrote, "The world would be a better place if you were dead," "Are you suicidal? You should be," and "You're a slut. You're a whore." Rose had no safe place to go at school, and she would "hide in the bathroom stall" during lunch. Although Rose had attended school in her small district since kindergarten, she and her mother, in their interview, attributed this harassment to Rose's lack of a "real social network" and to her status as "questioning" in terms of her sexual identity. They recounted that

Rose was targeted by straight and cisgender students, but because she was questioning, and eventually came out as bisexual, the out lesbian and gay students in her school doubted her legitimacy as part of the queer community. Therefore, Rose was too far out on the margins to be accepted by either camp. Rose's locker was defaced with the words "crazy bitch," and students came to her workplace, ordered food, and smeared it all over the dining room. Rose had pages of violent, homophobic comments that the students had posted to her online, including one that said, "People like you are the reason for genocide." In order for the school to intervene, Rose had to file harassment charges with the local police, so that is what she did. Neither the police, nor the school intervened in a way that helped Rose navigate the realities of being out at Granthaven, and she ended up choosing to leave her school to attend a queer-friendly charter school.

Under the circumstances described to us by students, it is no wonder LGBTQ and gender diverse young people struggle with coming out and/or being out at school. We know that labeling themselves presented challenges and created tensions between who they are and how that was represented at school. School policies and procedures that seek to categorize kids as a means of control often damaged these students. Sometimes, this was about space. Repeatedly, the LGBTQ and gender diverse students we interviewed were faced with dilemmas in choosing restrooms and locker rooms that were heteronormative and (cis)gender normative spaces. Other times, it was about real mental and bodily trauma. The emotional and physical violence that befalls these students is a result of the heteronormative, cissexist, and heterosexist structures of school and can lead to emotional and physical violence, like Chandler, Jeff, Tate, and Rose experienced. Even attending a "progressive" school did not assure safety in Rose's case, a reminder that being labeled as something (progressive, ally, etc.) is not a static thing. Rather, schools must continue to work actively at being safe, affirming places for LGBTQ and gender diverse youth.

Schools need gender-neutral spaces as options for students who are barred from using the gendered restroom of their choice, and educators simultaneously need to participate in ongoing discussion about opportunities to open up gendered options to student choice. And, in all of these instances, which are all too familiar, students need advocacy, which we turn to next.

The Complexities of Advocacy

Whether students advocate for themselves, peers advocate for their peers, or adults advocate for students, dedicated, purposeful time and space for supporting LGBTQ and gender diverse students, separate from vague anti-bullying policies and programs, is necessary in schools. Placing the harassment and victimization that LGBTQ and gender diverse students face under the ambiguous umbrella of "anti-bullying" initiatives washes away the critical attention the issue deserves. Jake addresses this trend of "bullywashing" in his interview:

when a lot of kids were being bullied via internet and then we had a big like seminar about it but uh, at the same time, I felt like it was kind of just like an honorable mention. Um, because within there, we talked a lot about um, sexting, how that affects people and, um, kind of bringing your school drama onto Facebook for the world to see. But there wasn't much about, gay students being bullied or anything like that. There wasn't, it just kind of felt like it was a—it just kind of felt like it was just like a little [false start] . . . like it was just there for a second and then it was gone.

Vague anti-bullying initiatives are not enough to address pervasive heterosexism and gender normativity. Often this kind of "catch all" work muffles the voices of, needs of, and threats to LGBTQ and gender diverse students. It is necessary to have dedicated space and specific support for LGBTQ and gender diverse students who experience higher incidences of bullying in schools (Kosciw, et al., 2016). Our educational outreach to both staff and students needs to value LGBTQ and gender diverse students enough to explicitly address the specific ways in which they experience bullying and oppression, both in school contexts and the larger world. Homophobia and transphobia are ubiquitous in our culture, particularly in the highly normative culture of high school; this warrants targeted attention and advocacy beyond more nebulous anti-bullying campaigns.

Our interviews with young people suggest that LGBTQ and gender diverse students appreciated even minor expressions of support even when such expressions failed to allow for things like attending school events with a same-gender date or to prevent things like fights grounded in homophobia. Students appreciated the attempts and the care and compassion these conveyed. But they deserve better, and educators can and should do better. Students made it clear that when they encountered more pronounced support, they were able to experience school in ways that were physically, psychologically, and emotionally safer and more academically productive. Some even managed to assert themselves in extending support to other LGBTQ and gender diverse students in their schools. Their stories suggest that the more teachers and administrators can do to support LGBTQ and gender diverse students, the more students can do for themselves. Even as we encourage youth to step up as advocates for LGBTQ and gender diverse students, we recognize the complexities of doing this in schools. In this section, we describe some of the missteps and missed opportunities we've faced in doing this complex work.

Adult non-advocacy. Opportunities for adult advocacy are abundant in schools. Whether through informal, hallway interactions or as part of the ongoing curriculum, teachers can and should address hate directly, such as homophobic and transphobic language, in classrooms, hallways, lunchrooms, and at extracurricular activities. Let's be honest. We know that for some teachers, the demands of the curriculum, teacher evaluations, special education, and the myriad other responsibilities of a teacher's daily job may make it feel necessary or even easy to pretend you didn't hear a student say, "fag" or "homo." In fact, you may be so busy at times, that you really don't hear it. But we see disrupting heterosexual hegemony as vital a responsibility as any other duty that a teacher has because students cannot ignore hate that directly impacts them on a daily basis. Teacher non-advocacy can include, but is not limited to: refusing to acknowledge or act on behalf of LGBTQ and gender diverse students, and/or intentionally or unintentionally harming them through inaction, language, curricular choices, and school policies and procedures.

At Williams High School, Leslie talked about how often she saw teachers advocating for students or disrupting hateful language in particular. She shared,

> I don't feel like it's addressed any less than anything else hateful or related to bullying or ignorance or anything like that. Like, whether it's like a racist comment or, like, sexist, or it has to do with someone's sexuality, people say things all the time, and teachers are just like, "Shh. Don't say that." Like, there's, like, I've really never seen anyone have a consequence for something that's said. Like, if a kid punches another kid in the face, there's always, always a consequence . . . If somebody says something that probably hurts as much as getting punched in the face, there's basically no consequence that I've ever seen. Or, like, the extent of it is the teacher pulling the kid out into the hallway, probably telling them that that's not acceptable, and then letting them come back into the classroom, but that's no consequence. Like, it's over, and they don't have to like, go home and tell their parent that, "Oh, I said such and such to whoever today," like, there's no . . . I don't know, if I punch someone in the face I know that my parents would know that it happened.

Leslie, who you'll recall is an out lesbian, made a valid and heartbreaking point: the old adage "sticks and stones will break your bones, but words will never hurt you" is absolutely false, although teachers can and do often ignore hurtful words. Teachers don't call parents to report when a student uses a homophobic slur, but a punch in the face requires the adult to take disciplinary action. This non-response occurs on a regular basis. In GLSEN's school climate survey, less than one-fifth of LGBTQ students reported that school staff intervened most of the time or always when overhearing homophobic remarks at school, and less than one-tenth of LGBTQ students reported that school staff intervened most of the time or always when overhearing remarks about gender expression. This is despite the fact that out of 7,898 students (ages 13–21) in the same school climate survey, 65% of LGBTQ students heard homophobic remarks often and 85% of LGBTQ students were verbally harassed (Kosciw, et al., 2016). Later in her interview, Leslie said,

> I feel like in general the most important thing, like, that you can do regarding discipline in students or discipline in kids, is to be consistent. Because if sometimes teachers or staff or whoever is lazy about it—like, sometimes they would call them out for it, or write them up for it, or whatever, but sometimes they have other paperwork to do, and the kid who they said it to doesn't seem like they're that upset, or whatever, and it's just blown off, like, that's what's not okay. You either have to always write someone up who says something offensive, or not.

Without a consequence for the harassing student and without adult advocacy for the victim, LGBTQ students bear the burden of self-advocacy and must do the work that adults should be doing. If educators do not advocate for our students, students are left to their own devices, which may be to internalize the fear and hatred they face, or in the most extreme cases, to deal with their oppression in violent ways. The words that "can never hurt you" actually destroy young people, and are generally even more prevalent than physical harassment. Tate highlighted this distinction:

> I came out in seventh grade. I didn't really come out to everyone, just my immediate circle of friends. I was pretty afraid to make it known, even though I feel like I was pretty bad at hiding it. I still somehow managed to draw a lot of attention to myself. And in ninth grade and part of tenth grade was when I started to receive not a lot, not as many as I think a lot of people would expect from someone growing up in a relatively conservative community, but a lot of negative feedback from my peers. . . . Negative feedback specifically because of a lot of it wasn't physical, and I think there's something telling in the fact that not all bullying is physical . . . There were a couple physical incidents. Um, there was a time in the hallway where I was shoved into a locker and I was tripped walking down the hallway on purpose. And the major incident was when I was walking to a friend's house, literally right across the street from the school, when I was jumped from behind. And the altercation only lasted for about 15 seconds, but—. . . I used to dress very, like, like, seen, like, straight long black hair, lots of bracelets, tight pants. Um, so I was pretty marked by as being different. Um, and I think that's probably what—That was where, I guess going back to earlier, is where I failed to hide very well.

Tate stressed that there was a higher incidence of "negative feedback," which we believe means he was verbally abused, bullied, silenced, and outcast at his original, suburban public school. Tate seemed to blame himself and his failure "to hide very well" for the hatred he endured. When he used the term "negative feedback," he indicated that he believed his choice in expression invited the harassment. Tate blamed himself for not silencing his expression enough in the heteronormative high school environment.

It's important to recall that Tate ultimately ended up leaving his public school district for a more accepting charter school culture because he did not feel safe. While this departure was unfortunate, Tate is fortunate that he had a place to go. Likewise, Rose, who we described earlier, also changed schools in order to find an educational space in which she could thrive. In both cases, adult non-advocacy was a significant factor in the decision to switch schools. And, although these stories have relatively happy endings for Tate and Rose, for many students, especially those in rural areas, there isn't a more accepting school environment to be found. Therefore, we believe that adult advocacy in every single school is paramount to creating safer and more secure environments for LGBTQ young people.

Regardless of whether students can or cannot advocate for themselves, we know that LGBTQ students who do not receive support in the face of verbal harassment are at higher risk of absenteeism, poor academic performance, dropping out, and self-injuring and/or violent behaviors (Kosciw, et al., 2016). Jake, for example, talked about dealing with bullies in ways that were "kind of illegal" because adults did not step up for him. Though many of our student participants, like Chandler, Jeff, and Rose, discussed the oppression they faced, they also did not let that oppression or their fear stop or change them. As adults, if our fear and our ignorance stymie our abilities to jump in and advocate for students, we fail them. Our advocacy may not always be perfect or exactly what a student needs in a given time, but the spirit of intent overrides our mistakes along the way. And each time we jump in, we have the opportunity to connect with students, call on their own expertise, and invite them to educate us in our own on-going efforts to grow as advocates.

Conflicting perspectives in advocacy work. Our interviews with students showed that adults' perspectives of their schools' climates for LGBTQ and gender diverse students drastically differed from the students' perspectives, causing disparities between what students saw and experienced within the school walls and what adults saw and understood about how students experienced school. For example, Dana, a straight, white, cisgender special educator, stressed the positive, inclusive environment for LGBTQ and gender diverse students at Mount Jeffery High School:

> Well, I guess, I mean at Mt. Jeffrey it's been positive. I've had, when we had one young student coming in, his parents, one of their biggest concerns was that their son is openly gay and he also has autism and they wanted to make sure that he wasn't going to be picked on. And he's had a very good experience at— at our school and the family was very happy at how open our school is and that their son would not be set—set apart because of his sexual orientation. And I've also had experiences with students doing research projects on gay rights. Students that—that were not gay. And had good experiences and their families embraced them, looking

> into equal rights for anybody. In my previous schools, I did not have as good of experience. We had, several students at my previous high school that were—were openly gay and—and even the staff weren't very welcoming to them. And it was pretty terrible . . . but I have not seen anyone set out set apart or discriminated against because of their sexual identity or because they have a disability or for—honestly for whatever reason.

Dana's words indicate that the perspective through which she observed her current school was colored by her personal experiences at her previous school. By comparing her past experiences to her current experience, she neglected to see how students had been experiencing and existing in her current school's environment. This comparison may have blinded her to the difficulties students were facing. This was made evident when, Shannon, an out gay (her preferred sexual identity) high school senior, conveyed a different view of the same school environment for LGBTQ students:

> Yeah, I think because it's like, OK, if a boy—if a group of boys was to find out a girl was gay they wouldn't talk about like 'em like "oh, that's nasty or whatever." And the girls, I mean, I don't know from what I've seen they don't really care. It's not me. And if a boy was to come out and say they were friends with that person or just friends like at school or whatever they would most likely have something to say like "that's nasty, you're gay," call them a fag and stuff. And nobody wants to, you know, have to go through that.

Though, in Dana's teacher eyes, Mount Jeffrey was safer than her former school, in Shannon's student eyes, Mount Jeffrey wasn't inclusive enough for students like her. If we take Shannon's word for it, and we do, queer students at the school did not feel the level of support that Dana believed existed there. What was better to this one adult was skewed, and simply gauging "better" based on her former school, or telling students that "it gets better," isn't good enough. These queer students experienced a high level of hostility and negative language from other students. When Jenell asked if she felt that the teachers at the school did what was necessary to create inclusive environments for LGBTQ students, Shannon said,

> No. I don't think it comes from any—I don't think the teachers acknowledge it. Like you're the first teacher that I've ever talked to that even acknowledged that there were gay people on campus . . . Not, I mean, I don't think they try to stop anything . . . I think if somebody like if a teacher was standing right there and somebody was like calling them a fag and they saw that it affected them then they'll say something. But like they would—I don't think they would go outta their way to make sure nobody's messing with somebody.

Sadly, although Dana felt that the Mount Jeffrey staff was visible, stepped in, and did a lot to protect and support queer students, Shannon felt invisible and unprotected. This gap in perspectives implies that even teachers who consider themselves to be allies need to listen harder, look more closely, and privilege the voices and experiences of students over their own perspectives.

In another instance of conflicting perspectives, administrative assistant Marge at Century High School indicated that Jake's changing into a white prom dress in the women's restroom was "making everyone uncomfortable." However, the principal of the school, Annie, recalled the students' reaction very differently:

> Marge had huge issues with Jake. Like when he came to in the prom totally in drag, she was like, well, this was an issue that we didn't know what to do. And Jake came and he was like "Well, Annie, I'm coming to the prom in my tuxedo, but I'm going to be changing. So should I go to the men's restroom, or the women's restroom?" And I was like "I don't know, let's ask Ms. Lester (another teacher)." And Ms. Lester was like, "Well, if you're going to come out of the restroom like a woman, you should probably go in the women's restroom because you don't, like in general a rule of thumb is you should come out of the restroom that looks like where you belong." So he was in there like changing, getting ready and stuff, and Marge was throwing a fit at prom. "Jake's in the women's restroom." "I know, he's changing." "Well, it's making everyone uncomfortable." "No, it's really not making anyone uncomfortable, except for you. Like, the kids never even blink or say a word or anything."

In his interview, Jake talked about having a great experience at prom and at school. What Marge saw as a problem was imagined. Her own bias against his gender creativity made her see something that wasn't there. When asked what he felt teachers could do or were doing to combat homophobia, Jake's response was quite different from Shannon's response to the same question. He said,

> honestly, I don't think it's up to you [teachers]. I really don't . . . I don't think it's up to the administration . . . I don't think it's up to the faculty. I think it's very peer driven. Because faculty can put in whatever rule that they want to, any kind of guidelines that they want to. But unless the student body . . . enforces it, then it won't work. That's, I mean, that's where we drive it. I think the power of your peer is much more, um, influential than the power of administration.

Some educators might agree with Jake, that the responsibility of peers in combating homophobia is paramount. We disagree and believe this puts too much of the burden on students. Whether they realize it or not, their teachers have a significant responsibility to create safer spaces and to teach students to honor diversity.

High school teacher Dana, offered this insight into why LGBTQ kids, especially those who are trans, experienced pronounced victimization in schools from peers and unfortunately, even adults,

> I don't know of many kids at school that walk around and actively tell their teachers that they're transgender. Like some people know, and then teachers might realize—that the student is gay or lesbian, but they may not know that. So I don't know how staff would feel about that, there's definitely a reason why kids aren't walking around telling all their teachers that though. Because we do have quite a few, you know, a handful of kids at—at our school that are trans—that identify as transgender, not everybody knows that. So if kids aren't going and—and telling their teachers that when they are open about it already. There—there's got to be a reason.

In other words, queer and gender diverse students, particularly transgender students, don't tell adults because they don't trust that the adults are going to be accepting (at best) or not hostile (at worst).

Peyton, a young trans woman, recounted a transphobic experience with a teacher who physically intimidated her and refused to use her accurate pronoun:

> He came up to me and he said he was—what did he say? I'm trying to remember. I remember vividly what he did and it was he was—he was like forcing me down the steps and I was just like, "Why, why, why are you forcing me? Why are you calling me this?" Because he kept saying "he" and I think by the time I got to high school it was very obvious whom I was going to become. Let's be real. Sorry, but let's be real. So it's like I'm not going to say I wasn't expecting him to have approached me in that way because maybe he didn't know who I was or what I was portraying to be, but it was just very offensive.

The harassment that Peyton experienced in this moment, and the fact that she wasn't surprised and even half expected this level of transphobia, indicates the danger that trans students face by being out. Particularly horrifying is that she was treated this way by an adult in a school. Regardless of whether a teacher knows that a student is trans or not, all students should feel safe and supported, not threatened or intimidated by any adult working in a school, but this often wasn't the case. Zachariah, an out gay young man and GSA member at Mount Jeffrey recalled an instance in which an administrator, who is a cisgender woman, misgendered a friend of his at lunchtime. The trans student refused to comply with the administrator's directions until she used the appropriate pronoun. The administrator said that she could not use a different pronoun because she had to abide by the pronoun on school records. The administrator then accused the trans student of being insubordinate and threatened them with suspension from school.

Acting upon his desire to educate the administrator and protect his friend, Zachariah later privately went to the administrator in an effort to help her understand why his friend was so upset. The administrator not only refused to listen to Zachariah, but also threatened him with consequences because she saw his agency and advocacy as disrespectful. Upon further investigation and after direct conversation with the district superintendent, we discovered that there was no such policy mandating that teachers and administrators solely use the names or pronouns in district databases. In fact, most teachers we know asked students if they went by another name or nickname on the first day of school, and these teachers committed to using those names throughout the school year and beyond.

When teachers and administrators do not or will not acknowledge the difficulties that LGBTQ and gender diverse students experience in schools, these spaces cannot grow to be more inclusive. Invoking a non-existent policy in order to harass LGBTQ and gender diverse students, like Zachariah and his friend, is not acceptable. Teachers must make space for inclusion and students must have the opportunity to advocate for themselves and one another. We believe it is necessary that teachers disrupt heteronormativity and create spaces for students to provide their correct pronouns, if they so choose, and for all adults in schools to honor these and to honor when these pronoun preferences change over time. Furthermore, when adults refuse to acknowledge queer students' realities and intentionally intimidate these students instead of support them, these adults become part of the problem, placing the burden of advocacy work solely on the shoulders of the very youth they are ignoring and intimidating. These students are left having to advocate for themselves and for one another, as we discuss next.

Youth advocacy in the absence of adult advocacy. In their candor, the youth we interviewed identified common themes across their experiences that have been central to their capacities to thrive in heteronormative and gender normative school spaces. They all spoke of an internal sense of autonomy, agency, and the right to self-determination. This was part of the reason Zachariah felt able to talk to the administrator and to stand up for his friend. Further, Peyton said, "I haven't really had many of those kind of run-ins because I like to think I handle myself very smoothly. And I think that's just a quality I just possess. It's very unique." Based on the accounts of Zachariah, Peyton, and other students we interviewed, we came to understand this confluence of qualities among some queer students as "smooth," a term we take from Peyton's use of the word, "smoothly."

Urbandictionary.com defines "smooth" as, "completing a task with such grace and fluidity that the onlooker will lose appreciation for how difficult a task it really was." This definition resonates with what we heard from many of the queer students we interviewed and whom we've taught. We understand it as the ability for some LGBTQ and gender diverse students to be so seemingly at ease in their own skin that they gain cultural capital (Bourdieu, 2011), which can be parlayed into social capital in high school contexts. Student interviews indicated that smooth can often impact the experience of coming out at school, the ability to hold high-ranking positions within the school community, and access to academic, economic, and other resources. Lack of smooth can subject LGBTQ and gender diverse students to higher incidents of harassment by other students and higher levels of indifference from teachers and administrators.

Though smooth may afford some LGBTQ and gender diverse students a seemingly richer and often less hostile experience in educational settings, it also comes with significant costs. Like "the mask" (Cassidy & Stevenson, 2005) or the "cool pose" (Majors & Billson, 1993) exhibited by some young, African American men, smooth often has to do with conveying an attitude to the outside world in order to survive. In this case, smooth is about being the "right" kind of gay. A form of homonormativity, rooted in homo- and transphobia and heteronormativity, students with smooth are often rewarded for fulfilling the expectations of straight, cisgender, and often white people who feel less threatened when experiencing queer people who seem just as "normal" as themselves.

Smooth is problematic for several reasons, then. On the one hand, it can be unattainable for some students. Take Rose, at Granthaven, for an example. As a freshman, Rose had no cultural capital that she could draw on to attain smooth. Her position, quite literally, in the lowest graduating class, was further exacerbated by her sexual fluidity. Her bisexual status, coupled with her class rank, gave her no capital and, hence, no opportunity to attain "smooth." She was neither gay enough to be accepted by the queer community nor "normal" enough to be embraced by the straight community, and ultimately, she was harassed, abused, and driven from the school. On the other hand, while having smooth may alleviate physical violence and other forms of harassment, it still comes with an emotional and psychological cost. Even the smoothest of students must wake up each morning and put on their "smooth mask" in order to traverse the heteronormative tightrope of school. Smooth is a tactic of self-protection and survival, then, but it is not the answer. In the midst of alienating, normative power structures that collude to rob LGBTQ and gender diverse students of voice, even these more-empowered youth are silenced. Chandler clarified, "I feel like I'm in a sound-proof glass box . . . that everyone sees my mouth moving, but they can't hear me talk . . . I feel like I never get anywhere with anyone . . . you get tired and sick of it."

Foregrounding barriers these students faced with the self-proclaimed agency they carved out for themselves reminds us of all the LGBTQ and gender diverse students whose voices, perspectives, and authentic performances of self are muted or silenced in high school settings. No student should have to rely on smooth to simply navigate school. It is not the students' responsibility to have smooth in order to advocate for themselves; it is the responsibility of adults in schools to ensure that the environment is not hostile and to advocate for youth against homophobia and transphobia. The stories LGBTQ and gender diverse students told us show that when there is no adult to advocate or in the face of adults who acted homophobically or transphobically, they step in and do the work themselves, like Zachariah.

Moreover, what students like Zachariah, Chandler, and Peyton really want are adults who try harder. They are not expecting perfection from adults. They are not even asking adults to be advocates, though all educators should be advocates. They are simply asking to be listened to, for their voices to be heard, to be honored and affirmed. Chandler addressed this same issue when she said:

> I wish people would just try harder. It's one thing I wish is just people would try harder, you know, from being called he or she, or you know even they. If that's what they want, just try harder. And, you know. It makes a difference, so you know. If I go to places, and I hear people say "she," I'm like, "oh my God! That's weird." You know, it's weird to hear people actually call me "she" because that's what I've been wanting all my life.

When students like Zachariah, Chandler, Peyton, and Rose share their stories of advocacy and resilience, we are amazed and humbled. But, let there be no mistake: even though students often advocated for other students and even for themselves, this does not excuse adult educators from their duty to protect and provide safe spaces for all students. When teachers do not advocate for queer and gender diverse students, they burden students with the responsibility of disrupting hate. This can be difficult and even dangerous work. Sometimes students did not interrupt hate because their concerns were dismissed by their peers. If the concerns they expressed did not warrant teacher intervention or support, then were their concerns even valid? Sylvia discussed this daily inner battle of advocating for other peers at Williams High School:

> I mean, every day is a constant decision of "Do I say something or don't I?" because there's always something. Like sometimes it's worse than others. But every day, it's the decision of whether I let somebody say something that I don't feel is right and that could hurt other people. Or I jump in and risk being looked at as the angry self-righteous lesbian-feminist. Those are just like synonymous here. It's really funny. I mean, they aren't, but they're perceived as. I'm like the angry self-righteous lesbian . . . It's just like every single day. And sometimes I'm tired. I don't want to deal with it so I just sigh and move on. Like—which I shouldn't. I mean, it's so hard to decide if it's worth it or not some days and if it's actually going to change anything . . . I mean, if there's someone who—if someone who I know is in a situation, like—if someone I know is in sort of like a personal situation where that language would damage them significantly, I usually say something. But—and a lot of the time, it just depends on how intense it is and where the language seems to come from. Like actually, I'm more likely to say something if it seems to come off of innocent, naïveté, and ignorance than hatred. Because naïveté and ignorance are much easier to deal with than hatred. And fix.

Though we admire Sylvia's willingness to step in, we further understand her desire to not be the one to stand up, especially in situations seething in hate. When she decided to interrupt, Sylvia did so from a place without any authority. She had knowledge and experience; however, without the adult authority in the room participating in the advocacy work, her words could be easily dismissed by her fellow students. She was not only burdened by the decision to disrupt, she was further burdened by the dismissal of her concerns.

We highlight these stories to show how difficult this youth advocacy is in the absence of adult advocacy. When LGBTQ and gender diverse students must adopt a mask of "smooth" to survive, go unheard by adults, or feel overburdened by the daily decision to step in, or not, in the face of hatred, it is exhausting. Students who acquire it might use "smooth" as a survival skill; however, as discussed above, smooth is a tactic, not a solution. Adults in schools are obligated not only to protect, but to not harm every one of their students. Instead of students doing this work and making these decisions alone, teachers must step up and advocate for and with LGBTQ and gender diverse students.

Out students as assumed advocates. Across our experiences as educators and advocates, we've noticed a pervasive expectation that our LGBTQ and gender diverse students will be allies to other members of the LGBTQ community. The hope is that these students, drawing on their own empathy, will necessarily stand up against homophobia and transphobia for themselves, and on behalf of others. But, this is not an assumption we can or should make. Again, we're reminded of David, and the consequences he suffered when he was pressured to be an ally to a younger, gay student because his teacher made this assumption. Educators cannot expect an LGBTQ or gender diverse student to play the role of experts for their gender or sexuality much less for those of other identities in the LGBTQ communities. For example, Kenyatta, a high school junior in a very public lesbian relationship, steered clear of the GSA at Mount Jeffrey. Though she accepted who she was and even faced extreme instances of homophobia, she did not want to be a part of the GSA due to the pressure she felt would follow, requiring her to educate and support the community in a more public way. She just wanted to be herself in her relationship like any other student couple. Even though her clothing blurred gender lines, she adamantly stated that she did not "get" trans people. "Why do they want to be something else?" she asked. Her expressed lack of knowledge regarding the transgender community is important and highlights our point that lesbian, gay, bisexual, transgender, queer, or questioning people do not automatically understand and/or support one another. Although we use LGBTQ all the time, as if this reflects one single, cohesive group, Kenyatta's response suggests that there may be underlying transphobia even from within a school's LGBTQ community.

In a meeting of our teacher inquiry group, the Pink TIGers, we discussed the importance of reminding ourselves that not everyone shares our same values of honoring diversity, and as adults, we know that not everyone in the world agrees with us. We recognize, as well, that we, too, have made the mistake of assuming that our students' shared struggles, shared discrimination would translate into empathy. As educators who value and honor diversity, what does this compel us to do? We must demand at minimum a tolerance of trans students in our schools and classrooms, and remind one another that every human being deserves safety and acceptance, especially at school. As allies and teacher activists, is it fair to expect our queer students to be experts on every identity or to assume that just because they are in the LGBTQ community, that they have adequate knowledge and share our values? We have to remember that they are kids, and if we want them to understand and gain empathy, we need to teach them rather than expect that they already know. All students are unique individuals with complicated advocacy needs that will vary and change depending upon their physical, social, and cultural contexts and their opportunities to learn.

Layers of advocacy. A lack of social, geographical, and racial privilege further complicates the struggles of LGBTQ and gender diverse students. We understand the word privilege to mean that some people benefit from unearned, and largely unacknowledged advantages, even when those advantages are not explicitly discriminatory. We cannot separate or isolate these three privileges because of the intersections of identities in time and space. For our students, their access to advocacy is also impacted by their intersecting identities. We recognize that these intersections of identities and privilege add to the complexity of advocating for students and have sometimes led to missteps and missed opportunities in our own work. Based on these experiences, we believe that sexual and gender diverse students need "layers of advocacy." Teachers need to be activists and work across spaces and places to coordinate the types of advocacy a sexual and/or gender diverse student may need. Here we discuss two trans students whose access to advocacy and resources, support, and safety was severely limited due to a lack of social, geographic, and racial privileges and what a layered approach to advocacy might have offered them.

Chandler: A special person in a small town. As you know from above, Chandler lived in a rural, small town in the Midwest and, in her interview, she did not identify with the LGBTQ community, but instead said, "I'm just a very special person." Doctors misidentified Chandler as a boy at birth and then later labeled her as intersex during adolescence, but, for all intents and purposes, Chandler was a girl. For Chandler, growing up, there weren't very many people willing to be kind to her. Even places where she should have found safety, such as school, church, and among family, were places of intense assaults on her being.

For Chandler, school was often a place where adults' transphobia was hidden behind so-called policies around the semantics of pronouns. Because she was identified as a boy on her birth certificate, the school not only refused to honor her pronouns, but also required that she participate in color guard as a boy. Additionally, because they did not see Chandler for who she was, teachers and other adults did not take any steps to protect her from bullying and harassment within the school. Instead, they allowed this transphobia to permeate every moment and space of her educational experience. During middle school, Chandler, who at the time had not transitioned in public spaces, found friendships within a church youth group; however, when she asked the group for their support during her transition, the adults in the group ostracized her and allowed the other young people to harass her. Chandler's great-grandmother was raising her, and though she loved her and bought her what would be considered girl clothing, she was still calling Chandler "him" at the time of the interview. Our interview with Chandler and her Mamaw was a few weeks before a very important appointment with a pediatric endocrinologist. At one point in the interview, when her great-grandmother said that the doctor could provide proof that she wasn't a boy, Chandler whispered, "I don't need proof. I'm living proof." Mamaw's optimism around the doctor's appointment was directly connected to the idea that possessing the documentation would provide agency for her to support Chandler. If the doctor proclaimed that Chandler was a girl, there would be no more of this trans stuff. Instead, the world that Mamaw and Chandler inhabited would fall back into order, with the gender binary strictly in place and enforced. But Chandler knew that it wasn't that simple. Medical documentation alone would not set things right. It wasn't about being a boy or a girl; it was about changing the mindsets of people at school. It was much bigger than a single piece of paper. Even if the doctor declared that she was a girl, Chandler would continue to be an outcast for not fitting neatly into a box. At this point in the interview, Chandler cried and said to her Mamaw, "What am I going to do, stand on the tables in the lunchroom with this piece of paper and wave it around?" Though Mamaw hoped medical evidence of Chandler's gender would force the school officials to treat her like a girl, Chandler knew it would not change the way the rest of the school population treated her. For Chandler, living in a conservative rural county meant that she did not have access to activist groups and allies or even relationships with people who shared similar struggles. The closest statewide organization for trans people was in an urban county over one hundred miles away, and Chandler did not have the means or mobility to get there. The layers to Chandler's identity were apropos to her need for advocacy. That is to say, Chandler lived a rich, complex life, which required rich, complex advocacy.

Daniella: A student who was wished away. The year 2016 was deemed one of the deadliest years on record for Black trans women and trans feminine people. There was a total of at least twenty-seven murder victims who were trans, with a disproportionate number being Black trans women and trans feminine people (Abeni et al., 2016). It is difficult to get accurate statistics for a number of reasons. For one, news outlets and scholars researching and reporting on this topic are few and far between. Second, the murders of trans people are often not reported as such due to misgendering of the victims. Finally, these deaths are simply not investigated. Online resources like "The Advocate" and "Black Trans Lives Matter" have taken up much of the advocacy work for these forgotten bodies. In the case of Daniella, a Black trans student at Atlantic High School, there was a tangible wish by her school that she would go away, and ultimately steps were taken to make sure that she did. Daniella attended an urban high school in a midsize Midwestern city that was almost 100% Black and where nearly every student qualified for free or reduced lunch. The school was located in a city center, generationally poverty-stricken, majority African American neighborhood. Despite the challenges, there was a lot of community pride in the neighborhood for its local music, resistance efforts, and Black-owned small businesses. The neighborhood was also heavily Christian, and there were several Black southern Baptist churches throughout the community. Many administrators at Daniella's school attended those churches. On the first day of school, Jenell, one of Daniella's teachers, greeted students at the door as a way to check attendance and make them feel welcome. Daniella made it to class last. On the roster she was Daniel, so when she introduced herself as Daniella, Jenell scoured the list and was about to ask to see her schedule when she pointed to the name "Daniel" and gave Jenell a knowing look. From this first day on, Daniella became the focus of several staff meetings and staff gossip. Daniella had been in and out of foster care, as her mother was in and out of prison for drug use and prostitution. At the time of Jenell's interactions with Daniella, she lived with her grandmother, who could barely read, did not have a job, and was severely overweight and homebound. These factors complicated her ability to navigate spaces in support of Daniella. Daniella was also in special education, identified as ED (emotionally disturbed). We know that students of color are disproportionately overrepresented as ED, and we also know that students who are LGBTQ and gender diverse are often labeled with mental health problems. These facts are problematic because they label something as deficient in the student—that there is something wrong with them—and we need to question whose standard their behavior is being held to. Is it just their behavior? The reality is that racism, homophobia, and transphobia are all at play here. It's a lack of understanding someone else's culture or gender or sexuality that leads them to being labeled as being deficient or even deviant.

Daniella did not want to conform, she refused to be silent, and she was often combative; her behavior was chalked up to her ED label. A decision was made by the administrators and lead intervention specialist to have Daniella re-assessed under special education and move her to a more restrictive environment, which was not a contained classroom but a separate contained school for students in special education. On paper, the decision appeared to be based on her learning needs and her own safety, but the unvoiced understanding was that she made everyone uncomfortable. The narrative constructed by the administrators during the meeting vilified Daniella and exonerated the school.

What was not addressed during the meeting was the fact that Atlantic High School divided lunch periods by gender, and that the administration forced Daniella to eat with the boys as her records indicated she was a boy. Similarly, the school's narrative failed to include the fact that Daniella was restricted from using the girls' bathroom since again, according to school records, she was not a girl. These actions, among many others, added to Daniella's already traumatic lived experience. As her case was considered by the school, no one gave a thought to the sort of trauma experienced by trans students, and in this case a young, Black trans woman in an inner-city school with no resources within in walking distance and no support within her school building aside from administrators praying for her to "accept Jesus as his savior" and "reject his devilish ways." There was no critique of the oppressive systems and structures in place at the school, nor were questions asked or concerns expressed around Daniella's lack of support or personal safety. Undoubtedly, these factors contributed to her chronic absenteeism, combativeness, and anger because who wants to be where they are not accepted? The school was only concerned with monitoring where she would pee or eat lunch, based on her gender designation on school records. No one considered her overall well-being or where she would feel safe enough to learn. Instead, they only enacted more trauma and pain on an already deeply marginalized human being. Unlike Tate and Rose, Daniella did not have the option of moving to a new neighborhood or attending a different school. For generations, her family had lived in the same impoverished neighborhood wrought with extreme racial disparities. And, as noted earlier, Daniella's mother was limited in her capacity to advocate for her. So where would this young, impoverished, Black trans woman go? Daniella did not need just a singular form of advocacy. She needed advocacy that addressed the fact that she was Black and trans; Black and trans and poor; Black, trans, poor, and in special education. She needed layers of advocacy.

Chandler and Daniella exemplify the complexity of advocacy work, particularly when issues of social, racial, economic, and geographical privilege intersect. Throughout this chapter, we have emphasized the need for advocacy to be individualized. Their stories demonstrate that a one-size-fits-all approach will not work. We know that stepping up for students in such complex and challenging situations can be risky, messy, and scary, but it is necessary. These young people are human beings that need advocates in their schools. For some of them, adult advocacy work is literally life or death. In a perfect world, every adult in the school would engage in this work in such a way that every student feels safe and secure. In the absence of that perfect world, LGBTQ and gender diverse students need you, the reader of these words, to decide today that you will take steps toward advocacy.

The Power of Advocacy

Advocacy can come in many forms, from small expressions of support to large investments of time and energy by both adults and youth. Regardless of the size of the expression, students report profound results when adults and other students make their support visible (Holmes & Cahill, 2004; Kosciw, et al., 2016;

Snapp et al., 2015). You don't have to become the leader of your school's GSA, though we encourage you to consider what impact that could have in your school, to engage in advocacy work that may be life-changing and life-saving. Below, we describe the ways, both large and small, in which adults and students advocated for one another and themselves, and the powerful outcomes of these efforts.

Visible supports. In several interviews, students pointed to that "one special teacher" who served as a harbor, who stood up against discrimination, who "fought tooth and nail," "who kids looked up to," and often other teachers did, as well, "who is willing to take you under their wing and make you feel comfortable with the situations you're going through." These teachers, who we see as trailblazers in their school contexts (see Chapter 3, this volume), serve as possible models for the kind of advocacy work that is needed to educate all teachers, staff, administrators, and fellow students as allies. Though we can allow ourselves to think that our support (no matter how small) does not matter, the fact is that we have youth voices saying that adult advocacy does matter. We cannot be afraid of the work. We cannot be scared to make mistakes. Being an advocate doesn't mean you have to get it right all the time. Many advocates misuse a pronoun or slip into heterosexism. Acknowledging these mistakes is a form of advocacy in itself.

Leslie showed appreciation for simple signs of advocacy, like classroom signage, but pointed out that more overt announcements of our advocacy positions would mean a great deal to LGBTQ and gender diverse students:

> I don't know. Like, pretty much all the teachers have the "I am an ally" like, signs, like, on their door, and all those things. But, like, at the beginning of the year, when teachers tell you like, "I have a dog, and I've been married for six years, and then I became a teacher, and this is my class, and I will let you turn in one assignment late every term, and we're going to have a lot of fun," like, no one ever says, like . . . like some teachers say, like, "If you ever need to talk to me about anything, you can," but no one ever like, points out that they are, like [advocates].

When asked about teacher allies, Peyton said, "I definitely would say that you will run into those ones who will be there for you." Chandler stated,

> There was one special teacher, and she was very understanding about everyone, and she didn't like bullying, and she didn't like being treated different, and you know, a lot of people didn't understand it. But, there were some kids that did, and some kids that looked up to her, and they needed that in the school.

And Jake referred to one teacher as the school's "gay advocate." Students also expressed the value of having visible peer allies. Student council president and straight, cisgender ally, Caitlyn, discussed her experience in realizing the great need to make changes to the traditions of the annual school dance in favor of inclusivity. She admitted,

> Well, to be honest, I was very oblivious to it, probably until the Sadie Hawkins dance, with all the stuff about, like, we need to be inclusive of them [LGBTQ people]. It's not really something that I have my eyes peeled for.

Like many straight, cisgender students in our schools, Caitlyn had the privilege of being oblivious. When asked what advice she could give to the council for the upcoming year on how to be more inclusive of the LGBTQ and gender diverse students in the high school, Caitlyn said,

> I think it'd be important for some of [the student council members] to maybe even go to GSA meetings or invite those people to the student council meetings when those things are being decided to make sure that they're including everyone. So I would say that's definitely the top advice, is talk to those people and ask, like, what is offensive and what isn't. Because it's hard to put yourself in those shoes when it's not something that's offensive to you and you're so used to, like, tradition, what's always been said. It's really hard to break out of that box, and you need other perspectives. You can't do that alone, I don't think.

Caitlyn's advice is for students with social capital, especially those in leadership roles, within the school to participate in GSA meetings and to learn from its members. Simply attending the meeting is not enough. Adults who advise these groups should prepare student group leaders to learn and listen when visiting. It's important for groups, like the student council, to understand that they represent every student in the school. The advisors of different student groups can help facilitate the connections between groups to create more allies and more understanding. Also, this shows that an adult in the school does not have to advise GSA to advocate for safer and more affirming schools for LGBTQ and gender diverse students; an advisor of a different student group can also do the work.

The appreciation of the visibility of student allies with smooth and social capital is also highlighted in David's interview. When discussing the Day of Silence,[2] he said,

> I saw some jocks do it [participate in DOS], some preppy girls do it. You know, some people that probably don't associate with other people like that, that did support it, which made me feel more comfortable, seeing that that many people were helping move it along.

Similarly, when Rose toured her new gay-friendly charter school, one of the student tour guides casually mentioned "[her] girlfriend," prompting Rose to ask, "Can you say that again?" When the student guide restated, "My girlfriend?" Rose said, "I'm in heaven!" This adventitious expression of a same-gender relationship made Rose feel like she had finally found a place where she belonged, a place where she could be her bisexual self.

Though our students don't always make a grand announcement of their gender and sexual identities—and, as we argue above, should not have to—adult allies need to make their advocacy overt, specific, and direct. As we know from Shannon's story, even when adults perceived that the school is a welcoming environment for LGBTQ and gender diverse students, it was not enough for students to just get lucky enough to run into one special teacher. Teachers, administrators, and school staff are vital agents of change to make schools safer for LGBTQ and gender diverse students, and the stories we have shared here underscore the work to be done.

Advocacy in the face of tradition. Many times, the problems that LGBTQ and gender diverse students face in schools are a result of "tradition." Often, these school traditions are deeply rooted in heteronormative structures, policies, and events (Pascoe, 2011). Sometimes unwittingly, sometimes not, adults in schools will use traditions, such as gendered dress codes for dances, or gendered homecoming courts to perpetuate heterosexual hegemony and hostility toward LGBTQ and gender diverse students. Chandler being required to participate in color guard as a boy, discussed above, is one example of this. We also know from experience, however, that space can be carved out within traditions for queer students to equally participate and thrive. When creative, caring adults step up, queer youth can be given supports that allow them to participate in these functions as their most authentic selves. Since tradition is so entrenched in school spaces, educators need to be knowledgeable and vigilant in monitoring school tradition for challenges that are unique to LGBTQ and gender diverse youth.

Jake's experience at prom, described earlier, provides an example. Recall that Jake was the gender queer, gay student at Century High School who wanted to wear a dress to prom. And Annie was the principal at Century High School who supported him. Even as Marge, Annie's administrative assistant, insisted that Jake's mode of dress was inappropriate, Annie held firm in her support of Jake. Annie understood that Jake's family did not approve of him wearing clothing made for women, and she allowed him space at the school to explore his gender expression. Even though Century High School observed a business casual dress code, Annie allowed Jake flexibility when he came to school in jeans because she knew that his father threw away his women's clothes that complied with the dress code:

> [Jake's] dad ended up going through his closet and taking all of his clothes that were not men's sizes. So then [Jake] didn't have any clothes to wear to school and so he was wearing jeans and it was this whole ruckus. But, so it

was really hard for [Jake]. But in that situation, I feel like a lot of his sorts of issues came from home, because they were very not supportive. And so he would come to dances or something and be like totally in drag. And then his mom would come and he would go in the bathroom and change back, and then, when she would leave, he would change back. It was really hard. And that's why I was telling the staff member like "I don't care that he's wearing high heels, just let him be alone, let's leave him alone."

This kind of advocacy from the school principal is powerful: Annie made clear to the teachers and support staff that the school was to be a safe space for Jake despite the traditional rules and policies.

Efforts to disrupt and change traditions related to dances and events at Williams High School provide additional examples. At Williams, a Sadie Hawkins dance (a traditional theme applied to formal dances where girls/women invite boys/men) was planned as a way to revitalize interest in the winter formal and boost ticket sales. However, this event presented a situation that was unwelcoming to LGBTQ and gender diverse students. For many Williams students, the Sadie Hawkins dance was a source of tension, with students questioning who was being excluded by this traditional dance and whether changes should be made. Some of the signs advertising the dance were changed to include the possibility of "partners" attending the dance. Regarding the Sadie Hawkins dance, Sylvia, explained

as a feminist, I was furious. As a lesbian, I was pretty mad as well. Because that is just not the most welcoming thing for anyone. And—but, it just sort of sets this precedent that, oh, of course the girl will want to ask the boy. It's old-fashioned.

Sylvia went on to express her anger, saying that she would "personally slash [the student council's] supply of crepe paper and balloons" if they held a Sadie Hawkins dance the following year, and that she looked forward to fighting over not having the dance if the student council chose to continue the tradition. Another student at Sylvia's school, Caitlyn, the student body president who identified as straight, approached the executive committee of the student council and started a dialogue regarding who was being excluded and why the traditional dance was an issue. When challenged, the committee organizing the Sadie Hawkins dance at this school questioned their assumptions and, according to Caitlyn, "got it to different degrees." Although the Sadie Hawkins dance presented a heteronormative and misogynistic tradition in the school, students worked together, along with teachers, and made attempts to include lesbian, gay, and bisexual students.

Similarly at Williams High School, teachers, administrators, and students advocated and supported a lesbian couple running for homecoming court. Terrence, whom you met in Chapter 3, was the faculty advisor for this event. When he learned that a same-gender couple would be on the court, he purchased two tiaras and two sashes reading "Homecoming Queen" just in case that the couple won. As Sylvia recalled,

> That was awesome. And that was really awesome that they were brave enough to [run] for that because [our school] hasn't had that before—ever. And they were on court and it was amazing. And Mr. T. even ordered an extra queen sash in case [they won].

Additionally, Caitlyn worked to make common the idea of a lesbian couple running for homecoming court. She decided not to broadcast the news of the couple running for court in hopes of making the situation seem normal:

> We didn't want . . . everyone to start forming opinions about it, and people to . . . take sides. We wanted to make sure that that was going to be something that was going to be okay, so we kept it between the two of us. Like, we don't want to give people the option to hate it. We're just going to be like, this is acceptable.

This advocacy, on the part of Caitlyn and Terrence, both combated homophobia and worked to destabilize assumptions about gender. And, these kinds of advocacy efforts led teachers, and administrators to question the traditions and social norms within their school. After these experiences, Caitlyn questioned whether the school should keep "imaging or idolizing this king and queen" and wondered aloud, "or can it be queen and queen?" Still, even after these experiences, Caitlyn recognized the deeply held practices related to such events in schools:

> This is tradition. Of course it's always going to be king and queen. This is classic. This is what I know . . . I really didn't want it to change. And, I was totally okay with the two girls running, but I didn't know what I would think if they won, you know?

Although Caitlyn was receptive to taking strides to advocate for her LGBTQ peers, she also recognized, and felt, the tensions that came with bucking tradition. Caitlyn's desire to preserve tradition is not unique. Schools across this country subject students to yearly traditions that not only exclude LGBTQ and gender diverse students, but may cause serious social and emotional harm as well. It is likely that efforts to change these traditions to make them more inclusive for all students will take great effort on the parts of adults and young people alike; however, tradition cannot be the excuse for further marginalizing these students.

LGBTQ organizations and events. Because there are so many "traditional" events and clubs that exclude LGBTQ and gender diverse students, it is important to have dedicated space and time to celebrate these students in schools.

At Mount Jeffrey High School, the Day of Silence and Week of Expression were both events that were particularly instrumental in providing a safer yet public space for LGBTQ and gender diverse students to use their voices and engage in powerful discussions around the many issues affecting them. Day of Silence is a nationally organized event in which students and school staff take a vow of silence to honor LGBTQ and gender diverse students who have been silenced by suicide and other acts of violence against them. Students may choose to wear tape across their mouths and attach signs to their shirts with messages of support for their peers. Mount Jeffrey students observed this day each year, ending the day with a "breaking the silence" ceremony, which included guest speakers and a question and answer session. Additionally, the Mount Jeffrey Gay Straight Alliance (GSA) students came up with the idea for the Week of Expression. They wanted to provide space for LGBTQ and gender diverse students to express themselves in various art forms. Each day during lunch, the GSA held different artistic events from music to poetry to chalk drawing messages of support on the sidewalks all over the school's campus. Both of these events were powerful for faculty and students. Events such as these also increased visibility and awareness around issues impacting LGBTQ and gender diverse students. The school's history department even recognized one of the GSA members for special achievement for bringing about social awareness on campus through her organizing the Week of Expression. That recognition emboldened the GSA members and encouraged other staff members and administrators to recognize the importance of LGBTQ and gender diverse student voices.

The success and recognition of these GSA sponsored events highlight the need for strong, LGBTQ-centered student organizations in every school, but there are myriad personal stories that show their value and limitations as well. Mount Jeffrey's GSA was the first place that Shane, a young African American, gay man felt comfortable to say what he truly felt and to be himself. This sacred space made school bearable for Shane and provided him with a place where he felt accepted and could thrive. He actively enjoyed planning and executing school wide events geared toward raising awareness and advocating for LGBTQ students and issues. Eventually, however, even GSA stopped serving as that space for Shane. Because he had fallen so far behind in his credits due to poor attendance and lack of effort, the weight of school infiltrated his once joyful space. Being at GSA became a reminder of how much he needed to accomplish in order to graduate. Every interaction he had was met with the question, "What are you going to do to graduate?" And for Shane, traditional education was not as important to him as his unfolding identity and surviving the forces he pushed against every day. For a while, Shane spiraled into a deep depression, refusing to get out of bed regardless of the truancy charges filed against him. Beyond traditional educational spaces, however, Shane encountered Rainbow Youth Center (RYC), an organization for LGBTQ youth that existed outside of school. Through involvement in RYC, Shane gained purpose and energy, and after a year, he assumed a position on RYC's Youth Leadership Council. At school, Shane felt stifled and oppressed by the one-size-fits-all structure, which, even at an arts-focused lottery school, did not allow him to grow his gifts and talents. Within the boundaries of school, what Shane was allowed to say and how he was allowed to say it were limited. Shane would not have blossomed, or perhaps even survived, without an outside of school space that allowed him to capitalize on his talent: public speaking. By assuming a very active and leadership-focused role at RYC, Shane found a less oppressive environment, a space where he could feel like he was reaching a magnitude of people and advocating for his community.

For some but not all queer youth, organizations within and outside of the school spaces provided avenues for self-advocacy as well as opportunities to work with adult advocates. These organizations are even more important in the face of national and global hostilities toward any bodies that are outside of the norm. These safe social spaces are where LGBTQ and gender diverse students can find strength and comfort in the midst of homophobia and transphobia, where they can collaborate on issues affecting their lives, or just hold space for one another to laugh, talk, and just be.

Conclusion. Much of our work focused on sharing the sad and isolating stories of LGBTQ and gender diverse students' experiences as they navigated being out. We shared these voices of students as a way to demand greater advocacy for them. Students are not asking for much; they just want to be treated as human beings, and to be respected and accepted for who they are. In order for this to happen, adults in education need to make spaces for all kids to be included just as they are. The Jakes of the world must be allowed the space to wear a dapper suit one day and playful prism pumps another. The Peytons can be the homecoming king as a freshman AND sport skirts as a senior. The Chandlers need adult support and advocacy to wear the color guard uniform, hairstyle, and makeup her peers are directed to wear. The Kenyattas need to know her teachers will see her when she chooses to write about lesbian human rights. The Davids should not be outed to make a teacher's life easier. The Cals need access to books that offer windows and mirrors and to restrooms that are consistent with his gender identity. The Shannons need to see adult advocates stepping up to disrupt hate. The Leslies need to be seen as more than just the lesbian. The Zachariahs need to be commended and not chastised for advocating for himself and for his friends. The Tates shouldn't have to change schools in order to feel safe. The Sylvias should not bear so much of the burden to interrupt hate. The Sammies' pronouns should be respected. The Daniellas need layers of advocacy. The Roses should have the space to question who they love. Through these stories we hope to reach and teach educators how to advocate for LGBTQ and gender diverse students, to be better allies, to develop safe, supportive environments, to establish more inclusive policies, to promote student groups and to educate and grow a school's ally base. As teacher allies it is our duty to realize how important these stories are in helping LGBTQ and gender diverse students navigate being out.

Advocates need not be perfect in each and every response, but should dive in, make an attempt, and correct course when necessary.

Teacher Take Aways

- Students need to be able to choose how, when, and with whom they come out, and they need to be able to advocate for themselves without the pressure of being positioned as an "expert." Students need the flexibility to explore and change their gender and sexual identities with the support of adults in schools.
- Adult advocates do not need to fear "messing up," for students appreciate adults trying and trying again. The smallest acts of advocacy can have big impacts on the lives of LGBTQ and gender diverse students. School should create space within school traditions to acknowledge and include the needs and layered lives of LGBTQ and gender diverse students. Schools must create and maintain gender inclusive physical, emotional, and intellectual spaces within the school, and establish school-wide clubs and events that celebrate the identities of LGBTQ and gender diverse students.

Notes

1 This chapter pulls from our interviews with secondary school students. See Chapter 4 of this volume for interviews with K-8 students and their families.
2 GLSEN's Day of Silence is a student-led national event organized in thousands of schools, bringing awareness to the silencing effects of anti-LGBTQ name-calling, bullying and harassment in schools. Students from middle school to college take a vow of silence in an effort to encourage schools and classmates to address the problem of anti-LGBTQ behavior by illustrating the silencing effect of bullying and harassment on LGBTQ students and those perceived to be LGBTQ (GLSEN, 2017).

6
STEPPING UP THROUGH CURRICULUM THAT IS INCLUSIVE OF SEXUAL AND GENDER DIVERSITY

We know that having curriculum that is inclusive of sexual and gender diversity in schools matters. In K-12 schools with such inclusive curriculum, queer and gender diverse students were less likely to hear "gay" used frequently or in a negative way; less likely to hear homophobic remarks like "fag" or "dyke"; less likely to hear negative remarks about gender expression or transgender people often or frequently; less likely to miss school because they felt unsafe or uncomfortable; more likely to report that their classmates were somewhat or very accepting of LGBTQ students; and overall felt more connected to their school community (Kosciw, et al., 2016). In short, queer students fared far better in schools where sexual and gender diversity were part of the curriculum. And students saw the difference. Students noticed when they saw themselves, or could be themselves, in the curriculum, and they could articulate the positive impact this had on their sense of safety and inclusion (Snapp, Burdge, Licona, Moody, & Russell, 2015). In spite of these clear benefits, however, only 22.4% of students experienced positive representations of LGBTQ people or topics in the curriculum, and 17.9% were actively taught negative content about LGBTQ people, with less than half having any access to LGBTQ-related materials in their school libraries (Kosciw, et al., 2016).

We also know that some of the best-intentioned teachers, including many whom we interviewed, still don't include sexual and gender diversity in their curriculum. As we noted earlier, some of this may have to do with how they define teaching. Teachers who saw teaching as "staying within the official curriculum" were less likely to integrate this content or even address related topics or questions in their classrooms. In contrast, teachers who saw teaching as "shaping youth as future community members" were more apt to take up sexual and gender diversity actively and explicitly as part of their curriculum.

138 Curriculum that Is Inclusive

In this chapter, we explore the curriculum as a place where teachers can step up in support of LGBTQ and gender diverse students. We start by defining curriculum and elaborating on how we understand it in our work. We then describe the most common ways that teachers included content related to and enacted curricula inclusive of sexual and gender diversity, recognizing that these are neither mutually exclusive nor better or worse than one another. Next, we explore what supported or hindered such curricular inclusion, examining the dispositions of teachers who integrated content inclusive of sexual and gender diversity and analyzing how theories of knowledge factor into their sense of buy-in and efficacy. Finally, we discuss the impact of teachers' curricular choices on students and argue for a conceptualization of curriculum that might better support LGBTQ and gender diverse students.

Conceptualizing Curriculum

For many educators, the idea of curriculum may seem clear-cut. It's the subject matter we teach, and in particular, the texts and materials we use to teach it. But curriculum is also a question of scale; it can be understood as spanning a year or several years, and it can encompass an entire grade-band or content area. Dig more deeply, and the definition becomes even more complex, comprising not only what we teach, but also asking what is most worth knowing and why. In this chapter, we focus most of our attention on the individual course curriculum, since this was the way it was most often talked about by teachers and the level at which most planning and debate occurs in U.S. schools (Applebee, 1996). For Applebee, questions around curriculum have been too rooted in static understandings of tradition, and dichotomies around whether to teach "this or that"—for instance, canonical literature or multicultural literature. And, as he notes,

> these arguments have been based on false premises and reflect a fundamental misconception of the nature of knowing. They strip knowledge out of contexts that give it meaning and vitality, and lead to an education that stresses knowledge-out-of-context rather than knowledge-in-action. In such a system, students are taught about the traditions of the past, and not how to enter into and participate in those of the present and future.
>
> (p. 3)

When he describes "traditions" as providing "culturally constituted tools for understanding and reforming the world" (p. 2), and a curriculum focused on knowledge-in-action rather than knowledge-out-of-context, we hear a call for teaching and learning as dialogic (Bakhtin, 1981) and curriculum as arcing toward activism and justice. Similarly, Applebee offers us language for understanding the relationship between teachers' ways of enacting curriculum, their reasons for these choices, and the consequences for students. We examine these enactments next.

Enacting Curriculum that Includes Sexual and Gender Diversity

Across grade levels, contexts, and content areas, we noted three predominate ways that teachers addressed sexual and gender diversity in their curriculum. Although we treat them separately here, we understand that they are not necessarily mutually exclusive. We also order them, here, but this ordering is not intended to suggest that one approach is better than another. Each approach has the potential to positively or negatively impact students.

One way of enacting curriculum inclusive of sexual and gender diversity was to focus on a particular text or topic, either for a single day or lesson, or when the topic arose. This stand-alone approach was inclusive, but the positioning of and consequences for students were complex and not always positive. Another way was for teachers to have texts and materials reflective of sexual and gender diversity present, visible, and available to individual students in their classrooms, an approach that we call "books on the shelf." This approach, too, was inclusive, but it tended to make inclusion optional for students and the consequences, again, were not always positive. A final approach, which we call "integrated," was to make sexual and gender diversity a regular topic or integral part of the curriculum. We discuss these three approaches in more detail below.

Stand alone topics or texts. One of the ways that teachers included sexual and gender diversity in their curriculum was by addressing topics in explicit, but relatively isolated, ways. While a few teachers did this intentionally, others took a less deliberate approach. For example, Dana, an intervention specialist at Mount Jeffrey who regularly collaborated with humanities teachers, understood some content areas as more suited to teaching about sexual and gender than others. For her, these topics were ones that could be addressed if or when they "come up," which she felt was more apt to happen in history or English, "because you're reading you know, a gay author, and you're reading about the author, or you're learning about a historical movement or, you know, in—in science and math I don't think it really comes up." In these other content areas, Dana felt sexual and gender diversity only came up in a "'Don't say those things to each other' kind of way." Similarly, Dave, an English teacher at Williams High School, addressed sexual and gender diversity on a "case by case basis" and often in response to a homophobic comment. Although he felt prepared and knowledgeable enough to do so, he never intentionally or proactively introduced sexual and gender diversity as topics:

> I think for me it's just, it's something that, I guess my hope is that it just becomes something that is just normal and isn't something to think about bringing up or to, you know. I certainly don't tip toe around it, but I guess, I guess because maybe I'm not thinking of ways to put, to put those discussions out there, to put those lessons out there, that maybe what happens is the kids kind of see, the kids kind of see what tone is going to be set based on maybe reactions to negative situations

For both Dana and Dave, sexual and gender diversity could and should be addressed, but only as they came up in the class and, ideally, from students. For Dana, this meant that these topics might arise in connection to a particular author or a moment in history, and therefore, be more evident, if not appropriate, in some content areas than in others. And for both of them, this often meant being educative in response to homophobic remarks from students. While both felt prepared to address these topics in their curriculum when they arose, neither of them intentionally executed curriculum that went beyond such stand-alone, reactive moments. Moreover, this approach tended to position the majority of their students as straight and homophobic and content related to sexual and gender diversity as focused on correcting or shutting down hatred rather than educating in queer-positive ways.

Two other Williams High School teachers, Fae and James, also addressed topics related to sexual and gender diversity in stand-alone ways. While both were more intentional in their approach, the consequences for students were still potentially problematic. For Fae, an English teacher, this happened through specific books, which were taught to the entire class. Fae said she liked to, "choose books to read that may be challenging," referring to these topics as "the squirmy stuff for me." This included books portraying different family structures and bullying, as well as "sexual trafficking and human trafficking," among other topics. Fae made these curricular choices so that, "we get a chance to kind of cast ourselves in different roles." As she noted,

> the kids are in a world where you have to give them a little bit of awareness of these things, or else they could find themselves involved in it or know people who get involved in it and won't know what to do or how to help them. So I feel like it's important to talk about, even if you don't think it might happen to them, so that they're aware that it's going on in their larger world.

Fae's stand-alone approach framed sexual and gender diversity among many issues to which she wanted to expose students through literature. The thread running through her curriculum was one of raising students' awareness around a changing list of social concerns. Although we understand Fae's approach as inclusive of sexual diversity in that it did, at times, address all kinds of families and homophobic-bullying, we also see it as stand-alone because these topics were options to be included, or not. Moreover, for queer and gender creative students sitting in Fae's classroom, her framing of these topics as "the squirmy stuff" or things that "may happen" to straight students, without explicitly naming and recognizing the presence of LGBTQ or gender diverse students, was dehumanizing.

Like Fae, James also took a stand-alone approach to including sexual and gender diversity in his government curriculum, but for quite different reasons. He explained that, generally, "I don't ever give my opinions. Like liberal, conservative, I won't tell them. I won't tell them my opinion of candidates, I won't tell them my opinion on anything that's related, really, to the curriculum." James made an exception to this stance, however, when it came to sexual and gender identity:

> I tell the kids, I say, "Listen. You want to know—all year you've been bothering me about what I think about certain things. I'll tell you: the 5th and 14th amendments protect everything except this. And it's not okay. And, at some point, it will change." But if you're going to say that inclusion—you know, inclusiveness and respect and equality are a way of life, but we make this one exception, you know? I don't care if it makes you—I don't know how to say it. I don't care if it makes you feel uncomfortable, it doesn't mean it's not right.

For James, explicitly teaching about LG-equality in his government curriculum is too important to be left up to chance, noting, "it's one of the very few things that I'll tell the kids my opinion on." He shared that students might push back, arguing, "Well, I think people choose it," while others will say, "Well, on this issue, you're telling us what you think. Why?' He shared his way of responding in some detail:

> I'll say, "Okay, ready. Close your eyes. You, now, because of something you picked, by some ignorant people, are going to be made a fool or made to feel inferior any time that you're in society by some people. People pick that. You're right. That's a really good take on that. People would want that. Go out just to be different. They want that." And then you can kind of see light bulbs start flickering, like, "Huh. Think about that. Maybe they're not just freaks that want to be different. Maybe they're just like me. Except just like some people have blond hair and blue eyes, some people . . ." And then I think then it kind of starts going, "Oh, if you take the other side then you are an ass."

For James, such explicit, direct instruction about LG-rights is critical. He was clear that he is not "teaching tolerance," but rather "breaking it down" and saying, "Here is how it is. You don't have your perspective. This is how it is. This is what is right." His approach is overtly LG-inclusive, but it is also stand-alone in that he addressed these topics in a way that was clearly different from other topics in his course, rather than integrated. In contrast to Dana and Dave, however, he did not wait for these topics to "come up," and unlike Fae, he always addressed LG-rights in his curriculum.

Addressing sexual and gender diversity through stand-alone texts or topics was the most common approach to enacting inclusive curriculum among the teachers we interviewed. This approach is important and demonstrates that teachers understand the value of addressing sexual and gender diversity through their curriculum. This approach, however, is also limited. As noted above, it is not an integrated approach but, instead, a relatively passive one. As enacted by Dana and Dave, this approach was often left to chance, with LGBTQ topics being addressed only if they happened to "come up." When such topics did come up, they were often the result of homophobic or transphobic comments on the part of students, not a generative choice by the teacher to be inclusive. As Dave noted, above, he was not really looking for ways to "put those lessons out there." While Fae and James were both more proactive in their stand-alone approaches to inclusive curricula, with James regularly voicing his opinions regarding LG-rights, neither truly integrated this content into their curriculum or framed this content in queer-positive ways. For teachers who took this approach, the positioning of sexual and gender diverse people was frequently problematic. In the curricula of the teachers described here, students were addressed as being straight and cisgender, if not homophobic, and queer students were presumed to be absent from the classroom and often dehumanized. Content related to sexual and gender diversity and queer people themselves were framed as problems, objects, issues, or outcasts, as when James asked his students to imagine themselves as gay or lesbian in order to understand why no one would possibly "pick that." This had the effect of further reinforcing negative tropes about the lives and opportunities of queer people, a framing that was potentially devastating to queer students and damaging to the humanity of all students (Blackburn & Schey, 2017; Clark & Blackburn, 2009).

Books on the shelf. Another way that teachers enacted curricula inclusive of sexual and gender diversity was by making books available to students. Trisha, for instance, a sixth grade teacher at Guthrie, was somewhat hesitant to center her teaching on sexuality or gender diversity, exclusively. However, she regularly displayed books, such as *Am I Blue?*, on her chalkboard tray so that students who wished to might select from these or other titles during choice reading times such as silent sustained reading (SSR). She also encouraged small groups of students to choose from these texts for literature circles or read-aloud groups, and during the time of this study, several sixth-graders in her class chose *Boy Meets Boy* to read in a small group, on their own, using a readers' theater approach. Dana also had a collection of books addressing sexual and gender diversity in her classroom. When asked about curricular inclusion, she responded, "Yes. I mean, I have, you know, books in my library of . . . written by people who are both . . . LGBTQ and have autism. We talk about it in the classroom when it's relevant." While both of these approaches are inclusive, both are optional, relying on the relevance of the topic or the interest of students and their willingness to share their independent choices to bring these materials into the wider realm of the classroom.

In contrast to Dana and Trisha, Anna, an English teacher at Williams High School, was more intentional and tactical in her use of inclusive books. She aimed to steer individual readers toward books that included representations of sexual and gender diversity in order for queer or questioning students to see themselves in texts and for straight and cisgender students to expand their reading repertoires. Additionally, she actively integrated discussions of sexual and gender diversity into her teaching, tapping into students' interests in order to point them toward inclusive texts that were thematically similar to the topic under study and also inclusive of queer characters. She attributed her capacity to do this to her knowledge of queer-inclusive literature, and her extensive, personal, classroom collection of books on the shelf. She also perceived that students trusted her judgment and recognized that she understood their tastes and would point them toward books they would enjoy. She described how she encouraged students to go beyond choosing queer-inclusive books for pleasure reading toward helping them select these books for academic tasks and, ultimately, for their literary quality:

> Or like giving—oh, I had—when they had to do their literary analysis, they had to choose an independent book. Tenth grade. I had a boy come to me. He was like, "I like sports books. But they always seem the same. I'd like something different." And I was like, "What do you feel about bullying?" And he was like, "Oh, yeah. I have a lot of friends who get bullied and picked on, and sometimes I feel like that too." I'm like, "Okay, here's *Crossing Lines* for you," which, you know, is from the perspective of a bully on a gay kid. And so, like, finding my ways of doing that and then them—and they tell me that it was good and that they liked it or that they didn't. But, at the same time, it's not because of the gay stuff. It's because of the writing or materials.

Anna's moves, here, echo calls for readers to embrace LGBTQ-themed books not only for their queer content, but also for their artfulness and their literary merits (Blackburn, Clark, & Nemeth, 2015; Cart & Jenkins, 2006). Like Anna, Jill, one of our co-authors and a Pink TIGer, has significant knowledge of queer-themed literature and, as a high school English teacher, kept many queer-inclusive books in her classroom library. Her rationale for encouraging students toward these texts went beyond allowing students to see themselves in texts or promoting them for their literary quality. She also wanted students to have access to "books and texts . . . that are not only inclusive of LGBTQ authors and characters, but ones that represent a variety of story lines. Like, they're not always tragic." Here, Jill was also tactical in her use of books on the shelf, working to expand the narratives to which students were exposed in order to move them beyond the common trope that gay and lesbian people are tragic figures who often die untimely deaths or end up alone (Cart & Jenkins, 2006), and instead, including texts that reflect stories of sexual and gender diverse characters living and thriving in queer communities.

Taking a "books on the shelf" approach to curricular inclusion was especially common among elementary teachers and English language arts teachers in middle and high school settings. As with stand-alone texts or topics, however, this approach to curriculum was not an integrated one and was generally optional, depending on students' interests and initiatives more so than on teachers' intentional inclusion. In the cases of Anna and Jill, however, both were tactical in using this approach, and both used this as a complement to their overall integration of queer content. In all cases, though, a "books on the shelf" approach, either alone or in combination with other approaches to curricular-inclusion, put the risks related to choosing these books on the shoulders of students, who, because of their choice, might be outed or targeted for being or being perceived as LGBTQ.

It's worth noting here that, when teachers did have books inclusive of sexual and gender diversity available in their classrooms, the queer students we interviewed noticed and felt supported. For example, Cal was not going to start the new school year with his old name and gender, in part because he read a book titled *Some Assembly Required: The Not-So-Secret Life of a Transgender Teen* by Arin Andrews. This book, a memoir of Andrews' transition from female to male, showed Cal a mirror of his own feelings and a window into the life he could be living. So many LGBTQ and gender diverse students never see themselves in literature or classrooms and so many cisgender and/or heterosexual students never see LGBTQ texts or learn about LGBTQ topics in the curriculum. Inclusion of these texts in a classroom library provides a small but important space to disrupt heteronormativity and gender binaries. How one chooses to organize such books may take different forms with different consequences, as noted above. One way is through spotlighting; that is, having a named LGBTQ section in the classroom library similar to other sections, such as sports, science fiction, and African American literature. This approach creates a clear, visible space on the shelf for these texts and makes it easy for students interested in reading them to find them. Conversely, though, such spotlighting may make these books easier for some students to avoid and may make others feel at risk of being targeted simply for perusing or selecting them. Another approach is to delineate genres with colored stickers. This method is a more subtle way to label books with LGBTQ topics, making them visible to students who take the time to notice this distinction, but not so obvious that the books are avoided or that selecting one may inadvertently out a student. The drawback, here, is that students may have to make a special effort to find these books. A final approach is to simply blend LGBTQ books into other sections, organizing them with no mention of or attention to sexual and gender diversity. For example, a teacher may choose to have sections based on authors instead of genre. Jacqueline Woodson and John Greene sections would both include LGBTQ texts, and a book like *I'll Give You the Sun* by Jandy Nelson could go in a LGBTQ section, but it could just as easily be shelved with realistic fiction or with books about the arts. There are positives and negatives to each of these approaches, and teachers will need to determine which method works best in their classroom and for their students.

In short, "books on the shelf" can work in both positive and negative ways, depending on the classroom context. It can be a proactive approach, enabling teachers to direct straight and cisgender students toward LGBTQ content that builds on their interests; to provide individual opportunities for LGBTQ and gender diverse students to see themselves in books; and to expose students to artful, LGBTQ-themed literature that provides positive queer content and disrupts negative, tragic tropes. Still, we believe that if teachers don't step up in other ways to make their classrooms safer, books on the shelf can be a risky choice that some students might not make on their own.

Including and integrating LGBTQ content. A final way that teachers made their curriculum LGBTQ-inclusive was by integrating and addressing sexual and gender identity throughout their course of study. In contrast to taking a stand-alone approach, these teachers tended to make LGBTQ content a regular, everyday topic, neither singled-out for special attention, nor excluded from the curriculum. And, in contrast to or in addition to steering students toward books on the shelf, these teachers brought LGBTQ content into their curriculum as a routine part of full class instruction.

As noted earlier, Anna, who had been teaching in the Williams district for seven years, was confident and unquestioning in making her curriculum LGBTQ-inclusive. In contrast to her earlier teaching, when she would gear up for resistance from students or plan for this inclusion as a special event, she now found that including LGBTQ content "doesn't even register" because "it's just a natural idea for me to include [it]." Anna had always been intentional about making her curriculum LGBTQ-inclusive, but over time she shifted from being more stand-alone in her approach to being more integrative. That is, instead of wondering and worrying about including LGBTQ content (in a way that we assume she did not wonder or worry about including content related to race, class, or Shakespeare, for instance), Anna simply included it as part of everything she taught, every day. In part, this shift was about knowledge and experience, as Anna noted:

> I think I've acquired so many more things in my repertoire of knowledge about authors or literature and things like that . . . [W]hen we're doing our literary analysis, talking about gender roles or sexual orientation of, you know—looking at it through a gay lens and that sort of thing. Teaching the kids to look at it and just putting it as a listing of things.

Knowing more about authors and their backgrounds and about literary theory and the use of critical lenses (see, e.g., Appleman, 2014) deepened Anna's knowledge and gave her more confidence in being LGBTQ-inclusive. Over time, she came to see possibilities for inclusion across texts and contexts, and encouraged her colleagues to do the same. When Anna's grade-level team chose to use the book *The Immortal Life of Henrietta Lacks* across all of their English classrooms in order to address the district's desire to include more non-fiction texts in the ELA curriculum in response to the Common Core, for example, Anna still found a way to leverage this required text in order to connect it to sexual and gender diversity. "[W]hen we were doing, with seniors, the Henrietta Lacks, there's so many, like thousands of issues to talk about." She shared how she encouraged her students to use the text as a point of departure for exploring race, class, gender, and sexual identity in their lives, making the book more inclusive by letting students bring their own experiences to bear. She noted how sharing this approach with colleagues teaching the same materials got it "to more kids than just my classroom. And so I think that's another strategic way to create more, you know, visibility in the classrooms without having to be in those classrooms."

It became clear to Anna that having these conversations and including this content had become an everyday, expected part of the curriculum based on her students' responses—or lack of responses. She described frequently bringing up gender and sexuality in relationship to texts, authors, articles, and other content and being, "pleasantly surprised throughout my teaching. Like the kids' ability to, like, I suppose, their lack of shock over the years. Like it's just become an, 'Eh,' sort of thing. And that's pleasing to me."

Maia, a physical activity, dance, and movement teacher at Guthrie, also took an integrated and inclusive approach with her curriculum, particularly in terms of gender identity. Teaching students in kindergarten through grade five, Maia saw it as, "my job to create a norm of being able to take risks, of being able to have multiple points of view . . . giving kids an opportunity to not just imitate but to create from themselves." Straight, white, and cisgender, Maia aimed to make her classroom a space where physical contact between students, including between boy students, was not only accepted, but also expected:

> You watch the boys and their inclinations as movers and stuff. They roll on each other. They wrestle with each other. They get very physical. And you know, and this [dance] gives them permission to do that. It's not just like a high-five. You have to have a physical interaction with someone else. It's athletic. It's creative. And it doesn't mean—the fact that you roll on somebody is not sexual. That's not a sexual action. You know?

A key goal of Maia's class, then, was to disrupt the heteronormative assumptions about physical contact between and within genders, and to give students the space to interact and create through their bodies and through movement, without fear of reprisal. Maia shared that she did not directly address sexual identity in her teaching because she did not feel like it was appropriate for her K-5 students. It's unclear whether her sense of what's "appropriate" is about sexual identity as a K-5 topic in general, or as a topic for dance class, in particular. Her later remark, though, indicating that she would be willing to collaborate with a teacher on a thematic unit where that might be part of the focus of study, suggests the latter, as does the fact that dance class and movement were often used as a means to deepen children's understandings of content under study in the general education curriculum at Guthrie. Maia's primary goal, however, was to create "a community that's about the normalizations. Accepting of all kinds of things. It's not about sexuality. I guess it's that." We understand Maia to mean "normalization" as ordinary or everyday, not standardized or restricted in a *normative* sense. Maia wanted dance class to be a place where things that are often seen as odd, out-of-place, or taboo—such as boys dancing with or touching other boys—as accepted. In addition to de-stigmatizing physical contact, especially among boys, Maia aimed to destabilize gendered assumptions about movement and dance in general. Like Anna, Maia explained how she tried to move the practice of dance outside of her classroom and into the broader school contexts by playing music and encouraging students to dance during lunch:

> [In my class] there's a norm that boys and girls dance. There's no—why would you not? . . . That's why we dance in the lunchroom. People say they think it's fun and everything, but part of that is to create an environment where they're in their normal life, and they're dancing. So, I'm not telling them what to do. Kids come. They see older kids coming up to dance. They say, "I want to do that." They get up. They start. So they're dancing. They're making a choice in a social community setting, to get up and dance. So they think that's what you're supposed to do.

Like Anna, Maia was seeking a non-response from her students. By regularly creating opportunities for students to dance in class and outside of class, it was her hope that for all of them, boys and girls alike, choosing to dance in public would not be questioned or frowned upon, it would just be "what you're supposed to do."

Although making content about sexual and gender diversity an integrated part of the curriculum was the least common approach among the teachers we interviewed, it was also something teachers seemed to desire. While very few teachers took this approach, many expressed some wish for this kind of content integration not only into the curriculum but, ideally, into other school contexts. As Dave noted, regarding LGBTQ-inclusive curricula, "I guess my hope is that it just becomes something that is just normal and isn't something to think about bringing up." It's unclear what Dave meant by "normal" here. Perhaps, like Anna and Maia, he wanted to destabilize heteronormative assumptions about who gets to be addressed in school and the kinds of things that boys and girls are allowed to do in school and elsewhere, a desire we support. Alternatively, it's possible that his wish is about wanting the concern to simply go away so he doesn't have to "think about" being queer-inclusive. Interpreted this way, his wish seemed to reflect not a disruption of the system, but a return to the status quo, in which heteronormativity, and gender-binaries are centered in the curriculum and other views are silenced. The granting of this wish would allow him to simply teach as he always has without having to address homophobic comments, a desire we do not support. Given these conflicting desires regarding curriculum integration among teachers, it's worth exploring what's behind them. Below, we analyze factors that seemed to support or hinder teachers' inclusion and integration of LGBTQ-content and the dispositions and knowledge that enabled these.

Why (Not) Inclusive Curriculum?

In talking with teachers, and reflecting on our own classroom practices, we noticed some patterns in terms of how teachers did or did not include LGBTQ content in their teaching. In looking across the ways of enacting curricula that are inclusive of sexual and gender diversity, we found that there were some necessary *dispositions*, which teachers had or needed to have, and we saw a relationship between these dispositions and various *kinds of knowledge*.

By dispositions, we mean that teachers needed to have a particular mindset or attitude about LGBTQ-content relative to the curriculum. First, teachers needed to have *buy-in*; that is, they had to believe that integrating content about sexual and gender diversity into the curriculum was necessary and important. Beyond buy-in, teachers needed to have a sense of *efficacy*; that is, they needed to believe that they could integrate these topics into their curriculum in ways that would positively impact their students. Both buy-in and efficacy, though, required teachers to tap into different types of knowledge. Teacher buy-in required *declarative knowledge*: teachers had to know *what to do* (include content related to sexual and gender diversity in their curriculum; stop and discuss homophobic remarks; make LGBTQ-themed books available) and teachers needed to know *why to do it* (to interrupt and prevent further hate; to allow LGBTQ and gender diverse students to see themselves in the curriculum; and so forth). Teacher efficacy in relationship to LGBTQ curriculum, however, required more. In addition to declarative knowledge, as outlined above, efficacy required *procedural knowledge*, that is knowledge of *how to do it*. Below, we unpack and analyze these dispositions and types of knowledge, and discuss examples of these in practice in order to better illustrate the relationships among them.

Buy-in. Whether approaching LGBTQ-inclusive curriculum through standalone texts or topics, books on the shelf, or integration, teachers who attempted to include content related to sexual and gender diversity in their teaching needed to develop "buy-in." By this, we mean that they needed to believe in the necessity for and the power of LGBTQ-inclusive curricula. To hold such beliefs, in turn, meant they must have two forms of *declarative knowledge*: teachers needed to know what to do and why to do it. As we can see from the examples above, teachers did not have to understand what to do or why to do it in the same ways in order to enact LGBTQ-inclusive curricula. Both Fae and James, for instance, implemented a stand-alone approach; but Fae did this through the use of books focused on issues in the world in order to prepare her students for the future, while James did this through explicit discussion of LG-rights in his government class so that his students would understand that "if you take the other side, you're an ass." Similarly, Trisha, Anna, and Jill all knew that it was important to make LGBTQ-themed books available in their classrooms; but Anna and Jill also knew ways to do this that would actively encourage more students to take up such texts, and they knew titles to include that would be reflective of positive, queer communities. Across all three ways of enacting curriculum inclusive of sexual and gender diversity, we found that buy-in and these two forms of declarative knowledge were essential.

To understand this better, let's look at Mallory, a teacher at Guthrie who did not develop buy-in. As a teacher of fourth and fifth graders, Mallory seemed to understand that making her curriculum inclusive mattered, and she shared this in her interview, noting that, "my job is to help kids who are either questioning or wondering now or will in the future" and "to help grow people who aren't going to have to wonder or question into people who accept other people's wondering and questioning." Despite this assertion, however, she had several reasons for *not* making her curriculum inclusive. When asked directly whether she supported sexual and gender diversity through her curriculum, she answered, "No." She attributed this, in part, to the fact that Martha, another fourth/fifth-grade teacher, already addressed these topics in her curriculum, and in part to the fact that "there is so much other stuff I want to do as far as literature." In spite of knowing that she should be supportive, and even naming this as "my job," Mallory chose to prioritize "other stuff" in her own curriculum and to leave LGBTQ content to Martha, her lesbian colleague. Whether Mallory knew what to do is unclear. What is clear is that Mallory knew that *someone* should make the curriculum LGBTQ-inclusive, but she did not know why *she* should.

Across all three ways of enacting curricula inclusive of sexual and gender diversity, then, declarative knowledge (knowing both *what to do* and *why to do it*) was essential. Whether taking a stand-alone approach, a "books on the shelf" approach, or an integrated approach, teachers needed to know what materials to use, what topics to address, what interests their students brought so they could build upon these, and what issues or language to interrupt. They also needed to know why this work mattered. And, most importantly, they needed both of these in order to have buy-in.

Efficacy. In addition to buy-in, efficacy was an important factor in terms of whether and how teachers enacted curriculum that was inclusive of sexual and gender diversity. In order to develop a sense of efficacy, teachers needed not just buy-in, based on declarative knowledge of *what to do* and *why to do it*; they also needed *procedural knowledge,* that is, *knowledge of how to do it.* Efficacy took a variety of forms among teachers. In part, it related to knowledge of LGBTQ-content and materials and knowing how to connect these to the broader curriculum and course of study. Anna, for instance, reached a point in her own teaching where, as she put it, "I think I've become so confident in including LGBTQ material in my classroom that I don't even question it." As discussed earlier, this sense of efficacy allowed her to use LGBTQ-content to disrupt heteronormativity and to make this an everyday part of her teaching. Additionally, it positioned her to provide support for colleagues who might, then, develop enough knowledge to achieve buy-in and efficacy themselves. Anna explained how she shared her knowledge, relative to LGBTQ-content, to achieve buy-in among her colleagues as they developed the sophomore English curriculum at Williams High School:

> [W]hen the English 10 [teachers] would be working on a short story unit or whatever, I would say, "Oh, this short story worked for me. I'd really like to include this." And it would be, like, a minority piece. Like a Sherman Alexie story. Or it would be "Am I Blue?" a gay piece. And they'd be like, "Oh, thank you. I just needed something right now." And so like just that cohesion, working together with materials and trying to save people time in finding materials, knowing what works and what doesn't, just saying, like, "This worked for me. Try it out if you feel comfortable," and that sort of thing.

In part, Anna nudged her colleagues toward being inclusive of sexual and gender diversity by using her declarative knowledge of LGBTQ content. "Am I Blue?" is a short story, so it fits their shared curricular work developing the English 10 unit. And, because Anna has used it before, she also has procedural knowledge about "what works and what doesn't."

In addition to knowing how to connect materials to the larger curriculum, Anna also knew *how to offer support to her colleagues*, another form of procedural knowledge related to efficacy. Here, she used this, in conjunction with her knowledge of how to connect LGBTQ-inclusive content to the curriculum, to assist Kassie, a colleague outside of English:

> I think building relationships, strategically building relationships, but also how it just happens. I'm friends with a lot of math people. And me being friends with Kassie, I know Kassie has been comfortable with making even story problems that have gender—like she's even told me she'll make gender equal names or whatever. Like it's just Pat and we don't know what gender Pat is. Or that she'll have two guys go out on a date. And it doesn't even register on the kids' radar half the time. But that she feels like that's something that she should be doing and is doing and not giving two shits about it or whatever. And so I think that's cool.

Anna's support of Kassie's LGBTQ-inclusive work in math led to Kassie's buy-in. That is, Kassie now had declarative knowledge regarding what to do—she could use gender-neutral names or same-gender couples in her math problems—and why—she knew it was important. Anna described this spreading of knowledge as "a cascade," and used her relationship with Kassie, who then shared with Darlene, another math teacher, as an example:

> Or like sharing the contact form that I give my kids that has "Parent 1" and "Parent 2" instead of like, "Mother," "Father," "Guardian 1 or 2." Just making it Parent–Parent or Guardian–Guardian or whatever. And, you know, that Kassie has taken that, and she's given it to Darlene, and they've given it to who knows how many people. But the fact that it has more gender-neutral terminology, things like that, I think it's just those tiny things that end up creating this atmosphere that allowed a lot of these things to happen.

Here, it's clear that Anna knew how to offer support to her colleagues, Kassie and Darlene, and she clearly felt efficacious in doing so and was aware of how her sharing with colleagues outside of the English department had an impact in other departments, like Math. We would argue, too, that beyond spreading buy-in, her efforts were also seeding efficacy in her colleagues, as when Anna noted, "and they've given [the gender-neutral contact form] to who knows how many people." We find this example particularly heartening. It shows that even small efforts at activism can create change and that both buy-in and even efficacy can be engendered in colleagues if teachers know how to offer support.

Another form of procedural knowledge, perhaps the flipside of knowing how to offer support, is when teachers *knew how to find help*. This kind of knowledge is often overlooked, but we see it as critical to developing efficacy in terms of enacting curriculum that is inclusive of sexual and gender diversity. Terrence, another Williams High School English teacher, described knowing how and where to find support in learning to use LGBTQ-inclusive language in his teaching, and how he engaged with Anna in doing this. And, during her interview, Sandra, a white, straight, cisgender English teacher at a high school in Hartville, actively demonstrated this way of knowing as she discussed her efforts to make one of her courses more LG-inclusive. When Jill asked whether her curriculum also included anything about transgender individuals, Sandra said no:

Sandra: It didn't, and I didn't bring it up because I don't feel comfortable, not with the, I don't feel comfortable with the language. I don't know what I'm saying. . . . So when you say transgender, I don't know if you mean people who physically have like because they were . . . ? Like a friend of my mom's child was born male and felt female kind of thing?

Jill: That's what I mean.

152 Curriculum that Is Inclusive

Sandra: So, there's that, but then, then I also know there are people who like to dress, you know—I don't know. All that. And so I feel ignorant, and I don't want to present things in a way that aren't, that isn't like, I don't want it to become a joke or because I don't know enough about it that if I say something like, you know, a man who likes to wear a woman's clothing, that becomes funny to them, or at least they talk about. And, I don't want it to be that way.

Sandra clearly has buy-in, which she demonstrated both through designing LG-inclusive curriculum and through her declarative knowledge that including transgender people in her curriculum is important. She also knows what she *doesn't know*; that is, she knows that she doesn't have enough knowledge to make her curriculum trans-inclusive and respectful of transgender people. Importantly, she is also developing procedural knowledge in terms of *how to ask for and find help*, in the form of Jill. What ensued between them, next, is an example of the interplay of Sandra knowing how to ask for help, and Jill knowing how to offer support, both key factors in developing efficacy:

Jill: I remember early in my teaching career, it's like you, you want to do it, you open that up and then, like I remember the first time I taught "A Letter to Harvey Milk."
Sandra: Yeah?
Jill: And Mary Faith [a more experienced English colleague] was like, "You know, here's what I do. Just do this." But I'd get to a certain point in the conversation where I would get emotionally worked up—
Sandra: Yeah.
Jill: —because some kid would say something.
Sandra: Yes!
Jill: And I wouldn't know how to address it in a way where I was being professional, that wouldn't shut the conversation down.
Sandra: Exactly!
Jill: And then the kids would be like, "Why the hell did you . . . ?" you know? "Why are we doing this?"
Sandra: Right.
Jill: And it would just be like, "All right." I would resort to, "I'm going to tell you what I want you to think about this."
Sandra: Right.
Jill: Instead of all of us kind of being in a community about it, and, and having the conversation. And, um, it took me a while to get, to get to where I have the confidence to do it. And, that takes a long time, I think.
Sandra: Yeah.

Here, in response to Sandra's asking for help, Jill, shared a detailed example of her own journey from buy-in—knowing the material to use and knowing why to use it—to efficacy—knowing how to integrate LGBTQ-content in a less didactic more dialogic way. When Sandra asked for help, and revealed her own limitations, Jill didn't offer support by telling her *what she should do*; instead, she shared her own challenges, confirming that the work is hard and takes time. Sandra's emphatic responses are moments of recognition as she saw her own concerns and struggles reflected in Jill's story. Together, they engaged in a form of mutual vulnerability not as a means of revealing individual self-consciousness about their practices but, instead, as a way of collaboratively naming and disrupting the cisnormative and heteronormative frames that limit possibilities for humanization in schools (Keet, Zinn, & Porteus, 2009).

A final form of procedural knowledge that was important for developing efficacy was teachers' *knowing how to have conversations with students about sexual and gender diversity*. This speaks to the concerns raised by Sandra, above, and also, perhaps, to why teachers like Dana, Dave, and Trisha found it challenging to move from a stand-alone or a books-on-the-shelf approach, to a more integrated one. James, who took a stand-alone approach to LG-inclusion in his government class, provides an example of this kind of procedural knowledge around having conversations with students:

> I think if in a setting where minds are so malleable, in a really, really tough age, I think if adults can't set up an infrastructure that makes people feel safe and okay to voice their opinion and not worry about backlash—back to what I said earlier: no matter how well you know stuff, you're going to fail. Because really talented kids, whatever the difference they have to somebody else, will not say anything because it's safer to not say anything than it is to say something if you don't know what's going to happen afterward. So I think setting up an environment where they know that there's not going to be any tolerance for any kind of ignorance is crucial. And I think that has to start on the very, very first day. And I think that has to be something that's talked about in terms of setting up a safe environment at this point.

Here, James articulates the importance of procedural knowledge relative to creating a classroom space where students are willing to share. Interestingly, he asserted that having declarative knowledge of content is not the key factor in creating these environments, but rather, it's about knowing how to make the space and have the conversations. Later in his interview, he named the specific ways in which he does this:

> One of the things that I do on the first day is—and obviously, you pass out the syllabus. And then I just tell kids, "Quit looking at the syllabus. Just listen." And I say, "This is my tenth year teaching here. And I don't know if

I've ever sent a kid to the principal's office. We're going to deal with things in here. But I do want you to know that, if I send you to the principal's office and you get down there, they're going to say, 'Mr. Jones sent you down here?' And they'll know that you screwed up. And if it's something that's a tolerance issue, or bullying, or being offensive to somebody based off what they believe because it's incongruent with what you believe, I'll find out what the worst punishment you can have is and I'll make sure that you get that." And it might be a scare tactic, but I also would do that. You know, if—I think it sets a pretty good standard early on that we're not going to deal with any of the bullshit. And you're here to learn and get better and you already know what you know. And the only way you're going to get smarter is to listen to other people. Or read. But you casting off your own opinion to other people as fact is not going to be something that's going to fly.

While some might argue with James's "scare tactic" approach, it is clear that he not only knew what he planned to teach and why it was important, he also had procedural knowledge in terms of how he set up a classroom in order to avoid any "bullshit." Whether this approach creates a sense of community, opens up dialogue, or even feels "safe" is debatable, especially when it is premised on potential punishment as a means to achieve his ends. But for James, that may be the point. If having an LG-inclusive curriculum requires creating an environment of potential threat for everyone as a means to curb ignorance and hate, and make things safer for a few, he was OK with that.

What it takes to enact curriculum that's inclusive of sexual and gender diversity. Based on our interviews with teachers and our own experiences, we can point to some specific factors, including teachers' dispositions and knowledge that are important to enacting curriculum that's inclusive of sexual and gender diversity, regardless of what this looks like. First, teachers need *buy-in*, which requires *declarative knowledge* about LGBTQ-content. Knowing both *what to do* and *why to do it* were necessary for teachers to have buy-in. Once teachers have buy-in, they can and often do go on to develop efficacy. This entails not only the declarative knowledge that is critical for buy-in, but also *procedural knowledge: knowing how* to do particular things relative to LGBTQ-inclusive curriculum. Teachers who exhibited efficacy knew how to connect materials to the larger curriculum, beyond their individual classroom or content areas. They also knew how to share their declarative and procedural knowledge in ways that were supportive of their colleagues, which in turn spread buy-in and potentially seeded efficacy. In order to build efficacy, teachers needed to know how and where to find support and how to ask for it, moves that sound quite simple but that, in fact, require vulnerability and a willingness to open up their curriculum to others. Finally, teachers who exhibited efficacy knew how to have conversations with their students around LGBTQ-content in ways that built trusts balanced risk and safety, and created a sense of community. We know that none of these are easy, but all of them are possible. We turn, next, to why they are important for students, looking again to the work of Applebee (1996) in arguing for curriculum that is inclusive of sexual and gender diversity.

Reframing Curriculum

As we noted at the outset of this chapter, having curriculum that is inclusive of sexual and gender diversity in schools is important and makes a difference in the lives of LGBTQ and gender diverse students across grade-levels and content areas. Arguing for expanding the curriculum beyond its white, Eurocentric focus to be more inclusive, Applebee asked,

> [W]hat happens to the students who find that their lives and values have been marginalized, if they have any place at all, in the curriculum we require them to study? What kind of multicultural society are we building that privileges one segment of society to the virtual exclusion of others?
>
> *(1991, p. 235)*

While Applebee was focused on race, ethnicity, and gender, his questions still resonate today, when we think about the importance of curriculum that attends to sexual and gender diversity. In response to these questions, Applebee (1993) argued for a transformation in how we think about and implement curriculum,

> a shift in emphasis from content knowledge to processes of language and thought . . . [where] conversations that take place within this classroom community are themselves framed within larger, culturally constituted conversations that take place across space and time—conversations about meaning and significance, about the nature of good and evil, about youth and aging, about gender roles and racial stereotyping, about canonicity and representativeness, among many others.
>
> *(1993, p. 200)*

Elaborating on this understanding of "curriculum as conversation," Applebee (1996) urged that students not only learn about and understand traditions of the past, or "knowledge-out-of-context," but that they also engage in "a variety of socially constituted traditions of meaning-making that are valued in the cultures of which they are a part," or "knowledge-in-action" (p. 17). Below, we discuss how these concepts connect to what we have come to learn about LGBTQ-inclusive curricula and the consequences for students. We close by offering a list of suggestions, based on our research.

Curriculum as coverage. In describing a knowledge-out-of-context approach, Applebee (1996) noted that teachers were overwhelmingly focused on curriculum as it relates to concepts and ordering, especially quantity and coverage. As experienced by many teachers, with so much content to cover and so much pressure to cover it, the only workable approach was to treat knowledge-out-of context as a scope and sequence of domain specific concepts and a related ordering of tasks to accomplish during the school year. So, even if a teacher believed that they *should* be more LGBTQ-inclusive in their approach (that is, declaratively, they *knew why* they should be inclusive), the pressure to cover all of the required material precluded it. As Applebee (1996) notes,

> If there is too much material to cover—and pressure for coverage is usually the villain here—dialogue is almost of necessity supplanted by monologue, in which the teacher reverts to telling students what they need to know.
> *(p. 56)*

This is not to say that the pressure many teachers feel to cover content is not real; we know that it is. But, we also see this pressure as related to a way of framing *what curriculum is*. When curriculum is about coverage, then knowledge is taken out of context and experienced as a list of disconnected concepts, facts, or literary works, often related to some measured outcome or test. This curriculum as coverage framing works against LGBTQ-inclusiveness in two ways. First, it's likely that these topics and content may not be a part of the given curriculum, particularly in disciplines beyond English and social studies, as Dana noted, above. Additionally, when framed this way, teachers may claim that they *want* to be LGBTQ-inclusive, as Mallory did, above, but they simply cannot be because they don't want to re-cover what another teacher is already doing or because there are so many other things to cover.

Curriculum as conversation. So, what if we reframe curriculum as conversation? What happens then? As Applebee argues, and as many of the teachers in this chapter illustrate, curriculum becomes less about coverage and more about creating a space for having "conversations that matter" (p. 52). In turn, knowledge is understood, not as decontextualized information, but as knowledge-in-action—that is, as information that is based in traditions of the past, but that will also have consequences for how students enter into and participate in traditions of the present and future (p. 2). We hear this in Jill, now a curriculum director for her district, as she described

> making the school more student centered instead of like creating this giant narrative of you know I guess patriarchy and heteronormativity and European literature—like a big cultural cannon that's never really represented anybody the way it should. But for some reason has been in place for a long time. Like even now, we're looking at course of study questions

and you know there's people like how—you know Shakespeare has to be in there. It has to be in there. It has to be in there. And I'm like well it doesn't really. You know like it—I—I like Shakespeare. But what—what happens if we take it out and we put something else in there?

And, we hear it in James, as he described the impact of making his government course LG-inclusive and insisting on open-mindedness from his students:

> I think that some of the kids who I've had in class change their take on homosexuals while they're in my class. And not just because of what I say. Because they start thinking, "Huh. This isn't what I've been taught, but this is not okay." And I think that's a cool part about growing up. . . . Of course, some people are just going to go with whatever is the most popular view. But I think that the fact that it's becoming more and more accepted, being accepting of homosexuals, I think that's something that people are noticing. Where it used to maybe, for some kids, be cool to make fun, now it's cool to embrace. You know what I mean? I mean, that's my take on it. I don't think that's only a Williams High School thing. I hope it's not.

When curriculum is framed as conversation, and information is understood as knowledge-in-action, then the work of teachers, with students, in classrooms, in schools, becomes not only about interpreting the past, but shaping our expectations about the future. Instead of framing sexual and gender diversity as problems or addressing students as mostly straight and homophobic, such a dialogic classroom space reveals knowledge as not simply out-of-context, static, traditions of the past, but as something that students come to understand, interpret, and change, through action, as they shape traditions of the future.

Teacher Take Aways

- Work toward building the knowledge to buy in. Read books, like this one and others (Blackburn, 2012) to understand why it's important to have curricula inclusive of sexual and gender diversity and what you can do.
- Team up with your school librarian to help build a collection of books that reflect the sexually and gender diverse students in your school. Build a collection for your own classroom as well.
- Read widely, and seek out materials that disrupt the standard, tragic tropes and, instead, show queer people thriving in queer communities.
- Be proactive in presenting positive portrayals of LGBTQ and gender diverse people in your curriculum. It's good and important to interrupt homophobic and transphobic language, but it's also important to be proactive and positive.

158 Curriculum that Is Inclusive

- Address students as possibly queer or questioning and as their best selves—not all straight and cisgender, and not all homophobic, transphobic, and cisheterosexist.
- If you have buy-in, work toward efficacy. Start by sharing what you've learned and how you've learned it with your colleagues.
- Work across disciplines. All curricula can and should be inclusive. Don't be afraid to ask a colleague how to do this. Everyone started somewhere.

7
STEPPING UP WITH SCHOOL LEADERS

School leaders who step up for LGBTQ and gender diverse people in schools make a difference in the lives of students. Two studies evaluating the effectiveness of the Massachusetts Safe Schools Program for Gay and Lesbian Students (Szalacha, 2003; Griffin & Ouellet, 2002), for instance, found that "the active support of key administrators (i.e., principals, district superintendents and school committees) was crucial to the success of safe schools initiatives," and that "Unanimously, study participants identified the active support of the school principal as the most important factor that made decisions 'stick'" (Griffin & Ouellett, 2002, p. 4). The GLSEN School Climate survey (Kosciw, et al., 2016) came to a similar conclusion nationally, noting,

> As the leaders of the school, school administrators may play a particularly important role in the school experiences of LGBT youth. They may serve not only as caring adults to whom the youth can turn, but they also set the tone of the school and determine specific policies and programs that may affect the school's climate.
>
> (p. 56)

Because they wield such power in setting policies and creating the environments in which all students are expected to thrive, we interviewed building principals, district superintendents, and administrative support personnel across schools. Understanding the perspectives of building and district-level administrators matters for how LGBTQ and gender-diverse students and families are supported in schools. Our aim for this chapter is to help you, as teachers, to better understand why some administrators do not or say they cannot step up for queer students;

knowing this might help you to persuade administrators in your own schools and districts to do otherwise. Moreover, reading about administrators who do go to great lengths to support queer students may offer exemplars so that when your colleagues ask, you can provide some concrete examples of what adults, beyond teachers, can do, and offer suggestions for how you can all step up together.

First, we discuss school leaders in broad terms, describing the people who hold most of these positions in U.S. school districts and the nature of their professional preparation for these roles. Next, we discuss how this context shapes how school leaders view knowledge—especially relative to difference—and, in particular, how their privilege and epistemic authority (Janack, 1997) shape how they see, recognize, and value (or not) what other people, often in less powerful positions, know and can do. Drawing from our interviews, we illustrate how superintendents' and principals' views of knowledge shaped how they understood sexual and gender diversity in schools, what they saw as problematic or challenging, what they experienced as positive change for LGBTQ and gender diverse students, and what counted as evidence of these things. Finally, we provide an in-depth example from one school setting to show how multiple adult personnel with varying understandings of difference, action, and support negotiated and affected the experiences of one gender diverse student in that school. To conclude, we discuss why theorizing adults' knowledge and recognition of difference in schools is important in terms of making positive change in the lives of LBGTQ and gender diverse students and make recommendations for how teachers can use these understandings in order to work with school leaders.

School Leaders and Leadership Preparation

To give some context for the views and voices of the school leaders we interviewed, it's important to know something about the makeup of school leadership in U.S. school districts and how principals and superintendents, in particular, are prepared to assume these roles. By and large, whether principals or superintendents, the vast majority of U.S. school leaders are white. From 2003–2012, for instance, 80% of public school principals, across elementary, middle, and secondary schools, were white (U.S. Department of Education, 2016). And, although women made up 52% of all school principals in 2012, they made up only 42% of public middle school principals and 30% of public high school principals (Department for Professional Employees AFL/CIO, 2016). The racial and gender disparity among school superintendents is even more stark. Of the 13,728 superintendents working in U.S. schools in 2000, 94% were white, and 91.9% were men (Glass, 2000). Finally, in 2017, the average annual salary for U.S. superintendents was $116,680 and for U.S. school principals was $78,000, placing both groups above the 75th percentile for average gross income nationwide. In short, based on these data, most school leaders in U.S. schools today are white men and financially comfortable if not well off.

Leadership preparation programs, in turn, mirror these statistics. Most school administrators, whether principals or superintendents, are prepared in programs that serve mostly financially secure men who are white and very few women or people of color (Brown, 2004; Lomotey, 1995). Moreover, the curriculum of leadership preparation programs often reflects and reifies the privilege that the majority of their students carry. As Poplin, Gosetti, and Rusch (1995) note,

> the texts, conversation, writing, and professional activities that construct our knowing and understanding of leadership come from an embedded privileged perspective which largely ignores issues of status, gender, and race and insidiously perpetuates a view of leadership that disavows diversity and equity.
>
> *(p. 12)*

More recent scholarship supports this claim. Despite calls in the early 2000s from groups such as the American Educational Research Association (AERA) and the University Council for Educational Administration (UCEA) to make "social justice a new anchor for the entire profession" (Brown, 2004, p. 80), there are very few leadership preparation programs that focus on social justice, and among those virtually none that recognize or address sexual and gender diversity in any focused or systematic way (O'Malley & Capper, 2015). Instead, in most leadership preparation programs, "professional practices based on the privilege and traditions of longstanding maleocentric and meritocratic society are common" (p. 19). This lack of diversity in both the make-up of school leaders and the preparation they receive has ramifications for students, families, and teachers in schools. Rather than entering schools prepared to recognize privilege and difference and work for social justice, "the picture we have is one of an educational hierarchy built on socioeconomic privilege that becomes whiter and more thoroughly male as levels of education increase" (Janack, 1997, p. 132).

This context of leadership population and preparation has consequences for minoritized people in schools. How principals and superintendents are prepared shapes what they come to know and value in schools, including social justice. Here, we understand social justice, in part, as recognition of and positive regard for social difference (Wang, 2015; Gale, 2000; cf. Patel, 2016) especially related to sexual and gender diversity. As Wang (2012) notes,

> Principals play a pivotal role in creating schools that promote and deliver social justice. Understanding the nature of their beliefs, attitudes and perceptions towards social justice is essential to understanding their choices, decisions, and practices in delivering social justice in their schools.
>
> *(p. 670)*

As, arguably, the most powerful individuals in schools and districts, principals and superintendents are "gatekeepers" for students seeking access, equity, and social justice through education; but as Rusch (2004) points out, "All too often, these young citizens are met by gatekeepers who have few skills, little understanding, and a tenuous commitment to multiculturalism, diversity, or equity in education" (p. 19).

In part, this is a function of epistemic authority (Janack, 1997). Based in Enlightenment constructions of rationality and objectivity, epistemic authority claims to derive, naturally, from a standpoint rooted in the privilege of royal or upper class bloodlines which carried with them traits such as intelligence, gentlemanliness, and overall "perceptual competence" (p. 134). In reality, however, epistemic authority is not natural or inherent in certain individuals; instead, it is "conferred on persons or groups through social, political, and economic practices, as well as through sexist, racist, and classist assumptions about reliability, intelligence, and sincerity" (p. 130). Currently, for instance, epistemic authority is granted, in part, to those who can access and afford prestigious educational credentials. As Janack points out, "People who appear to be white, male, upper middle class, and well educated generally carry more epistemic authority on their shirtsleeves" (p. 132). Based on the earlier profile, we could just as easily state that "*school principals and superintendents* generally carry more epistemic authority" as well. In short, because of whom they are and how they've been prepared, many school leaders come to their jobs unaware of their own privilege and epistemic authority, and they are either unable or unwilling to understand, recognize, and support sexual and gender diversity in schools. We turn to our interview data to illustrate these issues in more detail.

Principals, Epistemic Authority, and Privilege

Across interviews, school-leaders' views of knowledge and their awareness of their own epistemic authority and privilege mattered relative to sexual and gender diversity. Their views of knowledge shaped how they understood and recognized difference (or not), what they saw as problematic or challenging in their work, what they experienced as positive change for LGBTQ and gender diverse students in schools, and what counted as evidence of these things. Taken together, we assert that administrators' ways of knowing, naming, and recognizing difference shaped how they approached leadership, which, in turn, had significant consequences for queer students in schools.

Take, for example, Jeff and Kelly, two experienced public school principals. Both were white, middle class, cisgender, and straight. Jeff had served as principal at two different high schools, both predominately white, the first in a small mid-western city, Novack, with a single large high school; the other in an established, more affluent suburb, Granthaven, with a single small high school. Kelly had been a teacher before becoming principal at Guthrie, the K-8 lottery school described in several of our prior chapters. Comparing the two provides a good entry point for understanding how different enactments of epistemic authority and privilege shaped how school leaders recognized differences and worked for social justice.

Although Jeff and Kelly worked in different environments and across different grade levels, they both named themselves as supportive of LGBTQ and gender diverse students but in quite different ways. Jeff named other educators he knows as "more methodical about their advocacy," but said that he wouldn't put himself in that category. Instead, Jeff described his work supporting students as "more organic and just accepting of people." He noted, "In my years [being a teacher in a high school] I never did anything specific . . . other than just being an adult in a building [with whom] you could be who you want to be, or out." Later, as the principal at Novack High School, Jeff helped students start the school's first Gay–Straight Alliance by agreeing to be the faculty advisor and taking care of the "political stuff on the back end." Throughout the interview, Jeff reiterated that he got "too much credit for that," and that it was really a "phenomenal student, Lisa, who felt the need to start that sort of group." He repeatedly expressed feeling embarrassed to admit that, for him, helping to start the Novack GSA wasn't about advocacy, "it was just about a comfortable place for those kids to go so they knew they weren't in this alone."

> I get a lot of credit from folks, like "Oh the principal started this GSA group," but not really. I just supported a kid who wanted to do that because they saw a need. And frankly, if that kid had not been open enough to come to me I'm not sure that would have happened.

When asked for an example of "the political stuff," Jeff described that a Novack school board member had been "skeptical" of the GSA and had one of her friends, who was a library aide, "checking in on what we were doing in the meetings, sort of informally." Jeff never told the GSA student members about these things or had them formally approach the school board to receive an endorsement to start the group, since Novack allowed students to have any kind of club as long as an adult agreed to serve as a volunteer sponsor. However, he worried whether simply having "a comfortable place for kids to come" who were gay, or had gay friends or family members, was enough; or if, instead, he should have encouraged his GSA members to do more "politically or publically," noting, "I'm not sure that's right too. That might have driven some kids away that were really comfortable coming because they knew it was safe and what it was about."

As the principal, and a straight, white, cisgender man, Jeff had both the privilege and the epistemic authority to support LGBTQ and gender diverse students in co-founding the Novack GSA and to stave off any challengers who opposed the group's existence. Although he occasionally deflected his privilege, saying he did nothing "other than just being an adult in a building," he ultimately saw and owned his epistemic authority. And, importantly, rather than claiming credit for himself, Jeff was quick to point to the students as the ones who were "open enough" to ask for what they needed. In doing so, Jeff recognized and valued his students' differences and agency alongside his own privilege and epistemic authority. Jeff faulted himself for "fall[ing] short when it comes to really staunch advocacy." He indicated that if he were to face real obstruction from a school board or a superintendent for trying to support sexual and gender diversity, he would "find somewhere else to work, rather than fighting that battle there." Although he expressed embarrassment about this, his statement showed that rather than using his power and privilege to maintain the status quo, if such an instance were to occur, Jeff would walk away and "find a different situation" rather than stay and be forced to further an agenda of hate.

Throughout the interview, Jeff spoke frequently about "phenomenal students," including Lisa, the student who started the GSA at Novack High School, Stace, a transgender student who Jeff supported at Novack, and Chance, a student at Granthaven High School who was raised by two moms and was "just a phenomenal kid." He described these three young people in ways that showed appreciation for and recognition of their agency and that echoed our discussion of "smooth" gender diverse youth, as we discuss in Chapter 5, who navigated schools with enough confidence to get what they needed. Additionally, Jeff worried whether his "organic" approach was "good enough for the students that may just be more introverted and wouldn't be the type that would walk in and tell you. Is that enough to make them feel comfortable, is that enough?" In reflecting on his work with the GSA, Jeff equated the group to a counseling session, but quickly corrected himself:

> I think, when I look at GSA groups at high schools, not that I've looked at them closely but you know you see that sort of philosophical difference you know, like a GSA group will be in the Gay Pride parade or more public. But for me it was more like a, I don't want to say a counseling group cause nothing's wrong with these kids, it was just a comfortable place for them to come and we could build better relationships so students could come forward if they needed to.

Here again, Jeff owned his privilege and epistemic authority, but checked these as well, openly questioning whether he was doing enough to support the full range of young people seeking support around sexual and gender diversity. And Jeff continually wrestled with whether the group should be more public and active in local events like Pride or simply be a place where students could share their daily lived experiences. Recognizing their differences and their unique viewpoints, Jeff persistently positioned the GSA and the young people who populated it as normal, and often, extraordinary, but worried about supporting kids in school who may not have the same degree of "smooth," authority, and strength.

Like Jeff, Kelly also claimed the identity of ally but saw this as a stance that she "stumbled upon" when she became principal of Guthrie, a place where support for sexual and gender diversity was already in place when she arrived. She explained that because the district "had hired some openly LGBT teachers and supported their work that that was seen as a sign that nontraditional families would be supported" at Guthrie. Kelly shared how she "continued to support the work" which caused "the message to spread through informal structures that this was a place that nontraditional families would come, and their children would be supported." With all of her prior work in K-5 settings, Kelly acknowledged she had never really thought about sexual and gender diversity at the elementary level, but when she came to work with adolescents in a K-8 building, the need "became incredibly clear" noting, "I understand now, paying more attention, that, in fact, there are behaviors and opportunities from birth on." Kelly shared that regardless of the issue, "as long as it's focused on the needs of kids," people will get on board and it's not "pushing an agenda, or people thinking you're trying to orchestrate morality or religious education." Later in the interview, she reiterated that she didn't set out to intentionally support LGBT families,

> But the factors that I think influence, again, is that [Guthrie had] developed a reputation for being a safe place for LGBT families to come, and, frankly, for LGBT staff to work. And I didn't set out to do that, but because I think families here have been supported, they see others who look like them, for example, and are encouraged to participate in PTA activities and conferences and school-wide events. And what's curious here is that we attract a diverse population of folks in all kinds of nontraditional frameworks. Not just LGBT, but I think there's more racial diversity here than many people would expect to find. And there is even economic diversity that is also sometimes surprising to folks. We have a contingent of families who are actually very, very conservative in their religious beliefs, but, again, because they haven't been accepted someplace else, they do find acceptance here, where, again, I think it comes back to everybody here understands that it's about student achievement, in all facets of their life, and that's why they come here.

Like Jeff, Kelly had epistemic authority based on her position as the Guthrie principal. She also had privilege based in being white, straight, cisgender, and middle class. Although she didn't acknowledge this privilege explicitly, she repeatedly signaled it by referring to any families who didn't share these characteristics as coming from "nontraditional frameworks." Instead of naming and claiming these things, Kelly abdicated her epistemic authority and with it any responsibility she had for shaping the school into a "safe place for LGBT families," something she "didn't set out to do." Kelly's advocacy and activism as a school leader were rooted in the fact that she "continued to support the work," or, in essence, that she did not intentionally stop Guthrie from being a place that supported sexual and gender diversity. From Kelly's perspective, Guthrie's reputation as a supportive school came from the fact that there were some out, lesbian teachers there, which served as a sign that "nontraditional" families would be supported. The quality of these teachers and the fact that they were exceptional educators was not named, nor was the possibility that straight, cisgender teachers might also be supportive of queer families. Kelly lauded the fact that LGBT families "are encouraged to participate in PTA activities and conferences and school-wide events" as if not including them would have been acceptable, and she found it "curious" that Guthrie attracted a "diverse population of folks in all kinds of nontraditional frameworks." Rather than interrogating these curiosities and deeply recognizing, valuing, and responding to the diversity of families and their particular needs at Guthrie, Kelly drew on her epistemic authority as principal and her unacknowledged privilege to conclude that "everybody here understands that it's about student achievement . . . and that's why they come here," a claim that ran counter to many of the reasons that queer families gave for choosing to send their children to Guthrie.

Although Kelly expressed that she had a good deal of power and agency to support sexual and gender diversity and create change in the Guthrie building and "within these walls," she also suggested that she felt inhibited in supporting LGBTQ and gender diverse students and families because of the "political pressure, frankly, of always being afraid that somebody's going to complain about something." In addition to fearing complaints, Kelly worried about spending "time educating the naysayers." Although she expressed hating to say that she constantly had to "choose which battles" to fight, she acknowledged that there were times when, "maybe you don't take as strong a stance on a particular issue because it's going to cause so much distraction from what is our essential work here, and that is the student achievement piece." Asked if by "essential work," she meant "academic" work, Kelly responded

> Holistically. But we have a responsibility to educate children. And there's a curriculum that has to be followed, and there's standardization, and testing, and all of those things. And we want our kids to be best able to thrive, then, at whatever secondary program the family selects. So there are times when you don't spend as much time on the social-emotional piece, because you've got to get through the curriculum too. And so I would say it's that balance of constantly trying to decide what it's going to be. There's never going to be enough time in the day, or enough resources to do everything.

Although Kelly clearly acknowledged that she had the power and authority to create change on behalf of queer families within her building, she was reluctant to do so because of internal, political pressures in the form of complaints from parents, from staff, or from both—a stance that was striking since, frequently, teachers who were trying to support LGBTQ and gender diverse students through pedagogical and curricular changes often said that one of the things they feared the most were negative repercussions and resistance from their principals. Instead, Kelly used her epistemic authority as a means of self-protection and justified this decision with her assumption that she was focused on what all families cared about, student academic achievement. Although she used the phrase, "we want our kids to be best able to thrive," we understand the word "thrive" here to mean "succeed academically," particularly in terms of covering the curriculum and performing well on standardized tests. By abdicating her epistemic authority to these external forces, Kelly failed to recognize the different needs of LGBTQ and gender diverse students and queer families and the importance of "the social-emotional piece," among other factors, in their overall thriving.

Throughout the interview, Kelly framed LGBTQ-headed households as "non-traditional," and positioned LGBTQ and gender diverse students as potentially tragic or in crisis. In reflecting on her experiences with some of Guthrie's middle grade students, Kelly described "the extreme behaviors" and "some really potentially tragic situations with kids who were wrestling with their own gender identities, and some of the mental health issues around that, with depression and a couple suicide attempts, actually, with students." Kelly described these events as sparking an epiphany for her, and she realized "we have to do more than just be accepting. We have a responsibility to protect and educate and help kids really find their voice and identity, whatever that is." Having had a few 12 and 13-year-olds students "who really seemed to be in crisis," Kelly also felt obligated to help parents "who may or may not understand the struggles that the kids are going through, helping them get to resources to support the whole family."

Although Kelly expressed these positions from a place of concern, they also revealed how she understood her own privilege and wielded her epistemic authority without recognizing the epistemic privilege (Collins, 1993; Harding, 1993; Janack, 1997) that others might bring to bear, specifically the epistemic privilege that marginalized people—especially those who will be disproportionately impacted by a decision—bring to social situations. Kelly characterized her middle school students as in crisis relative to their sexual and gender identities. She referenced "extreme behaviors" such as depression and suicidality, which we agree are cause for alarm. However, Kelly located these problems within individuals and her response was to focus on these students and their behaviors, as opposed to focusing on the school community as a social context that needed to change, and which she had the power and authority to change. She failed to acknowledge what her middle school students could teach her about the ways that adults and young people in the school collectively perpetuated these dangerous situations; instead, she centered the "damage" (Tuck, 2009) she perceived as defining the experiences of queer youth.

Similarly, Kelly framed the parents of these students as unable to understand their children's struggles, a move that re-centered her privilege and epistemic authority as someone who "knows better" (Janack, 1997). In part, her discourse reflects what Lesko (2012) calls "confident characterizations" of adolescents. These taken for granted, naturalized conceptions are especially concerning when they are imposed on LGBTQ and gender diverse adolescents, positioning them in a persistent state of inadequacy, inferiority, helplessness, and need, which can lead to a failure to recognize their agency and the legitimacy of their actions and desires.

Kelly and Jeff provided important insights into how school leaders' views of knowledge and their awareness of their own privilege and epistemic authority mattered relative to sexual and gender diversity in schools. As school principals, both expressed commitments to supporting queer students and their families, but how they acknowledged privilege, wielded epistemic authority, and recognized and valued difference shaped and constrained their commitments in significant ways. For instance, Jeff valued the insights that queer adolescents brought to the table. They helped him see ways that he could step up and advocate with and for queer students, such as by facilitating the creation of a GSA. His actions focused on modifying the school's offerings to reshape that context. In contrast, Kelly positioned queer students as primarily able to teach her about their own victimhood and pain. While she felt bad about these experiences, they revealed little to her about the social context of her school or possible ways that she could innovate and step up. The same held true for the district superintendents we interviewed.

Superintendents, Epistemic Authority, and Privilege

Oscar, Leo, and Rufus worked in very different contexts, but they shared much in common as district superintendents. All were white men, middle or upper-middle class, and cisgender, and all were experienced educators and school leaders, having decades of experience. All had been teachers and administrators across a variety of districts before becoming superintendents, with Rufus also having served in the military and continuing to do so as a reservist. Oscar was the superintendent at Hartville and Rufus at Williams. In contrast with these two public school districts, Leo had worked as an integral part of founding and developing a grassroots public chart school district, Guilford.

All three of these men identified themselves as supporting sexual and gender diversity through their work as superintendents, and their supportive actions looked surprisingly similar in practice, despite the differences in their contexts. Leo, for instance, identified himself as a straight ally, and when asked whether combatting heterosexism and homophobia was important to his work as an educational administrator, he said,

> Well it's as important as promoting a sense of acceptance and equality for all people. Whether it's based on race, gender, or where people come from in terms of their origin or their country, in terms of poverty, in terms

of LGBTQ. So in all of those areas, I don't know that I would say that's more prominent than other values of equality, but the value of equality is really something that does matter to us.

Leo framed his support for LGBTQ and gender diverse students as no different and "no more important" than other differences. Rather than recognizing and valuing any distinctions among the many people who embody these differences, Leo centered the more generic value of "equality." When he asserted this as a value that mattered to "us," Leo claimed epistemic authority as the school superintendent and spoke for everyone involved with the Guilford schools. Leo used his own personal acceptance of sexual diversity and his own lack of homophobia to justify this stance. Throughout the interview he persisted in calling sexual and gender diversity a "non issue" because of his personal stance that "I just never ever, ever thought that there was anything about being gay or questioning that was an aberration. Ever!" While his lack of personal bias is laudable and supportive in some ways, by focusing on his individual perspective over what actual LGBTQ and gender diverse people experience, Leo privileged his own knowledge and experience over the daily, lived experiences of queer people. Because of his epistemic authority and unacknowledged privilege, he failed to recognize the social climate of the school, the community, or broader systems at play, hence limiting the kinds of actions he might take, or not, as the superintendent.

Like Leo, Oscar framed sexual and gender diversity in generic rather than particular terms. When asked whether he saw combating homophobia as part of his job as superintendent, he said,

> I think combatting any phobias is a big part of what I try to do. But it doesn't seem to be this central concern for our student body anymore. They're more concerned with other kinds of harassments it seems than harassment based upon a particular orientation or where they exist on some continuum.

Like Leo, Oscar treated all "phobias" equally and drew on his epistemic authority as superintendent to justify his claim and speak for the entire student body when he asserted that homophobia was no longer a concern for the students in his district. Although Oscar initially resisted identifying himself relative to the LGBTQ community, stating, "I don't see myself on that continuum somewhere," he later shared that he had been with his partner, who is a man, for 25 years, and finally said, "So . . . myself? Yeah, I get it, gay." Oscar's reluctance to place himself on some "continuum" may have informed his sense that Hartville students were, likewise, not interested in doing so. We cannot say for sure. What we do know, however, is that both Leo and Oscar privileged their own experiences and used these to claim epistemic authority for what people in their districts valued and what students in their districts needed in terms of support.

As with Leo and Oscar, Rufus also expressed his support in terms of "people" in general, rather than queer people specifically. When asked how he included LGBTQ or gender diverse people in his work, Rufus responded, "I think you just include people as you find them, as they are." He later invoked the Golden Rule, something he felt was "cliché to talk about" but then asserted, "there's a reason it shows up in every religion and organizational paradigm, treating people the way you'd want to be treated. And in so many cases, it's not the first thing you know about a person." Here, the "it" to which Rufus referred, is sexual identity. For Rufus this "it," while present, was never singled out or named specifically, and as with Leo and Oscar, "it" was seen as no more important than any other "value of equality" and as a "non-issue." Although Oscar, after some probing, ultimately named and identified himself as gay, all three men privileged their own, personal perspectives and experiences above others and presumed they had the epistemic authority to speak for, or instead, of others; that is, "treating others the way you'd like to be treated" without recognizing that "you," as a queer parent or gender diverse student might want to be treated quite differently from "you," as a white, cisgender, financially secure man or even from other queer people.

Later in his interview, Rufus described a system, beyond education, where he felt that addressing and supporting the needs of LGBTQ people had worked well—the military. As a reservist, Rufus was knowledgeable of this system and referenced it frequently throughout his interview. He lauded "the power in 'Don't Ask, Don't Tell'" (DADT), an approach that he said, "absolutely worked" because "you got to know people as soldiers before you got to know whether they were lesbian, gay, bisexual. And by knowing them as what they could do and what they could add value on." As he praised DADT, Rufus persistently re-centered his own unacknowledged privilege and re-asserted his own epistemic authority stating, "I got to know soldiers as who they were in terms of the mission and the unit before I knew anything about their background." DADT served as a touchstone for how he thought about including LGBT people in his work as a superintendent. When asked about any explicit efforts of his to be inclusive, Rufus noted,

> I don't know if I've actively tried to build a blended team that has people from varying backgrounds, including L, G, B, you know, T, but we seem to, it seems to happen spontaneously as long as you have an open culture where people can be themselves.

Here, Rufus again expressed support, in general, but it was clear that he did not actively seek to be inclusive; rather, he saw his "blended team" happening "spontaneously" and attributed this to having an "open culture." Although he indicated that this was a culture where people could "be themselves" the unspoken caveat seemed to be *as long as they blend in and keep parts of themselves hidden so that I don't have to recognize any differences or that these differences matter.*

Although Oscar, unlike Rufus, did not invoke the military's DADT policy, he did advocate for a similar kind of silence and invisibility in terms of LGBTQ people. He repeatedly rejected the importance of recognizing LGBTQ people, or any particular group, as unique in terms of their diversity, including himself, stating, "I've always struggled with—what does 'out' mean? . . . I just, I want to affirm everyone's right to be who they are. I just kind of live my life." In terms of specific district-level actions of support, he pointed to the International Festival at one of the district high schools as a "student driven" initiative that was supported by the district and inclusive of all students, including LGBTQ students in the school's diversity club and noted, "I think they [the LGBTQ kids] had a presence there as almost their own nation. It's cute because it was recognizing that these people have this commonality." Oscar laughed when he made this comment and noted that, as the superintendent, these initiatives were "fun to watch." He shared that "since I'm a hugger I generally go to those and make sure I hug every kid that's involved so that they know the superintendent blesses this or whatever they're looking for." In language that felt similar to Rufus's in its opacity, Oscar never named LGBTQ kids explicitly, or even recognized them as a group relative to their sexual or gender identities. Instead, he referred to them as "almost their own nation" within the diversity club, a reference that seemed aimed at explaining why queer kids would participate, as a group, in an international festival. And, as discussed above, his expressions of support were neither systemic not specific. Instead, he drew on his epistemic authority as the superintendent and leant his personal affirmation through hugging, which presumably conveyed his support "or whatever they're looking for," which he characterized as being about personal relationships rather than systemic change.

In their roles as superintendents, Leo, Oscar, and Rufus all named themselves as supporters of sexual and gender diversity in their districts. The way they recognized or expressed knowing about LGBTQ and gender diverse people, however, revealed much about their own privilege and epistemic authority. All of them employed direct and indirect silencing through the use of catch-all, non-specific terms like "diversity" and "equality," and each of them made general claims of support that were rooted in their privileged experiences as white, cis-normative men rather than naming the significance of race, class, gender, or sexuality in precise ways. Finally, in terms of their claims to knowing how to be actively supportive, all of them framed their understandings through their own, individual experiences: Leo in terms of being personally anti-homophobic and defining sexual identity as a "non-issue"; Oscar in terms of not characterizing his own sexual identity as significant; and Rufus in terms of his positive experiences in the military. So, despite their espousing support, their sense of epistemic authority and their failure to acknowledge their own privileged identities or recognize the epistemic privilege that others might bring limited their actions to act supportively and was sometimes even explicitly non-supportive.

Take Rufus, for example. Rather than acknowledging his epistemic authority as superintendent and his multiple privileged identities, he seemed oblivious to the risks of coming out and being out, a position he reiterated in the interview. When asked whether staff in the Williams school system felt comfortable being out in the district and community he responded, "within the organization, I get the sense, yes. I think in the community, it's a little harder." Rufus, however, characterized these challenges as not about the district and the community as related systems in which he held a powerful, leadership position, but, instead, as simply about the individual choices that people made to reveal themselves, or not.

> I think it's an independent decision that each person has to make. I know of those who become comfortable, but I know of some who aren't still, you know? And the nice part is it's, it's one of those things all of us have the freedom to share as much as we want to. I mean, there are people on my team that I don't know anything about their husband, their significant other, their partner. Where there are others where I know everything about their personal life because they're the type that share. I think we're in such a role that we can be as open as we want to be. The sense I have is that those that have become more open have not seen a lot of pushback, but it doesn't mean that everybody's as comfortable to make that step.

His stance here was interesting for several reasons. First, through the use of the pronouns "we" and "us," Rufus again claimed the epistemic authority to speak for queer people, along with every other person in the district and community, without recognizing their unique differences or acknowledging his own privilege. Instead, he suggested that coming out and being out was something that everyone does, including him, not something specific to queer people. As he noted, "all of us have the freedom to share as much as we want to," which might be read as, a) a suggestion that queer people are free to hide or cover (Yoshino, 2006) their sexual identity if they choose to; and b) coded language (Castagno, 2008) for race insofar as most people do not have the freedom to share (or not share) their racial or ethnic identities. This stance, too, failed to see the misogyny and sexism resting below the surface of homophobia, and the fact the men who perform their gender in less masculine ways are often read as gay whether they identify this way or not. Moreover, as Rufus discussed it, coming out and being out was solely up to the individual and how "comfortable they are to make that step." The particular environment in which this happened, and the responsibility of community members, policy makers, or himself—as arguably the most powerful person in the district—for making places open and accepting for queer people, were not key factors in the process.

Like Rufus, Leo expressed support for sexual and gender diversity in similarly generic, and self-privileging ways throughout his interview. He viewed identity, for example, as an issue for all youth, not just LGBTQ and gender diverse youth but noted, "I don't want this to sound like I don't get that there is an issue. I get that there's an issue." For Leo, however, he did not recognize any differences among *how* "people agonize about their own identity." Instead, he maintained that "figuring out" one's identity was an individual pursuit, not something rooted in systemic privilege for some identities. As he saw it, "this is for kids who are part of the majority, who are white, who are middle class, who feel that they're straight" and he stated, "identity matters for humans as they grow" and "we need to be addressing and making people feel good about the people who they are." In his efforts to be universally supportive, Leo consistently failed to recognize any distinctions among young people and noted "every teenager questions his or her identity" and "they need to be made to feel that that's okay, that there's nothing wrong with you because you have a lot of angst over who you are in this crazy social setting that we call school." Although Leo seemed to give some attention to the social context of schools, his lack of attention to the specific needs of LGBTQ and gender diverse students and his dedication to the notion that identity is purely developmental led him to abdicate his epistemic authority as the superintendent to make change and simply attribute what was happening to "this crazy social setting that we call school."

In his interview, Rufus responded similarly to Leo. When asked about homophobic bullying, and whether it affected the students in the Williams school system, district-wide, he was quick to focus on general bullying, as an issue for all kids. Like Leo, Rufus saw homophobia as a general developmental problem within all people that "will always be a challenge in those middle school, early high school ages." Rather than recognizing the particular experiences of LGBTQ and gender diverse students as the targets of homophobic and transphobic bullying and the students who attack them as enacting violence rooted in hate, Rufus saw the issue as developmental, "because every kid is trying to figure themselves out and trying to figure out who they are as a sexual creature and how do I deal with these thoughts and feelings and urges that I haven't had to before."

Both Leo and Rufus made a generalized claim that "all" students were working out their identities and "trying to figure themselves out," echoing again a confident characterization applied across adolescents (Lesko, 2012). As in their earlier comments, both of these men, who held powerful positions in dramatically different school settings, failed to acknowledge their own privilege as white, heterosexual and cisgender men, and, instead, used their epistemic authority to generalize the experiences of all students rather than recognizing the particular—and the challenging and at times hate-filled—experiences of people based on race, class, gender or sexual identity, or any combination of these and other identity markers.

In spite of his differently intersecting identities compared to Rufus and Leo, Oscar took a strikingly similar stance when it came to recognizing and understanding the impacts of difference. Although he expressed that "combatting phobias is a big part of what I try to do," he persisted in seeing homophobia as far less prevalent or important in schools, relative to other forms of "harassment." When asked about heteronormativity in his district, and attention to gender identity, particularly concerning feminine acting men, masculine performing women, or young people who might not identify with a particular gender in a strong way, he stated, "At the high school level I haven't noticed that so much. Our student body seems to embrace students a little differently." He cited "Challenge Day," a national organization that the district hires to run an annual assembly for students aimed at combating bullying, as one way of addressing heteronormativity and something that "helps to some degree." He noted that, although "it doesn't mean that a male that has more effeminate characteristics or attributes will be invited to sit with the football team at lunch" he also doesn't "see them actively harassing or discriminating." Ultimately, he re-centered his own perspective and noted "I don't think it's as big an issue as maybe—maybe I'm just naïve. It seems to be a bigger issue for the teachers, but again, I begin to wonder if that's generational." As he did earlier, Oscar again suggested a "generational" difference in terms of how sexual identity and gender expression are viewed and treated in schools, without specifying precisely what he meant. Whether he just didn't get teachers' concerns because of the age difference between him and some of them; or whether teachers didn't get that homophobia and heteronormativity didn't "seem to be a central concern for our student body anymore" was unclear. What was clear, however, was that Oscar did not view homophobia, heterosexism, or transphobia as issues in his district. Moreover, when asked about the role of policy in supporting LGBTQ and gender diverse people, Oscar, expressed that it had little influence on practice. He shared that "teachers are very cognizant of when we don't have a policy that offers those sorts of protections," and "when we haven't included gender orientation, sexual orientation policies" they seemed to be "more assertive in ensuring that those rights are codified." But for himself, "pragmatically, I'm not so certain it changes anyone's practices at all" and moreover, he noted "I haven't necessarily observed that there are a lot of discriminatory practices either." Here, despite his epistemic authority as the district superintendent, a role in which policy work is central, Oscar abdicated his authority and capacity to make change and justified his position in his own, personal, privileged perspective.

Later, Oscar expressed enthusiasm for the work that some teachers have done in the district to combat homophobia and heterosexism, but continued to convey his doubts about the impacts of policy. He shared that in his first year in the district, there was a group focused on "LGBTQO—whatever and I attended that one to try to get a better understanding of what their concerns were." This group of teachers had proposed that the district revise their policies to include specific, enumerated language that recognized sexual diversity. Oscar noted the success of the group, but added, "then they wanted to go to the next step, and make certain we had included gender orientation, and other vernacular," another policy step he described as "all well and good, we're codifying it, but does it really change dispositions and behaviors? And does that really need to be our focus?" Oscar suggested that individual students and teachers were really the key sources of support, as opposed to a more system-wide approach that might be led by policy or by himself as the superintendent. When asked about the Day of Silence, a nationwide event aimed at helping non-queer people understand the impacts of silencing LGBTQ and gender diverse people in schools, and whether the district is fully behind that event Oscar replied, "I don't think they're fully behind it. I think it's more student-driven. And I think that's okay. Those things tend to have more meaning and sustainability than those top-down sort of initiatives so, I think it's a good thing." He noted that each school seemed to have adult advocates that students knew about and that this was "very, very clear." He also noted that some teachers used signage, such as the rainbow triangle "right in the classroom" to signal their support of sexual and gender diversity and that "there are teachers that are very explicit about their sexual orientation with students. They let them know, you know, 'I am a lesbian.'" Although he wondered aloud that he didn't know "why it's critical that you share that," he acknowledged that, "for some students, that might help them feel safe in who they talk to."

Oscar's recognition of the work that some teachers did to support LGBTQ and gender diverse students was both laudable and problematic. On the one hand, it was important that he knew that there was a group of teachers who were actively engaged in supporting queer students and that in general he supported their efforts. On the other hand, it was troubling that he abdicated his epistemic authority and ceded this work to some teachers rather than seeing it as an expectation for and the responsibility of all teachers, something he could have codified and required in his role as superintendent. Moreover, he continued to seem somewhat baffled as to why a queer teacher might choose to be publicly out to their students and failed to recognize the risks involved for the teachers themselves, suggesting, again, that his own power and privilege affected and limited his work in support of sexual and gender diversity.

In a similar vein, Rufus suggested that the real work to actively support sexual and gender diversity in the district rested on the staff and students. He noted that, "I couldn't be more proud of the team that we have. I think it's just continuing to develop that ethos among the staff and their students that we are going to treat every person with whom we interact with respect." Rather than recognizing the epistemic privilege of people whose daily lived experience might differ dramatically from his own, Rufus referred to sexual and gender diversity as part of "all those other differences that don't make a difference in terms of who somebody is" or their "character." Instead, he asserted that differences in race, class, gender, or sexuality "are just going to be part of what we know about somebody not part of how we judge somebody" a statement that again revealed the limitations in his capacity to recognize or deeply understand the experiences of queer people in schools.

Their epistemic authority as superintendents and their unacknowledged privilege as white, cisgender, financially secure men limited Leo, Oscar, and Rufus in recognizing and valuing difference and, hence, in their work for social justice. Instead, they positioned LGBTQ and gender diverse students and families in some troubling ways. Across and throughout their interviews, none of them recognized or valued the unique differences among students, families, and their own staff in these terms. This persistence rendered LGBTQ and gender diverse students and their families invisible. Despite overt claims to the Golden Rule and equality, all three failed to acknowledge LGBTQ and gender diverse youth as uniquely different from straight and cisgender youth and from either other, and, instead, re-centered their own privileged perspectives as universal and used "diversity" and "social justice" as blanket statements to capture all differences without recognizing or valuing the specific nuances of any of these differences. Such a stance refused to acknowledge the privilege that accompanied all of their identities and roles and rendered opaque an actual hierarchy of differences. As O'Malley and Capper (2015) point out,

> A tempered social justice discourse that normalizes attention to particular aspects of identity while legitimizing the layers of silence vis-à-vis others carries the risk of devolving into an alternate mechanism of colonization . . . and fundamentally fails to disrupt the foundational cultural logic that produces and sustains inequitable structures and practices.
>
> *(p. 319)*

For all three, their failure to acknowledge their privilege and recognize difference furthered their confident sense of epistemic authority. Rufus, for example, expressed that coming out, or not, is an experience and choice shared by all people. Leo stated that all students struggled to "figure themselves out." And Oscar felt sure that students in his district were not concerned with homophobia or heteronormativity.

Our claim, across all of these school leaders, superintendents and principals alike, is that their privilege and epistemic authority as school principals and district superintendents mattered in the lives of LGBTQ and gender diverse students in schools. Their perspectives affected whether schools even acknowledged particular identities and differences among students and, by extension, recognized related problems of homophobia, transphobia, racism, misogyny, and heteronormativity. Moreover, their perspective resulted in an erasure of the generative potential of difference, such that approaching it as a resource could be a way to reexamine and transform social structures such as schooling. Instead, they positioned queer people as invisible or as victims, not as agents who could act and even teach them about how to improve their school communities. In doing so, they reaffirmed their own knowledges and ways of knowing as definitive and static, unable to take up a stance of inquiry, learning, and change. Likewise, the epistemic authority of these school leaders affected other educators' sense of power relative to intervening in these problems. As noted in earlier chapters, some teachers claimed to not have the expertise or knowledge to be able to intervene in problems facing LGBTQ and gender diverse students and were seeking guidance in learning more or at least permission from school leaders to do more. In other cases, administrators' failure to recognize difference led them to not see a need for action or intervention. A closer look at how three adults working in the same school environment, responded to an African American queer, gender-nonconforming student helps to support our claim that school leaders privilege and epistemic authority matter in the lives of queer students in schools.

One School Context

Annie, Marge, and Craig all worked at Century High School, a STEM-focused lottery, early-college high school in a midsize mid-western city. The school was quite diverse, with 8% of students identifying as Asian, 29% as Black, 4% as Hispanic, 54% as white, and 6% as bi- or multi-racial. In total, 49% of the students were identified as male, and 51% female, with no data available on the proportion of students who identified as transgender or queer. The school had an active Gay–Straight Alliance (GSA) as well as a state-mandated anti-bullying policy. Annie was a white, straight, cisgender woman and the principal of Century High School. Marge was a bi-racial, cisgender woman and the Administrative Assistant at Century, attending and helping coordinate all school events, including orientation, prom, and graduation. With her desk directly inside the entrance to the school, Marge was the first person to interact with people as they entered the building. Craig was a straight, white, cisgender man with a genetic disease that affected his eyes. At times, this disability was very apparent because of what he called a "wandering eye." As a teacher and member of the leadership team, his administrative work focused on "the nuts and bolts of attendance and test coordination, but also discipline."

Although Annie, Marge, and Craig all worked in the same school, their roles in the school, and their epistemic authority and privilege varied, as did their recognition of difference; that is, how they named and expressed knowing about differences of race, class, sexuality and gender, both their own and others. Annie, for instance, stated right away,

> Well, I mean, personally, I'm straight. I have friends who—that's what everyone says, right? "I have friends who are Black. I have friends who are LGBTQ." But I definitely have friends, close friends that I would travel with, that know my kid.

Annie positioned herself as a straight ally, and even though she stated that, "pretty much people get along" and that having a "culture and climate of acceptance" is something that "Century does really well," she also noticed problems in how some staff treated LGBTQ people:

> I've seen staff here more willing to verbalize their displeasure or discomfort with LGBTQ staff and students than they would be with students, if they were talking about students that were poor, or students of color, or students who believe something different.

Annie not only saw differences among Century students and staff, but she named these differences explicitly. Moreover, she was aware of how staff members took up differences, noting some who treated LGBTQ students and staff in more openly disapproving ways than they did students based on class, racial, or religious identities.

In contrast to Annie, when Marge was asked how she identified herself in relationship to the LGBTQ community, as either a part of it, or as an ally, she was flummoxed.

> I don't know that I would use any of those labels because that subject matter doesn't come up in any of my interactions with students. I feel like I would be supportive of a student regardless just because my role here is to help them, period.

She then stated,

> I've never seen where that becomes an issue as to determine how I would interact or how I would relate to any of the kids. So, I'd never even thought in those terms. Like how would it, and would I do things any differently if I knew a student fell in into one of those categories? So, it's interesting to even consider. Like, what is my relationship to it? I, I wouldn't even think in those terms.

Unlike Annie, Marge asserted that she had no place in relationship to the LGBTQ community because "the subject matter" didn't come up. Moreover, she was oblivious to race, class, gender, and sex, claiming to never recognize "those categories" or any other differences, and asserting that she knew little to nothing about them. In fact, throughout the entire interview, she never explicitly named race, class, or sexual identities with any specificity either in reference to herself or others.

Finally, in contrast to both Annie and Marge, Craig recognized differences, but felt that in order to support and advocate authentically for LGBTQ students, adults in schools had to have some direct personal experience with feeling different themselves and noted, "the only thing that helps me be empathetic with things that I don't know firsthand is to have some sort of emotional connection." Craig argued that one had to reach "a similar emotional level" with people, because one never wants to say, "'Well, I know how you feel,' cause that's bullshit, short of like living that exact same experience." Instead, he argued that educators could use their own experiences of being different to connect and relate to others and shared, "I think what you could say is like, 'I know what it's like to feel out of the mainstream. I know what it likes to feel out of place.'" Craig drew explicitly on his visual impairment to illustrate his point and shared a story of being mocked when a photo was circulated among colleagues and students that showed that "my eye was a little bit wandering." A mass email was sent out "to every Century person, even like graduates and kind of highlighting, like one is calling me Robocop, and they had superimposed some things and really highlighting my, my weird eye." Craig described that story of harassment as an example of having his own differences used as a reason to abuse him and also the reason he believes in connecting to students through differences. He asserted that to be an educator, "you need to have somebody who's empathetic" and suggested that, if he were a teacher educator, he would start by asking, "When have you ever felt different?" In spite of his cis- and heteronormativity and other privileges, Craig recognized the ways in which specific differences mattered, noting that being gay and having a disability are distinct, and that claiming that a person knows how anyone else feels is "bullshit." He also recognized that knowing how it feels to be different, regardless of the specific difference, was critical if a teacher were to connect to students emotionally and empathize with them.

These contrasting views of privilege and difference affected how Annie, Marge, and Craig positioned Jake, who you will recall from Chapter 5, is a Black out, gay student at Century. It's worth noting here that Century had a "business casual" dress code, which basically meant that students could not wear jeans, leggings, short skirts, tank tops, or athletic shoes to school. Annie described Jake as a student, "where his home situation was in no way accepting of his sexuality." She shared a story of how troubled Marge was by Jake's dress:

> And then he started to come in high heels during his, with his outfit. So he would wear dress shirt, dress pants, women's high heels. So I had a staff member who was really bothered by that. And I said "OK we're not," we actually had a direct conflict about it because I said, "OK we're not addressing that with him right now. We're just going to let it go." And [Marge] was like "Fine."

Annie shared how, later, on a day when she was out of the building, Jake was sent to the office for something else, and Marge raised the issue of dress code with him. This was memorable for Annie because, "as far as I could remember, that's the only thing that I've ever given a direct, 'We're not doing that,' [to a staff member] and [she] did it anyway." Caroline asked Annie, "And when you say 'We're not addressing that,' were you saying we're not going to call that out as problematic. Or we're just not even going to comment on it?" She responded:

> I was saying we're not going to have a conversation about dress code with that kid because we're just, like if he wants to wear women's shoes right now . . . and he's got a lot of other stuff going on, no one else has any problems with this, right? Like none of the kids are even phased by it. All the other teachers are fine with it. You have an issue with it. I get it. I get it. Right. I understand that in a business world, probably men who want an office job are not wearing high heels to work. Like I get that. But this kid is 16. We have two more years to have that conversation with him. We are not doing it right now. I just want him to come to school. I want him to do his work. . . . No one's bothered, except for you. So we're not going to talk about it.

Annie described how Jake had been collecting dress code clothes that were really women's clothes, but that after Jake tried to come out to his parents, his father went through his closet and threw out all of the clothes that were not men's sizes, forcing Jake to come to school in jeans, and as Annie put it, causing "this whole ruckus":

> So it was really hard for Jake. But in that situation I feel like a lot of his sorts of issues came from home, because they were very non-supportive. And so he would come to dances or something and be like totally in drag. And then his mom would come and he would go in the bathroom and change back. And then, when she would leave, he would change back. It was really hard. And that's why I was telling [Marge] like, "I don't care that he's wearing high heels, just let him be, let's leave him alone."

Because Annie had epistemic authority as the principal and recognized Jake, as a queer, gender non-conforming student, she could take specific action to support and advocate for Jake, including not enforcing the school dress code and directing staff to do the same. However, not all adult staff members recognized and valued Jake's differences and did not follow Annie's lead. In telling her own story about Jake, Marge recounted,

> Yeah, when I think of him, and specifically, like he's such a funny character. So much of the attention that he brought on himself is because he's such a charismatic and in-your-face kind of person. Whereas other students who've come through the program who maybe were like in the exact same position, you know, like—not that no one knew, but they never got any negative attention.

Rather than recognizing and naming Jake as either queer or gender non-conforming, Marge referred to him as "charismatic" and "in-your-face," comparing him to students in "the exact same position," who remained unseen, unknown, and thus, did not bring "any negative attention" on themselves. While she acknowledged, later in the interview that, "I think he had struggles," she attributed these as, "things, temperamentally, that it was just who he was." She went on,

> And that had nothing to do with, 'How are you identifying yourself?' So, even with him and that he was so flamboyant, I've never seen that there was an issue within the school community of anybody singling him out for mistreatment, or exclusion, or anything of that nature.

When Marge was asked whether she had known other students who were out at Century, she responded,

> Probably nobody as flamboyant as Jake. [Chuckles] Uhm, yeah, we had others. And everybody was aware. And like I said, I don't think it's ever become an issue that impacted them like within the educational environment or socially. And even this year we have. Actually, well, I think we've had every year since then. Uhm, everyone gets along well. I just—and I mean either I'm blind. But I'm out in the open. And I see them interact every day. Oh, really, they don't make an issue of it. And I think it's because people just get along. And that's a choice.

In contrast to Annie, Marge did not recognize or value Jake's perspective and experiences as a queer, gender non-conforming Black student, and, instead, named him as charismatic, in-your-face, temperamental, and flamboyant, comments that framed his vocal queerness and visible Blackness as negative, rather than generative, disruptions. Marge saw Jake through a lens of problematic behaviors rather than recognizing him as a unique person. As a result, Marge only saw Jake as an outlier from all of the other students at Century who, unlike Jake, "choose" to get along.

Craig, by comparison, did see Century students acting in ways that were homophobic, heterosexist, and transphobic, and he worked to respond educatively. He noted that, in his work as an administrator, "anything that smacks" of homophobia, heterosexism or transphobia, "that's a big no-no. I will drop everything with that. That never gets swept under the rug." He described intervening when students used terms like "That's so gay," by asking, "Really? What does that mean? Let's break that down. What are you trying to say?" and forcing them to say it out loud, "Oh, I just meant like that's weird or strange" and then him responding, "Oh, so you're saying that gay people are weird or strange." He contrasted himself to another teacher, Delia, who was "so much better at this" because she would innocently say to students, "Oh, I don't know what you mean. What do you mean by that?" whereas Craig was "a little bit more aggressive, like you should, you should frigging know better" because he never wanted students to play as if "I just didn't' know."

Like Annie and Marge, Craig had also worked with Jake and had frequent run-ins with him about dress code. Craig described how he tried to tell Jake that he should "embrace who he was" because "who he was, was fine," but also how he tried to give Jake "the same logic that I give a lot of other kids," that "your culture's fine, but not at all times. Like the way you dress and the way you talk is fine, and I honor that, but like you should dress and talk different here." With Jake, however, he felt that these conversations put him in an "emotional danger zone." Here, Craig seemed to be describing the way that he talked with students about language in and out of school, and urging them to see that there are different discourses and ways of speaking that are expected and required in different settings for different occasions. When asked if he thought about Jake's dress as a kind of code switching, Craig initially agreed and noted that "it's okay to be different things at different times." But when he commented on Jake's dress, as part of the dress-code policy, he recognized that it was "very dangerous to say that to him without creeping into saying, like, 'Well you should be, that means that maybe you should be straight, or less of who you are.'" Here, Craig seemed to be questioning the use of code switching as a metaphor in terms of Jake's choices to wear women's clothing and the dress code. Craig seemed to understand and accept language and discourse as something that can change from context to context, and he was comfortable with talking to students about this. But, he worried that if he talked to Jake about dress code in that way, he would be challenging Jake's fundamental identity as a Black, queer, gender non-conforming young person, and he did not want to do that. Craig struggled with his desire to both honor who Jake was and affirm that his identity as a Black gay, gender diverse young person was just fine, while also pointing out the expectations of society, as he understood them. Craig noted that he also had to "change and modify" to fit in, but then quickly recognized that "who I am is largely, society is largely cool with who I am." Although Craig didn't "love being, you know, the dress code guy," he also saw dress code as "a big deal" because other teachers never dealt with it, which he saw as a "cop out" and which he felt was "selling kids short." Craig wondered,

> What if you let Jake do whatever? And just let him go, and then go out in the world? The world as it is now, not some pie in the sky, what we really wish it could be, or what it maybe should be [world]. But what if we never had a conversation?

Craig decried people who might say that ignoring the dress code was a way of "caring about the child," and instead argued that these people "actually care about themselves and not wanting to have a very challenging conversation." He noted that, even though he was "Mr. Business Casual, Jake knew that I cared about him." Craig described his experiences with Jake as a struggle; he struggled to care about how he felt in the short term, but also what skills I could arm him with for the long run. I was doing that because I knew it was the right thing, because I know about life.

However, he named his direct interactions with Jake as the only way he might approach supporting him with respect to his sexuality, gender expression, and race, whether in the short or long term, and did not consider other actions, such as impacting the school or even society.

In part, because of his own difference, Craig recognized and worked hard to understand Jake's experiences as a queer, gender diverse student at Century. In contrast to Marge, Craig's visual impairment positioned him to recognize, and address, homophobia among students at Century, and to humanize Jake rather than view him as the problem. That said, unlike Annie, Craig used his epistemic authority to enforce rather than overlook the dress code, believing that was the most caring thing to do for Jake. In doing this, Craig re-centered his own privilege and perspective, believing that he "knew better" how to prepare Jake for a complex, often cruel world that might not support him in the ways that he, Annie, and other Century staff and students did.

Looking across the three adults, and their varying responses to Jake, reveals how epistemic authority and recognition and valuing of difference led to different kinds of action (or inaction) among adults in schools. In this case, Annie, Marge, and Craig all shared the same school and community context. And while all of them saw Century as a welcoming and supportive place for students, both Annie and Craig understood that the culture occurred through the intentional actions of staff, students, and policies. As the principal, Annie not only used her epistemic authority to enforce the rules and policies of Century, she also used it to modify and change them when they were not in the best interest of students. Likewise, Craig saw that part of his job as an administrator was to educatively combat homophobic language among all students. And, while he saw the differences among students, and related these to his own, he also recognized his privilege as a straight, white, cisgender man, and struggled to both honor students' identities and freedom to express themselves while also preparing them for places and people who might not do the same. In contrast, Marge characterized the majority of students at Century as fitting in and "getting along well," and Jake as the exception. When asked in her interview what made the school this way, Marge indicated that it "just happens . . . people just get along." Unlike Annie and Craig, Marge did not see the school culture as something that was intentionally created by people or policies. Moreover, because she was oblivious to race, class, gender, and sexuality, Marge failed to recognize how Jake's identity as queer, Black, and gender non-conforming affected his experiences at Century in ways both similar to and different from all of the unique and varied students there. Instead, Jake's visibility was discomfiting to Marge, leading her to position Jake as the problem. Choosing to ignore Annie's directive to leave

Jake alone, an action that would have supported him, Marge, instead, enforced the dress code in an attempt to force Jake to fit in.

Enacting Leadership

Like Kelly, Jeff, Leo, Oscar, and Rufus, how the administrative staff at Century viewed knowledge and recognized and valued differences affected their support of Jake and of LGBTQ and gender diverse students and families in general. Across adults in schools, we noticed that how administrators recognized and harnessed their own power to make change, based on their awareness of their own privilege and epistemic authority, shaped their stances as leaders. As school principals, for instance, Kelly, Jeff, Craig, and Annie fit fairly neatly into two conceptual leadership models. With her focus on student achievement and improving educational outcomes, especially in a distressed, urban district serving racially and economically diverse families, Kelly was an instructional leader (Hallinger, 2003); for principals like Kelly, student academic outcomes are the key goal, which often narrows their mission and focus (Hallinger, 2003, p. 332) and depends on outside indicators of success, such as standardized test scores. Annie, Craig, and Jeff, however, focused on relationships, a word that Jeff used 21 times in his interview. Knowing and working with students, families, colleagues, and staff throughout the school system, modeling desired behaviors for others, and addressing "school conditions that produce changes in people rather than promoting specific instructional practices" (Hallinger, p. 339) were paramount to Jeff, Craig, and Annie. While all three recognized their own power and privilege, they were more apt to use their power in concert with others, or re-shape policy in response to student and community needs, rather than generalize their own experiences to everyone. All of these are essential features of a transformational leader (Leithwood et al., 1996).

As district superintendents, Leo, Oscar, and Rufus presumably had even more power and epistemic authority than Kelly, Annie, Craig, or Jeff. While they may have had to answer to elected school boards and other constituents, they also had the capacity to set policy, guide curriculum decisions, and reward building administrators and teachers who demonstrated positive support of sexual and gender diversity in their schools. Given this, we were especially curious to know if they recognized this power in themselves or if they, too, felt limited in their ability to take action. It's important to note that, in some instances, superintendents were not aware of particular issues related to homophobia and transphobia. And, to be fair, if they were not aware of a problem, then they were also unlikely to recognize it, acknowledge it, or taken action in response to it.

Rufus provided a good example. In describing what schools might do, specifically, to support LGBTQ and gender diverse students, he raised the work that positive signage, such as No Hate posters or rainbow stickers, might do and how these would be received. "I think it would be less well received if we had as much signage at the middle school from a parent perspective, because they're not comfortable with any sexual discussions, to include sexual orientation." He expressed feeling good about the current status quo and stated, "And I have to say I have not seen anything end up on my desk as the superintendent." The ones that did end up on Rufus's desk were "the big ones . . . Because what I see then are the suspensions and expulsions, I see every one of those reports, that have been triggered by bullying related to homophobia." He asserted, "I don't know what you're hearing through the grape vine, if that's something you're seeing at the high school, it's certainly not ending up on the big ones that end up on my desk." Here, although Rufus did not explicitly express fear or a sense of powerlessness around his supportive actions, he clearly recognized limits in the kinds of actions that could and should be taken in particular contexts, noting that middle school parents would see pro-LGBTQ signs as indicative of "sexual discussions" and would be against them. Additionally, Rufus noted that only certain kinds of issues, "the big ones," ended up on his desk. In other interviews, and in our own experiences, we recognized and understood his point. In most schools, a clear goal was for teachers to manage behavior and discipline issues at the classroom level. And, for some teachers, like James who you read about in earlier chapters, never sending a student to the office was a badge of honor and indicative of how well they did their job.

Unfortunately, homophobia, transphobia, and heterosexism, and the daily impacts of these, are rarely "the big ones" until they lead to significant tragedies. Instead, they are the countless microaggressions that queer kids face on a daily basis,

> the way homophobia and sexism interact, the way the fear of being labeled gay or lesbian pushes people into conforming to traditional sex role expectations . . . the 'million little suicides' children and young people experience when they are prevented by teaching or by their own fears from trying something they would like to do.
>
> *(Rensenbrink, 1996, p. 267)*

So, perhaps it's no wonder that so few superintendents or even school principals notice the day-to-day harassment faced by LGBTQ and gender diverse students in schools. Still, although all three men recognized that some of their staff, particularly teachers, were concerned about serving and supporting LGBTQ and gender diverse students and families, none of them actively rewarded these efforts, acknowledged the risks of these efforts, or deeply embraced policy as a viable solution or mechanism for change. Again, we contend that this was, in part, due to their unacknowledged privilege and epistemic authority and their failure to recognize difference. As noted earlier, all of them filtered their understandings of race, class, sexuality, gender, and gender expression through their own personal experiences of oppression and difference. Oscar saw no need for specific policy-level responses because he viewed these not as systems of oppression, but instead, as individual beliefs. Likewise, for Rufus, any policies or intentional action was not necessary since, in his experience, inclusivity "seems to happen spontaneously" as long as you have a culture "where everyone can be themselves"—never mind the privilege and power attached to some identities and not others.

This focus on individual identities, people, and beliefs oblivious of race, class, gender, or sexuality, reflects what Mayo (2014) calls, "the inability to see diversity as more than one aspect of identity at a time" (p 40). She goes on to state, "too often discussions of diversity seem to assume that all people have one identity, not that they might live complex lives in which their multiple differences intersect and affect one another" (p. 40). For these three superintendents, their unacknowledged privilege, epistemic authority, and failure to recognize difference, in turn, shaped and limited their actions as leaders. Rather than lead collective responses to homophobia, transphobia, or heterosexism at the district level, they saw individual teachers or students as the solution. Each repeatedly pointed to individuals rather than policies and assumed that students will know who the supportive teachers are and how to find them, ultimately putting much of the burden of advocacy and action on those with the least amount of power: teachers or queer students themselves.

Enacting Leadership for Social Justice

Given their privilege, power, and epistemic authority, school leaders can and must do more to enact leadership for social justice. The work of supporting sexual and gender diversity in schools should not fall on the shoulders of young people or teachers alone. As noted earlier, principals and superintendents are "gatekeepers" for students seeking access, equity, and social justice through education. But, when gatekeepers can't or won't acknowledge their own privilege and epistemic authority and fail to recognize and value differences, "fault lines" (Smith, 1987) emerge. These "points of rupture between socially organized practices and daily lived experience" (p. 52) are common experiences in the lives of LGBTQ and gender diverse students in schools (Kosciw et al, 2016; Rusch, 2004). They occur whenever school leaders use their own privileged lives as the basis for school rules, regulations, and structures rather than recognizing the daily, lived experiences of queer students and families. And, they happen whenever school leaders abdicate their epistemic authority and power to make change and look to outside indicators of "thriving" in the form of test scores, instead of looking inside and recognizing the social, emotional, and other needs of LGBTQ and gender diverse students. And although school leaders like Jeff, Craig, and Annie provide exemplars of what is possible, we worry that without significant shifts in how school leaders are prepared there is little hope for real change. As Rusch (2004) notes, "Sadly, the gatekeepers seldom facilitate talk about the inequities. In fact, silence, blindness, and fear frequently mediate the discourse about diversity and equity among educators" (p. 19).

We know that administrators play a key role in the school experiences of LGBTQ youth; but we also know that very few leadership preparation programs address LGBTQ content, even when those programs identify as social justice oriented. Moreover, most leadership preparation programs focus on developing instructional leadership rather than transformational leadership. We contend that focusing on instructional leadership alone is not enough if we want more adults who will take action on behalf of queer people in schools. School administrators therefore are important, but they cannot do the work alone. As O'Malley and Capper (2015) note, administration licensure and leadership preparation programs need to "shift . . . away from notions of the social justice leader as a solitary or uniquely heroic figure advocating for particular marginalized groups within schools" (pp. 301–302). Instead school leaders, and all adults who work in schools, need to acknowledge their own privilege and epistemic authority and recognize and value differences as emerging from intersecting roles, places, and identities, acknowledging that epistemologies are not neutral and cannot be oblivious to race, class, gender, or sexuality, but, instead, are produced by and often advantageous to people who are privileged in terms of any or all of these. Working from a humanizing paradigm (Paris & Winn, 2014), administrators and other adults in schools might then be able to recognize and learn from the "epistemic privilege" (Collins, 1990; Harding, 1993; Janack, 1997) of minoritized people, including people of color, women, and queer people, as holders and creators of knowledge unique from dominant epistemologies. In this way, adults in schools might then be positioned to work both individually and collectively for social justice, facilitating alliances across difference, to take action in new, more robust ways in support of queer students, and all students, in schools.

Shields (2004) argues that what is needed is a new conceptual model of leadership: transformative, dialogic leadership. In this framework, administrators attend to both social justice and academic achievement (p. 110) by examining inequities inherent in the status quo and challenging current practices and beliefs through dialogue across communities of stakeholders within schools. Key to such leadership is the need for educators, and especially principals, as school leaders, "to acknowledge and validate difference without reifying or pathologizing it" (p. 113) and for educators to learn, "that difference is normal. It is neither to be celebrated or denigrated. It just is" (p. 127).

Imagine what a leadership shift such as this might enable for queer families at Guthrie. Such a leadership stance might open up spaces where "visibility as queer would not mean vulnerability, and visibility as straight would not mean security," as we said in chapter four. And, imagine what dialogic, transformative leadership might have afforded Jake and other LGBTQ and gender diverse students in schools. What would their school lives have looked like if they had principals who sought not only to transform the practices of schooling but also to transform the deeply engrained ways of perceiving LGBTQ and gender diverse people in schools? If school districts are embracing and supporting such work, as Kelly suggested, then administrators, administrative staff, and leadership preparation programs must follow suit and work not only to lead, but also to transform school spaces in order to better support LGBTQ and gender diverse students and families.

Teacher Take Aways

- Talk with people, not simply about them. Seek to learn from and with them. Make time to communicate in person at least as often as you do by email.
- Acknowledge privileged identities and how these affect marginalized identities. Neither is totalizing or wholly who we are.
- Ask for help. Request opportunities to (re)educate yourself about diversity in authentic and specific ways, including topics related to sexual diversity, gender expression, race, class, and the intersections among these. Invite your superintendent, principal, and other adult staff beyond teachers for their input and participation.
- Work on broadening the circle of people you know and connect with queer communities and communities of color, among others. Invite parents, families, and community members into schools spaces so that their views and voices are part of the ongoing conversation.

8

STEPPING UP

What It Takes and Why It Matters

Every day, there are teachers, families, students, administrators, and other school personnel who choose to step up and advocate for LGBTQ and gender diverse people in schools. Each time they make this choice, they also make a choice to learn, reflect, and connect. And every day offers a new opportunity to step up. Each time someone does step up, they must act, in a humanizing way and with an awareness of and respect for intersecting identities. They must make safe enough spaces for LGBTQ and gender diverse people in schools. And, depending on who they are and where they come from, they must acknowledge their own privilege, power, and authority and use these in ways that recognize and value what people who are different from them may know instead of assuming that because of their privilege and power, they know better. Stepping up, though, increases visibility of LGBTQ and gender diverse people as well as those who step up on their behalf. With increased visibility comes increased vulnerability, which may be risky but can also be a springboard for change. With practice, stepping up gets easier. Each time, new information is gleaned, new opportunities for growth reveal themselves, and new occasions for recognizing and connecting across differences can occur. But the learning never stops, the reflecting never ends, and the connecting is never finished.

Stepping up for LGBTQ and gender diverse people in school requires learning about queer communities in and around your school and more broadly speaking, including in your discipline. Some of this learning can come from listening to queer students and parents, among others. Some of this learning can come from reading about queer people and lives, especially texts created by queer people and queer people of color. Pay particular attention to learning about a wide diversity of people in a wide range of contexts and from a variety of sources, including non-fiction—like news outlets, essays, biographies, and films—and fiction—particularly that representing people who are in some ways like your students. One can also learn by seeking and attending professional development opportunities that pertain to LGBTQ and gender diverse people in schools. Learning relies on practice, that is trying, making mistakes, receiving feedback, and trying again (and again).

So, for example, if a straight kindergarten teacher has a student coming in who has two moms, and as far as she knows, this is the first time, she might watch *It's Elementary*, a video about talking about lesbian and gay people with younger students, and *That's a Family*, a video that explores a wide range of families in schools, including those with same-sex parents. She might even watch these with colleagues and school principal and talk about how to best meet the needs of the incoming family as a way of learning how to step up. She might take what she learns and apply it to her curriculum but also in her conversations with the student and her moms. Think about how having this teacher might have improved the experience of Mollie's child, whose kindergarten teacher failed to acknowledge and therefore engage the more androgynous of her two moms.

Related to learning, is reflection. People who step up for LGBTQ and gender diverse people in schools reflect on the biases they carry with them and the consequences these biases have for queer people with a particular awareness of the diversity—racial, ethnic, class, religious diversity, among other kinds of diversity—among queer people. Further, they reflect on their own privileges, as well as their vulnerabilities and risks, recognizing that these are not all they are, but they are a part of who they are; and this is the case, not only for them but others as well. There is also a need to reflect on one's authority, acknowledging that one has it and considering how one uses it. Finally, there is a need to reflect on what one does not know, helping propel one into further learning.

Consider a white gay high school teacher who is fairly discrete in terms of his sexuality at his school. He may keep a journal of moments that just feel tense for him as a way of exploring those tensions, so perhaps moments like when homecoming or prom kings and queens are elected or when his students, who he really likes, use the term "gay" in a derogatory way. He might write about what he feels and write through why he feels that way, but he might also challenge himself to write about how his whiteness allows him to see himself in popular culture in a way some of his students of color who he perceives as queer might not. He might explore, through his journaling, how his class status allows him to be out in his personal life since he no longer depends on his parents' approval for a place to live. In these ways, he reflects on the complexity of his stepping up. Think about how having this teacher might have impacted the school life of Jake, a Black and out gay student, who struggled with the dress code at his school in part because of his parents' rejection of his desire to wear women's clothes.

Just as important as learning and reflection is connection. Building individual relationships with LGBTQ and gender diverse people is strengthened when it draws on love, compassion, and a commitment to justice. One might better connect with students when actively rejecting assumptions that all students are straight, cisgender, homophobic, and transphobic. One might better connect with parents when listening and receiving feedback with patience and a desire to hear and learn. It is also valuable to foster connections among others. Students might better connect to one another when they are provided opportunities but not obligations to share about themselves and their families. Parents might better connect to one another when they are invited to work together on something for their children.

Imagine a high school teacher who has noticed a student who expresses her gender in stereotypically feminine ways but is called by most people—teachers and students alike—by a stereotypically masculine name and is referenced using he/him/his pronouns. The teacher noticed, in particular that she sits alone in the hallway during lunch. He introduces himself to her and asks her name. He regularly speaks to her in the hallways, using the feminine name with which she introduced herself. He has a copy of *Beyond Magenta* and *Rethinking Normal* and tells her about them. She seems interested, so he lends them to her. They discuss the books as she returns them, well read. Think about how Chandler's school experience, as a girl who was misidentified at birth as a boy, might have been improved by such a teacher.

Beyond learning, reflecting, and connecting, advocating for LGBTQ and gender diverse people in schools demands action. Specifically, teachers must understand their teaching as activism. They must seek opportunities to act for social change rather than perseverating on the barriers that hinder such action. Further, when seizing those opportunities, they must be both purposeful and tactical, but not in a cold and calculating way, instead, in a humanizing way. This requires engaging in the work with love and respect, but also with humility and a desire and willingness to improve. Imperative in engaging in humanizing work, too, is understanding people's multiple and variable identities. We sometimes use the term intersectionality to refer to where these identities converge, knowing that any one—be it sexuality, gender, race, among many others—is not adequately represented by a line that intersects with others. Still, it is a reminder that people cannot be understood as only gay or only trans or only any single identity. Stepping up compels an understanding of LGBTQ and gender diverse people beyond their sexual and gender identities. It depends on the drawing on these aspects of identities as resources, strengths, or, in Lena Waithe's words, "superpowers" (Bliston, 2017). This should be evident in curricular and pedagogical choices as well as interpersonal moves.

Imagine the possibility of a cisgender middle school physical education (PE) teacher who expects a student who she knows to embody gender in fluid ways to be coming to her class. She reads GLSEN's Model District Policy on Transgender and Gender Nonconforming Students created with the National Center for Transgender Equality (2016), but her district has not approved such a policy. She thinks through a variety of possibilities for the student, such as having the freedom to use the locker room of their choice, knowing this might vary across the school year; the option of using a single stall "handicapped" restroom; and the option of dressing in the nurse's office. All of these choices have pros and cons related to students' potential reactions, locations relative to the gym, among others. So, she meets with the student in advance to discuss the possibilities and to listen to their hopes and concerns related to PE. Think about how having this teacher might have influenced the school life of Kai, an Asian American gender queer student, who actively avoided using lavatories and locker rooms in school because their peers' reactions to their gender expressions were amplified in those contexts.

Queer people need space to make choices about coming out, being out, and being activist. They need space to embody and enact multiple and variable sexual and gender identities, among others. Young people need support in these efforts, particularly since such space can be made hostile with mundane things, such as lavatories and locker rooms, and even with cherished traditions, like homecomings and proms. To expect these spaces to be safe is unrealistic since what is safe for one person is not necessarily safe for another, and even what is safe for one person at one moment in time is not necessarily safe for that same person at another moment. But it is reasonable that spaces in schools be safe enough for them to learn and live in ways that are consistent with who they are and strive to be. It is important to create contexts in which queer people can see themselves, in schools in general and in curriculum more specifically. They must see themselves in ways that are positive, healthy, and diverse to counterbalance the many images that suggest otherwise.

Consider a sponsor of a high school GSA who is a bisexual woman. Although she is not out to her classes, she is out to the students in her GSA. They have a lot of questions about her sexuality, and she answers all of the questions that are, in her mind, appropriate. (She chooses not to answer any questions about sexual behavior.) She tells them about significant relationships she's shared with both men and women and talks about the tensions she's negotiated as a result. When students in the GSA introduce themselves, she never asks them to identify in terms of gender and sexuality, but she invites them to tell stories about their lives with one another. In these stories, the members begin to understand fluidity in desire and identity. They also learn about ways of responding to the ignorance, fear, and hatred they experience, not just individually but also collectively. Think about how having such a teacher and group would have benefitted Rose, a bisexual student who was, essentially, harassed out of her neighborhood school and in turn sought out a queer-friendly charter school.

We recognize, though, that with all of this connection, action, and space comes visibility. Visibility is, we know, a double-edged sword. As queer people are visible to one another and those stepping up on their behalf, they are also visible to those whose actions are homophobic and transphobic. Thus, their visibility is tied to their vulnerability. And though vulnerability to fear and hatred are not desirable, vulnerability among queer people and their advocates has some promise. There is vulnerability in holding one another accountable. There is vulnerability in hearing criticism as an invitation for improvement and with an openness to learning. This requires gratitude, humility, courage, trust, and forgiveness, and it offers promise.

Consider an afterschool care provider at an elementary school. There is a child in the program who is sometimes picked up by a cisgender woman and other times by a parent who he knows as a woman but who seems to be transitioning toward being a man. The care provider is always warm and friendly to the parent but cautiously avoids names and pronouns. One day, though, he notices that the child calls the parent "Daddy." The care provider says to the parent, "I notice that your child calls you 'Daddy' now. Is there a name you would prefer for me to use when addressing you? Should I use masculine pronouns?" Although the care provider was very nervous about asking questions, the parent's generous response assured him it was OK. The parent asked the care provider to call him by his masculine name and to use masculine pronouns. Afterwards, the two were much more likely to share extended conversations about how the child was doing in afterschool care, including how his peers seemed to be reacting to the parent's transition. Think about how having such a care provider would have changed the school experiences of Dylan, whose father transitioned during one of his elementary school years.

We challenge you to step up. We challenge you to learn, reflect, and connect. We *then* encourage you to act and to create space. We know this will make you visible, we know it will make you vulnerable, but your learning, reflection, and connection will prepare you. You will be prepared to step up for LGBTQ and gender diverse people in schools, and you will do it because it matters.

REFERENCES

Abeni, C., Malpani, A., Brighe, M., Ring, T., & Ennis, D. (2016). These are the trans people killed in 2016. *The Advocate.* www.advocate.com/transgender/2016/10/14/these-are-trans-people-killed-2016

Ahmed, S. (2013). Feeling depleted? Retrieved from https://feministkilljoys.com/2013/11/17/feeling-depleted/

Airton, L. (2013). Leave "those kids" alone: On the conflation of school homophobia and suffering queers. *Curriculum Inquiry, 43*(5), 532–562.

Anderson, M. D. (2016, November, 15) How discrimination shapes parent–teacher communication. *The Atlantic.* Retrieved from www.theatlantic.com/education/archive/2016/11/which-parents-are-teachers-most-likely-to-contact/507755/

Applebee, A. N. (1991/2014). Literature: Whose heritage? In E. H. Hiebert (Ed.), *Literacy for a diverse society: Perspectives, practices, and policies* (pp. 228–236). New York: Teachers College Press.

Applebee, A. (1993). *Literature in the secondary school: Studies of curriculum and instruction in the United States.* Urbana, IL: National Council of Teachers of English.

Applebee, A. (1996). *Curriculum as conversation: Transforming traditions of teaching and learning.* Chicago, IL: The University of Chicago Press.

Appleman, D. (2014). *Critical encounters in secondary English: Teaching literary theory to adolescents* (3rd Edition). New York: Teachers College Press.

Atkinson, E. (2001). Deconstructing boundaries: Out on the inside? *Qualitatives Studies in Education, 14*(3), 307–316.

Atkinson, E. & DePalma, R. (2009). Un-believing the matrix: Queering consensual heteronormativity. *Gender and Education, 21*(1), 17–29.

Bakhtin, M. M. (1981). *The dialogic imagination: Four essays* (C. Emerson & M. Holquist, Trans.). Austin, TX: University of Texas Press.

Blackburn, M. V. (2010). Learning to b/se(e) an activist community: The importance of differences in working for change. In M. V. Blackburn, C. T. Clark, L. M. Kenney, & J. M. Smith (Eds.), *Acting out: Teachers combating homophobia and becoming an activist community* (pp. 143–159). New York: Teachers College Press.

References

Blackburn, M. V. (2012). *Interrupting hate: Homophobia in schools and what literacy can do about it*. New York: Teachers College Press.

Blackburn, M. V. (2014). (Re)writing one's self as an activist across schools and sexual and gender identities: An investigation of the limits of LGBT-inclusive and queering discourses. *Journal of Language and Literacy Education, 10*(1), 1–13.

Blackburn, M. V., Clark, C. T., Kenney, L. M., & Smith, J. M. (Eds.) (2010). *Acting out: Combating homophobia through teacher activism*. New York: Teachers College Press.

Blackburn, M. V., Clark, C. T., & Nemeth, E. (2015). Examining queer elements and ideologies in LGBT-themed literature: What queer literature can offer young adult readers. *Journal of Literacy Research, 46*(14), 11–48.

Blackburn, M. V. & Schey, R. (2017). Adolescent literacies beyond heterosexual hegemony. In K. Hinchman & D. Appleman (Eds.), *Adolescent literacy: A handbook of practice-based research* (pp. 38–60). New York, NY: Guilford Press.

Blackburn, M. V. & Schey, R. (in review). The importance of vulnerability: Collaborative composition and the interrogation or reification of oppressive values in a high school LGBTQ-themed literature course.

Blaise, M. (2005). *Playing it straight: Uncovering gender discourses in the early childhood classroom*. New York: Routledge.

Bliston, J. (2017, Sept. 18). Watch Lena Waithe's inspiring Emmys 2017 speech for 'Master of None.' *Rolling Stone*. Retrieved from www.rollingstone.com/tv/news/lena-waithes-emmys-2017-speech-for-master-of-none-watch-w503785

Bourdieu, P. (2011). The forms of capital. In I. Szeman & T. Kaposy (Eds.) *Cultural theory: An Anthology* (pp. 81–97). West Sussex: Wiley-Blackwell.

Bourdieu, P. & Passeron, J. (1977) *Reproduction in education, society and culture*. London: Sage.

Bronfenbrenner, U. (1976). The experimental ecology of education. *Educational Researcher, 5*(9), 5–15.

Brown, K. M. (2004). Leadership for social justice and equity: Weaving a transformative framework and pedagogy. *Educational Administration Quarterly, 40*(1), 77–108.

Butler, J. (1990). *Gender trouble: Feminism and the subversion of identity*. New York: Routledge.

Butler, J. (1993). *Bodies that matter: On the discursive limits of "sex"*. New York: Routledge.

Cart, M. & Jenkins, C. (2006). *The heart has its reasons: Young adult literature with gay/lesbian/queer content, 1969–2004*. Lanham, MD: Scarecrow Press.

Cassidy, E. F. & Stevenson Jr., H. C (2005). They wear the mask. *Journal of Aggression, Maltreatment, & Trauma, 11* (4), 53–74.

Castagno, A. E. (2008). "I don't want to hear that!": Legitimating whiteness through silence in schools. *Anthropology & Education Quarterly, 39* (3), 314–333.

Clark, C. T. (2010a). Inquiring into ally work in teacher education: The possibilities and limitations of textual practice. In M. V. Blackburn, C. T. Clark, L. M. Kenney, & J. M. Smith (Eds.), *Acting out!: Combating homophobia through teacher activism* (pp. 37–55). New York, NY: Teachers College Press.

Clark, C. T. (2010b). Preparing LGBTQ-allies and combating homophobia in a US teacher education program. *Teaching and Teacher Education, 26*(3), 704–713.

Clark, C. T. & Blackburn, M. V. (2009). Reading LGBT-themed literature with young people: What's possible? *English Journal, 98*(4), 25–32.

Cohen, C. J. (1997). Punks, bulldaggers and welfare queens: The radical potential of queer politics? *GLQ, 3*, 437–465.

Collins, P. H. (1990). *Black feminist thought: Knowledge, consciousness, and the politics of empowerment*. Boston, MA: Unwin Hyman.

Collins, P. H. (1993). New vision: Race, class, and gender as categories of analysis and connection. *Race, Sex & Class, 1* (1), 25–45.

Crenshaw, K. (1991). Mapping the margins: Intersectionality, identity politics, and violence against women of color. *Stanford Law Review, 43*(6), 1241–1299.

Deleuze, G. & Guattari, F. (1987). *A thousand plateaus: Capitalism and schizophrenia*. Minneapolis, MN: University of Minnesota Press.

Department for Professional Employees AFL/CIO. (2016). School administrators: An occupational overview. *Fact sheet 2016*. Retrieved from http://dpeaflcio.org/programs-publications/issue-fact-sheets/school-administrators-an-occupational-overview/

Espelage, D. L. (2014). Ecological theory: Preventing youth bullying, aggression, and victimization. *Theory Into Practice, 53*(4), 257–264.

Fecho, B. (2001). "Why are you doing this?": Acknowledging and transcending threat in a critical inquiry classroom. *Research in the Teaching of English, 36*(1), 9–37.

Ferguson, R. A. (2004). *Aberrations in black: Toward a queer of color critique*. Minneapolis, MN: University of Minnesota Press.

Foucault, M. (1975/1995). *Discipline and punish: The birth of the prison system*. New York: Vintage Books.

Gale, T. (2000). Rethinking social justice in schools: How will we recognize it when we see it? *International Journal of Leadership in Education, 4*(3), 253–269.

Glass, T. (2000). "Where are all the women superintendents?" Retrieved from http://aasa.org/SchoolAdministratorArticle.aspx?id=14492

GLSEN definition of Day of Silence. www.glsen.org/day-of-silence

Greytak, E. A. & Kosciw, J. G. (2013). Responsive classroom curricula for lesbian, gay, bisexual, transgender, and questioning students. In E. S. Fisher & K. Komosa-Hawkins (Eds.), *Creating safe and supportive learning environments: A guide for working with lesbian, gay, bisexual, transgender, and questioning youth and families* (pp. 156–174). New York: Routledge.

Griffin, P. & Ouellet, M. (2003). From silence to safety and beyond: Historical trends in addressing lesbian, gay, bisexual, transgender issues in K-12 Schools. *Equity and Excellence in Education, 36*(x), 106–114.

Hallinger, P. (2003). Leading education change: Reflections on the practice of instructional and transformational leadership. *Cambridge Journal of Education, 33* (3),329–351.

Harding, S. (1993). Rethinking standpoint epistemology: What is "strong objectivity"? In L. Alcoff & E. Potter (Eds.), *Feminist epistemologies* (pp. 49–92). New York: Routledge Press.

Holmes, S. E. & Cahill, S. (2004). School experience of gay, lesbian, bisexual and transgender youth. *Journal of Gay & Lesbian Issues in Education, 1*(13), 53–66.

James, S. E., Herman, J. L., Rankin, S., Keisling, M., Mottet, L. A., & Anafi, M. A. (2016). *The report of the 2015 U.S. transgender survey*. Washington, DC: National Center for Transgender Equality.

Janack, M. (1997). Standpoint epistemology without the "standpoint"?: An examination of epistemic privilege and epistemic authority. *Hypatia, 12*(2), 125–139.

Jorgenson, J. (2011). Reflexivity in feminist research practice: Hearing the unsaid. *Women & Language, 34*(2), 115–119.

Keet, A., Zinn, D., & Porteus, K. (2009). Mutual vulnerability: A key principle in a humanising pedagogy in post-conflict societies. *Perspectives in Education, 27*(2), 109–119.

References

Kosciw, J. G., Gretak, E. A., Giga, N. M., Villenas, C. & Danischewski, D. J. (2016). *The 2015 National School Climate Survey: The experiences of lesbian, gay, bisexual, transgender, and queer youth in our nation's schools.* New York: GLSEN.

Leithwood, K., Tomlinson, D., & Genge, M. (1996). Transformation school leadership. In K. Leithwood, J. Chapman, D. Corson, P. Hallinger, & A. Hart (Eds.), *International handbook of educational leadership and administration* (Part 1) (pp. 785–840). Dordrecht, the Netherlands: Kluwer Academic Publishers, Inc.

Lesko, N. (2012). *Act your age! A cultural construction of adolescence* (2nd Edition). New York: Routledge.

Lomotey, K. (1995). Social and cultural influences on schooling: A commentary on the UCEA Knowledge Base Project, Domain I. *Educational Administration Quarterly*, *31*(2), 294–303.

Lugones, M. (2003). *Pilgrimages/peregrinajes: Theorizing coalition against multiple oppressions.* New York, NY: Rowman & Littlefield Publishers.

Majors, R. & Billson, J. M. (1993). *Cool pose: The dilemmas of Black manhood in America.* New York: Touchstone.

Mayo, C. (2014). *LGBTQ youth and education: Policies and practices.* New York: Teachers College Press.

McCready, L. T. (2010). *Making space for diverse masculinities: Difference, intersectionality, and engagement in an urban high school.* New York: Peter Lang.

Melvin, A. (2010). Choosing to stay "in" and the significance of race for lesbian teachers in urban classrooms. In M. V. Blackburn, C. T. Clark, L. M. Kenney, & J. M. Smith (Eds.), *Acting out!: Combating homophobia through teacher activism* (pp. 127–142). New York: Teachers College Press.

Muñoz, J. E. (1999). *Disidentifications: Queers of color and the performance of politics.* Minneapolis, MN: University of Minnesota Press.

Model District Policy on Transgender and Gender Nonconforming Students, Model Language, Commentary and Resources. (2016). Model language commentary and resources. *GLSEN and National Center for Transgender Equality.* Retrieved from http://glsen.customer.def6.com/sites/default/files/Trans_ModelPolicy_2013.pdf

Murdock, T. B., & Bolch, M. B. (2005). Risk and protective factors for poor school adjustment in lesbian, gay, and bisexual (LGB) high school youth: Variable and person-centered analyses. *Psychology in the Schools*, *42*(2), 159–172.

Nealy, E. C. (2017). *Transgender children and youth: Cultivating pride and joy with families in transition.* New York: W.W. Norton & Company.

O'Malley, M. P. & Capper, C. A. (2015). A measure of the quality of educational leadership programs for social justice: Integrating LGBTIQ identities into principal preparation. *Educational Administration Quarterly*, *5*(2), 290–330.

Paris, D., & Alim, H. S. (2014). What are we seeking to sustain through culturally sustaining pedagogy?: A loving critique forward. *Harvard Educational Review*, *84*(1), 85–100.

Paris, D. & Winn, M. T. (Eds.) (2014). *Humanizing research: Decolonizing qualitative inquiry with youth and communities.* Thousand Oaks, CA: Sage.

Pascoe, C. J. (2011). *Dude, you're a fag: Masculinity and sexuality in high school.* Oakland, CA: University of California Press.

Patel, L. (2016). *Decolonizing educational research: From ownership to answerability.* New York: Routledge.

Pollock, M. (2004). *Colormute: Race talk dilemmas in an American school.* Princeton, NJ: Princeton University Press.

Poplin Gosetti, P. & Rusch, E. (1995). Re-examining educational leadership: Challenging assumptions. In D. Dunlap & P. Schmuck (Eds.), *Women leading in education* (pp. 11–35). Albany, NY: State University of New York Press.

Pritchard, E. D. (2013). For colored kids who committed suicide, our outrage isn't enough: Queer youth of color, bullying, and the discursive limits of identity and safety. *Harvard Educational Review, 83*(2), 320–345.

Rensenbrink, C. W. (1996). What difference does it make? The story of a lesbian teacher. *Harvard Educational Review, 66*(2), 257–270.

Rusch, E. A. (2004). Gender and race in leadership preparation: A constrained discourse. *Educational Administration Quarterly, 40*(1), 14–46.

Ryan, C. L. (2011). Talking, reading, and writing about lesbian and gay families in classrooms: The consequences of different pedagogical approaches. In C. Compton-Lilly & S. Greene (Eds.), *Bedtime stories and book reports: Connecting parent involvement and family literacy* (pp. 96–107). New York: Teachers College Press.

Schniedewind, N., & Cathers, K. (2003). Becoming allies for each other: An inclusive approach to confronting heterosexism in schools. *Equity and Excellence in Education, 36*(2), 184–193.

Shields, C. M. (2004). Dialogic leadership for social justice: Overcoming pathologies of silence. *Educational Administration Quarterly, 40*(4), 111–134.

Smith, D. (1987). *The everyday world as problematic: A feminist sociology*. Boston, MA: Northeastern University Press.

Snapp, S. D., Burdge, H. Licona, A. C., Moody, R. L., & Russell, S. T. (2015). Students' perspectives on LGBTQ-inclusive curriculum. *Equity & Excellence in Education, 48*(2), 249–265.

Swearer, S. M., Espelage, D. L., Vaillancourt, T., & Hymel, S. (2010). What can be done about school bullying? Linking research to educational practice. *Educational Researcher, 39*(1), 38–47.

Szalacha, L. (2003). Safer sexual diversity climates: Lessons learned from an evaluation of Massachusetts safe schools program for gay and lesbian students. *American Journal of Education, 110*(1), 58–88.

Tuck, E. (2009). Suspending damage: A letter to communities. *Harvard Educational Review, 79*(3), 409–427.

U.S. Department of Education, Office of Planning, Evaluation and Policy Development, Policy and Program Studies Service (2016). *The state of racial diversity in the educator workforce*, Washington, D.C.

Wang, F. (2012). *Leading diverse schools: Tempering accountability policy with social justice.* Dissertation: Ontario Institute for Studies in Education, University of Toronto.

Wang, F. (2015). Conceptualizing social justice: Interviews with principals. *Journal of Educational Administration, 53*(5), 667–681.

Winn, M. T. (2014). "Epilogue: Reflecting forward on humanizing approaches." In Paris, D. & Winn, M. T. (Eds.), *Humanizing research: Decolonizing qualitative inquiry with youth and communities* (pp. 259–251). Thousand Oaks, CA: Sage.

Yoshino, K. (2006). *Covering: The hidden assault on our civil rights*. New York: Random House.

CONTRIBUTORS

Mollie V. Blackburn is a Professor in the Department of Teaching and Learning in the College of Education and Human Ecology at the Ohio State University. Her research focuses on literacy, language, and social change, with particular attention to LGBTQ and gender diverse youth and the teachers who serve them. She lives with her partner and two children in Columbus, Ohio.

Caroline T. Clark is a Professor of adolescent literacies and English education in the Department of Teaching and Learning at the Ohio State University. Her research focuses on language and literacy practices in and outside of school and collaborative research with teachers, young people, and families for social action. Currently, she is analyzing data from her work with teachers and families involved in community-based teaching and teacher education in local schools in Columbus, Ohio.

Courtney Johnson, a National Board Certified English teacher, now works as a middle school librarian in Columbus City Schools. During her 15 years in the classroom and now as a librarian, Courtney's work focuses on giving young people choice in their reading lives. She has been a member of Pink TIGers and a co-advisor of her school's GSA. She lives in Hilliard, Ohio with her husband and son.

Jenell Igeleke Penn is a doctoral student in adolescent literacies and Program Manager in the English and Social Studies teacher education programs at the Ohio State University. She researches the literacy and language practices and school experiences of culturally and linguistically diverse people. She taught English for ten years and co-sponsored her school's GSA. She resides in Reynoldsburg, Ohio, with her husband and their daughter.

Ryan Schey is a doctoral candidate in the Adolescent, Postsecondary, and Community Literacies program at the Ohio State University. He has recently accepted an Assistant Professor position at Auburn University. His research explores literacy and language practices and social change in schools, focusing on LGBTQ and gender diverse young people. Previously, he taught high school English for seven years and co-advised his school's Gay–Straight Alliance.

Dorothy Sutton teaches Integrated Language Arts and centers her teaching pedagogy on building community and equity. She lives with her partner in Columbus, Ohio.

Kim Swensen teaches high school English, specifically AP Language and dual enrollment courses through Columbus State Community College. Her pedagogy is informed by social justice and the simple idea that we must want for all children what we want for our own children, and she advises the GSA and the Young Feminists club. She lives with her husband and two sons in Columbus, Ohio.

Lane Vanderhule is a fifth-year teacher at Hilliard Davidson High School, where she teaches general and AP English from a social justice perspective and works to create a culturally diverse and inclusive environment in her classroom. Additionally, Lane advises the school's GSA and the Gender Equality Club and creates and provides LGBTQ-related professional development sessions for her colleagues throughout the Hilliard City Schools. Lane lives with her wife in Columbus, Ohio.

Jill M. Williams, Ph.D., works as an English Language Arts and Social Studies curriculum specialist for Westerville City Schools and teaches Education classes at the Ohio State University. She is also a member of the Pink TIGers and was a Gay-Straight Alliance adviser. She taught high school English at Westerville City Schools for 18 years and this is her 21st year as a classroom teacher. Jill lives with her husband and 2 children in Clintonville, Ohio.

INDEX

academic content 20–22, 23–27, 34, 35
acceptance 32
action, queer parents' 81–84
activism 19, 191–192; courageous 60–61; definitions of 19, 27–33; as a humanizing act 35–37; relationships between teaching and 33–35; seeing possibilities in 19–37
administrators *see* school leaders
adult advocacy: non–advocacy 114–117; youth advocacy in the absence of 121–124
advocacy 113–136; complexities of 113–128; conflicting perspectives 117–121; in the face of tradition 131–133; layers of 125–128; out students as assumed advocates 107, 124–125; power of 128–136
agency 121
Ahmed, S. 9
allies 6; visible supports 129–131
Am I Blue? 142, 150
American Educational Research Association (AERA) 161
And Tango Makes Three (Richardson and Parnell) 47, 82
Andrews, A. 144
anti–bullying initiatives 113–114
anti–work approach 30–31, 35
anxiety 79
Applebee, A.N. 138, 155, 156
athletes 104

Atkinson, E. 13
authenticity 97–98; living as authentic self 51, 55–57
authority: claiming 23–27, 36–37; epistemic *see* epistemic authority
autonomy 121

bathrooms 77, 78, 86, 111–112, 119, 192
being informed 46–48
being out 172; complexities of being out at school 103–113; out students as assumed advocates 107, 124–125; realities of 109–113; vulnerability to risks 51, 55–57
Blackburn, M.V. 19
Blaise, M. 95
blind spots 9–11
books 81–82, 92; in the library 51–52; stand–alone texts 139–142, 149
books on the shelf approach 142–145, 149
Boy Meets Boy 142
Bronfenbrenner, U. 11–12
bubble, insulating 67–68
bullying 6, 12, 113–114
'bullywashing' 113–114
buses, problems on 78
buy–in 148–149, 151, 152, 154

Capper, C.A. 176, 187
Castagno, A.E. 9
Catcher in the Rye, The 110
Cathers, K. 6

censure 50, 51–53
Century High School 15–16; school leaders 177–184
Challenge Day 174
charisma 180–181
choices, individual 172, 192
claiming authority 23–27, 36–37
class 9–11, 65–66
classism, reacting to 88–90
coalition building 61
code switching 182
cognitive dissonance 26
collaborative inquiry 58, 60
Collins, J. 104
Collins, P.H. 12
coming out 172; complexities of coming out at school 103–113
community 69–71
competition between teaching and activism 34
concentric circles model 11–12
confident characterizations 168
conflicting perspectives in advocacy work 117–121
connecting LGBTQ content to the broader curriculum 149–150, 154
connection 190–191; emotional 178–179
consistency 116
Constitutional amendments 35
content: connecting LGBTQ content to the broader curriculum 149–150, 154; including and integrating LGBTQ content 145–148, 149; official academic content 20–22, 23–27, 34, 35
contexts 14–17
continual process of learning and doing 57–61
conversations: about family structure 93–94; about sexual and gender diversity 153–154, 154–155; curriculum as conversation 155, 156–157
courageous teacher activism 60–61
coverage, curriculum as 155, 156
covering 75
criticism 50, 51–53
Crossing Lines 143
cultural capital 121–122
curriculum 137–158; books on the shelf approach 142–145, 149; conceptualizing 138; as conversation 155, 156–157; as coverage 155, 156; dispositions and kinds of knowledge needed by teachers 148–155; enacting to include sexual and gender diversity 139–148; integrating LGBTQ content 145–148, 149; reframing 155–157; stand–alone approach 139–142, 149; staying within the official academic curriculum 20–22, 23–27, 34, 35; week–long curriculum celebrating individuality and diversity 83

daddy–daughter dance 86–87
dancing 146–147
Day of Silence 130, 134, 136, 175
decisions to step up: impact of 38–44; knowledge and 44–50; vulnerability to risks 50–57
declarations about sexual/gender identities 108
declarative knowledge 148–149, 150–151, 152, 154
dedication page 84–85
Deleuze, G. 13–14
developmental theory 11–12
dialogic transformative leadership 187–188
dialogue, opportunities for 61
difference: helping children understand it in family structures 92–94; helping children understand individual difference is OK 91–92; valuing 33
dispositions 148–155
district superintendents *see* superintendents
diversity, honoring and valuing 124–125
diversity club 171
'do no harm' ethic 42
documentation: legal 71, 74, 82; medical 100–101, 126
doing more, continual process of 57–61
Don't Ask, Don't Tell (DADT) approach 170
dress code 179–180, 182, 183
Dutro, E. 98–99

ecological systems theory of human development 11–12
effectiveness of stepping up 43–44
efficacy 148, 149–155
embracing vulnerability and risk 56–57
emotional connection 178–179
emotionally disturbed (ED) 127
empathy 125; building 26
epistemic authority 162–184, 187; principals 162–168; and privilege in one school context 177–184; superintendents 168–177

Index

equality 35, 168–169
Espelage, D.L. 12
Everywhere Babies (Meyers and Frazee) 81–82
exclusion 86–87, 132
expectations, academic 23–24
experts, same–gender parents positioned as 82–83
extreme behaviors 167

familiarity 69–71
Family Book, The (Parr) 81, 92
family structures 72–73; helping children understand difference in 92–94
fault lines 186
first impressions 71–72
focusing on individuals 27–28
focusing on structures and patterns 28–30, 36
fold, the 13–14
football 51
forgiveness 60
Foucault, M. 12
freak factor 67–68

gatekeepers 161–162, 186
Gay, Lesbian, Straight Education Network (GLSEN): Day of Silence 130, 134, 136, 175; School Climate survey 1, 115, 159
gay rights 35, 141
Gay–Straight Alliances/Genders and Sexualities Alliances (GSAs) 1, 4, 16, 17, 28–29, 130, 134; school leaders and 163–164
gender fluidity, teaching children about 94
gender markers 91
gender–neutral spaces 86, 112, 113
generational difference 174
geographical privilege, lack of 125–128
Golden Rule 170
Greene, J. 144
Griffin, P. 159
Guattari, F. 13
Guthrie School 14–15

Hansberry, L. 58, 59
Harding, S. 12
Hartville School 17
hatred, activism against 30–31, 35
Heather Has Two Mommies 92
hegemonic masculinity 95, 96, 97

help: queer parents helping their children 90–95; straight parents helping their queer children 98–101; teachers' knowing how to find 151–153, 154
heteronormativity, as protection 95–99
homecoming court 29–30, 59, 132–133
human development theory 11–12
humanizing paradigm 14, 187, 191; teaching and activism as humanizing acts 35–37

ideal schools, for queer parents 65–67
ignorance: activism against 30–31, 35; teachers' and the decision to step up 44–46
I'll Give You the Sun (Nelson) 144
Immortal Life of Henrietta Lacks, The 145–146
impact of decisions 38–44
inaction 49–50
inclusive curriculum *see* curriculum
individuals 186; choices 172, 192; focusing on 27–28
informed decisions 46–48
inquiry 57–61
instructional leadership 184, 187
integrating LGBTQ content approach 145–148, 149
International Festival 171
intersectionality 9–11, 42, 61, 89–90, 191; and layers of advocacy 125–128; vulnerability to risks 50–51, 53–55
invisibility 73; *see also* visibility
invisible lines 13
'It Gets Better' project 6
It's Elementary 83, 190

James, S.E. 57
Janack, M. 162
job security 55–57
Jorgenson, J. 10
journaling 190

knowledge: continual process of knowing more 57–61; kinds of and LGBTQ–inclusive curriculum 148–155; lack of 44–46; teachers' and the decision to step up 44–50
knowledge–in–action 155, 156–157
knowledge–out–of–context 155, 156
Kosciw, J.G. 1–2, 57, 137, 159

labels 104–109
language 182; homophobic 30–31, 39
layers of advocacy 125–128
leadership 159–188; enacting 184–188; in one context 177–184; principals 159, 160, 162–168, 184; superintendents 159, 160, 168–177, 184–186
leadership preparation programs 160–162, 187
learning 189–190; continual process of 57–61; stepping up for 50
legal documentation 71, 74, 82
lesbian couple running for homecoming court 29–30, 59, 132–133
Lesko, N. 168
LG–rights 35, 141
LGBTQ–inclusive literature 47, 81–82, 142–145, 149
LGBTQ organizations and events 133–135
library, books in 51–52
lines of flight 13
lines of force 13
Little Mermaid, The 108
living authentically 51, 55–57
locker rooms 78, 86, 111–112, 192
lottery system 65
love 93

male cheerleader 27–28
Mayo, C. 186
medical documentation 100–101, 126
mental health problems 127, 167
microaggressions 185
military, the 170
Miller, T. 6
misgendering 120–121
misrecognition 50–51, 53–55
mistakes 60
moral character 35
Mount Jeffrey High School 15
movement 146–147
murders of trans people 126–127
mutual enrichment 34–35
mutual vulnerability 153

navigating student responses 41–42
neighborhood values 65
Nelson, J. 144
networking by queer parents 75
normalcy, claiming 75–76
normative, visibility as 78–80

Obergefell versus Hodges 71
official academic curriculum 20–22, 23–27, 34, 35
O'Malley, M.P. 176, 187
open culture 170
'organic' leadership approach 163–164
Ouellett, M. 159
out students *see* being out, coming out

paperwork *see* documentation
paradox of visibility 76–80, 103
parent/teacher conferences 84–86
parent–teacher groups (PTGs) 73–74, 83
parents 43, 63–102; criticism from 25, 52; queer *see* queer parents; straight parents trying to help their queer children 98–101; who unintentionally harm experiences of queer families 63–64; with children performing heteronormativity 95–99
Paris, D. 9, 14
Parr, T. 81, 92
pattern-focused activism 28–30, 36
peer advocacy: in the absence of adult advocacy 121–124; out students as assumed advocates 107, 124–125
peer allies 129–131
performing heteronormativity 95–99
perspective 12
physical contact 146–147
Pink TIGers 2, 3–7, 124–125; blind spots 9–11; research project 7–9
policy 174–175
political pressures 166–167
Poplin Gosetti, P. 161
positive signage 184–185
possibilities, seeing 19–37
poverty 127–128
power 12; of advocacy 128–136
presence, asserting by queer parents 71, 73–76
principals 159, 160, 184; epistemic authority and privilege 162–168; *see also* school leaders
privilege 50; and blind spots 9–10; and epistemic authority in one school context 177–184; lack of and a layered approach to advocacy 125–128; principals and epistemic authority 162–168; school leaders 160–161, 162–184, 187; superintendents and epistemic authority 168–177

proactive approaches 39, 47
problematic behaviors lens 180–181, 183–184
procedural knowledge 148, 149–155
pronouns 108, 120–121
protection: heteronormativity as 95–99; vs support 39–41

queer parents: establishing a presence in schools 71, 73–76; getting started in schools 71–73; helping their children 90–95; ideal schools for 65–67; paradox of visibility 76–80; reacting 84–90; seeking welcoming schools 67–71; taking action in schools 81–84
queer-positive activism 31, 36, 61

race 9–11, 40–41, 42, 53–55, 65–67; layered approach to advocacy and 125–128
racism, queer parents reacting to 88–90
Rainbow Youth Center (RYC) 134–135
reacting, by queer parents 84–90
reactive approaches 39
reading through a queer or gay lens 31
realities of being out in school 109–113
reflection 190; on decisions 43
reframing curriculum 155–157
rejection 50, 51–53
relationship building 61
religion 42, 50–51, 53–55, 66, 127
Rensenbrink, C.W. 185
reporting of harassment or assault 1
resources: provision by queer parents 81–82; queer parents as 82–83; *see also* books
respect 69–71; as resistance 45–46
responsibility for knowing 48–50
restrooms 77, 78, 86, 111–112, 119, 192
risk: embracing and sharing vulnerability and 56–57; vulnerability to risks 50–57
Rusch, E. 161, 162, 186
Ryan, C.L. 73

Sadie Hawkins dance 132
safety 69–71; safe spaces 133–135, 192; unsafe spaces 78, 111–113
same-sex marriage, legalization of 71
Savage, D. 6
Schniedewind, N. 6
school buses 78
school contexts 14–17

school leaders 159–188; enacting leadership 184–188; lack of diversity 160; and leadership preparation programs 160–162, 187; one school context 177–184; principals 159, 160, 162–168, 184; social justice 186–188; superintendents 159, 160, 168–177, 184–186
security 78–80
Sedaris, D. 58, 59
self-determination, right to 121
sexual fluidity, teaching children about 94
shaping students' lives 22–27, 34, 35
sharing vulnerability and risk 56–57
Shields, C.M. 187
signage, positive 184–185
silencing 170–171
single-factor identity 106–107
Smith, D. 186
smooth 121–122, 124
social capital 130
social change, teaching for 22–27, 34, 35
social justice 161; enacting leadership for 186–188
social privilege, lack of 125–128
social relationships 58
Some Assembly Required: The Not–So–Secret Life of a Transgender Teen (Andrews) 144
space: gender-neutral spaces 86, 112, 113; problems relating to bathrooms and locker rooms 78, 111–112, 192; safe spaces 133–135, 192; unsafe spaces 78, 111–113
spotlighting 144
stakeholders 7–9; expectations 23–24
stand-alone topics/texts 139–142, 149
starting school, queer parents and 71–73
straight parents' helping their queer children 98–101
structural activism 28–30, 36
students 103–136; complexities of advocacy 113–128; complexities of coming out/being out at school 103–113; navigating student responses 41–42; power of advocacy 128–136; teaching as shaping students' lives 22–27, 34, 35
suicides 6
superintendents 159, 160, 184–186; epistemic authority and privilege 168–177; *see also* school leaders
support: for colleagues 150–151, 154; leadership based on supporting nontraditional families 165–168; for

other students 107; vs protection 39–41; straight parents supporting and helping their queer children 98–101; visible supports 128–131
support groups: LGBTQ organizations 133–135; for queer parents 94–95
suppression of gender expression 108–109
switching schools 117

teachable moments 19
teacher allies 129
teaching: definitions of 20–27; as a humanizing act 35–37; relationships between activism and 33–35; seeing possibilities in 19–37
tension between teaching and activism 34
terminology 2–3
texts: stand–alone 139–142, 149; *see also* books
That's a Family 190
time 34
tolerance 32, 34–35
topics, stand–alone 139–142, 149
tradition, advocacy in the face of 131–133
trailblazer teachers 48–50, 58, 129
transformational leadership 184, 187–188
treating others the way you'd like to be treated 170
trial–and–error 58–59
trying harder 123
'two girls together sexy' trope 110

underlying theories 11–14
universalizing approach 32–33, 36
University Council for Educational Administration (UCEA) 161

values: neighborhood 65; U.S. 35
valuing differences 33
violence 111–113
visibility 189, 192–193; paradox of 76–80, 103; queer parents in schools 73–75; visible supports 128–131; vulnerability and 50–51, 53–55
vitalism 13–14
vulnerability 78, 80, 189, 193; embracing and sharing 56–57; mutual 153; queer parents noticing vulnerable students 81; to risks 50–57

Wang, F. 161
Week of Expression 134
weighing the impact of a decision 39–41
welcoming schools 67–71
Williams High School 16–17
'wince factor' 68
Winn, M.T. 9, 14
Woodson, J. 144

Yoshino, K. 75

zero tolerance policies 106